E-Learning and Disability in Higher Education

Most practitioners know that they should make e-learning accessible to students with disabilities, yet it is not always clear exactly how this should be done. *E-Learning and Disability in Higher Education* evaluates current practice and provision and explores the tools, methods and approaches available for improving accessible practice.

Examining the social, educational and political background behind making e-learning accessible in higher and further education, this book considers the role of, and provides advice for, the key stake-holders involved in e-learning provision: lecturers, learning technologists, student support services, staff developers and senior managers.

Key topics covered include:

- the opportunities that e-learning can offer students with disabilities;
- the impact of accessibility legislation, guidelines and standards on current e-learning practices;
- the reliability and validity of accessibility related evaluation and repair tools;
- practical guidelines for 'best practice' in providing accessible e-learning experiences.

E-Learning and Disability in Higher Education is valuable reading for all practitioners and researchers involved in the design and delivery of accessible e-learning in higher, further and distance education.

Jane K. Seale is Senior Lecturer in Educational Innovation in Higher Education at Southampton University. Her research interests include accessibility and assistive technologies and she has published and presented widely in these areas. Jane's recent work includes *The Development of Accessibility Practices in E-learning: An exploration of communities of practice* (Association for Learning Technology Journal, 2004).

E-Learning and Disability in Higher Education

Accessibility research and practice

Jane K. Seale

Routledge
Taylor & Francis Group

LONDON AND NEW YORK

First published 2006
by Routledge
2 Park Square, Milton Park, Abingdon, Oxon OX14 4RN

Simultaneously published in the USA & Canada
by Routledge
270 Madison Ave, New York, NY 10016

Routledge is an imprint of the Taylor and Francis Group, an informa business

© 2006 Jane K. Seale

Typeset in Times by RefineCatch Ltd, Bungay, Suffolk
Printed and bound in Great Britain by
Antony Rowe Ltd, Chippenham, Wiltshire

British Library Cataloguing in Publication Data
A catalogue record for this book is available from the British Library

Library of Congress Cataloging in Publication Data
Seale, Jane K.
    E-learning and disability in higher education : accessibility
research and practice / Jane K. Seale.
        p.   cm.
    Includes bibliographical references and index.
    ISBN 0–415–38310–2 (pbk.) – ISBN 0–415–38309–9 (hbk)
    1. Education, Higher – Computer-assisted instruction.
    2. College students with disabilities – Effect of technological
    innovations on.   3. Computers and people with disabilities.
    I. Title.
    LB2395.7.S42 2006
    378.1'734 – dc22   2005034183

ISBN10: 0–415–38309–9 (hbk)
ISBN10: 0–415–38310–2 (pbk)
ISBN10: 0–203–96959–6 (ebk)

ISBN13: 978–0–415–38309–7 (hbk)
ISBN13: 978–0–415–38310–3 (pbk)
ISBN13: 978–0–203–96959–5 (ebk)

Contents

Figures

Tables

Chapter 1

Introduction

Magic fairies and accessibility dust

> While it is physically possible to read and reply to discussion board contributions with a screen reader, it is not practical. . . . Just because something is possible does not make it practical. Perhaps there is a magic solution for this problem that we haven't encountered yet, but we fear that until the Fairy of Learning Technology raises her magic wand to sprinkle accessibility dust all over the VLE, our students who use screen readers will not be able to take part in online discussion. Surely, if this is the case, instead of widening participation and enhancing accessibility – we are narrowing it.
>
> (Nicole Kipar, ALT-N Newsletter, July 2005)

Introduction

At this point in time, most practitioners in higher education know that they should make e-learning accessible to students with disabilities. Very few practitioners however, know exactly how to make e-learning accessible. This is despite the fact that tens, if not hundreds of accessibility related 'tools' exist supposedly to assist practitioners in the development of accessible e-learning material. This situation is bemusing many accessibility experts and advocates. Despite the presence of a multitude of tools, why do practitioners appear to some to be waiting for the magic fairy to miraculously transform all e-learning material with one wave of her magic wand? The purpose of this book is to seek to answer this question by addressing accessibility from a practitioner's perspective. The focus of this book therefore is on accessible e-learning practice and not on the products of this practice.

In order to address accessible e-learning practice, this book has been organized into three sections entitled: Contextualizing the scene, Surveying the scene and Conceptualizing the scene. The chapters presented in part 1: 'Contextualizing the scene', address why accessibility is important and relevant to practitioners working within higher education. The chapters presented in part 2: 'Surveying the scene', explore the perspectives of the different stakeholders that practice within a higher education institution. Finally, the chapters in part 3 seek ways of conceptualizing accessible e-learning practice, with a view to helping practitioners gain an understanding of what has happened, what is happening, what needs to happen in the future and how to ensure that it does happen.

Contextualizing the scene

Many commentators have sought to convince higher education practitioners that accessibility is important and that it is something they need to address in their own practice in relation to e-learning. The reasons given are varied and include:

- legal reasons: make e-learning accessible or you will be punished;
- business reasons: make e-learning accessible and you will make a profit;
- moral reasons: make e-learning accessible because it is the right thing to do;
- pedagogic reasons: make e-learning accessible and students will have a better learning experience.

Sloan *et al.* (2000) make a distinction between selfish and altruistic reasons and from this list it would appear that there as many selfish reasons for making e-learning accessible as there are altruistic ones. The most compelling and eloquently published arguments for accessible e-learning however, typically centre on moral or altruistic reasons:

> None of us would knowingly build a course Web site that students of color, or students who are women, or students who are men, would be unable to use simply by virtue of their racial or ethnic status or their gender. It should be equally unthinkable for us to design web resources for our classes that are inaccessible to students or colleagues with dis-abilities simply because of those disabilities. It's no less morally wrong to discriminate against individuals on the basis of disability than on the basis of race or gender or creed, and it's no less against the law.
>
> (Slatin 2002)

Such arguments however appear to have done little to increase the level and spread of accessible e-learning within higher education. One purpose of this book is to consider why this might be. Such a consideration will involve an exploration of what accessibility is (chapter 4) and particularly what it means in the context of disability (chapter 2) and e-learning (chapter 3).

Surveying the scene

In the accessibility field it can be very tempting to place all the responsibility for delivering accessible e-learning onto the shoulders of one person, usually the designer or developer. Opinions within the literature suggest however, that the responsibility needs to be more evenly distributed. In the commercial world, Paciello (2000: 5–6) argues that the responsibility needs to be shared between the engineers, the designers and content creators, the standards organizations, the disability organization and the assistive technology corporations: 'There's no rocket science here, everyone shares a measure of the responsibility.' Within higher education, there is also growing recognition that responsibility needs to be shared between all relevant stakeholders. The IMS Global Learning Consortium (2004b) for example, identifies stakeholders who are both external and internal to a higher education institution including: courseware and software vendors; educational publishers; authoring tool developers/vendors; authors/content developers; educational institutions (including administrators); educators/instructors; administrative staff and students.

In thinking in more detail about those stakeholders that exist within an institution (virtual or physical), many people recognize that key stakeholders are disabled students, lecturers, disability support services, IT and computing departments, administrators and managers (e.g. Sanda 2003). Opinions vary however as to which stakeholder should take the brunt of the responsibility for ensuring accessibility and what the different roles of the stakeholders might be. For example, some people consider that accessibility is the sole responsibility of specialists such as disability service providers and assistive technology specialists (Burgstahler and Cook 2005; Anderson 2004) and that part of their role is to develop strategic partnerships with those who make technology and planning purchase decisions and those who provide services to students such as libraries, counselling and registration.

For the purposes of this book the key stakeholders in the development of accessible e-learning within a higher education institution will be considered to be: disabled students, lecturers, learning technologists, student support services, staff developers and senior managers. Chapters 5 to 10 will explore the perspectives of these stakeholders in turn and attempt to give a voice to the issues and concerns that each stakeholder is facing as well as address the roles and responsibilities that each stakeholder is taking or could be taking towards developing accessible e-learning.

In the context of this book, learning technologists will be defined as anyone who has formal responsibility for: the development and maintenance of a university or departmental website (e.g. webmasters); the development or maintenance of university or department-wide courseware systems or virtual learning environments (VLEs and learning management systems (LMS); the development and maintenance of electronic information systems (e.g. online library databases); the development, production and maintenance of learning objects (e.g. Java applets, Flash animation); the development, production and maintenance of portal and repositories; or development and maintenance of support resources (e.g. study skills websites). In the context of this book senior managers will be defined as anyone who has a responsibility for managing the provision of learning and teaching (e.g. Deans, Pro Vice Chancellors), support services (e.g. libraries, disability offices) or Information Technology and Computing Services.

If accessible e-learning practice is to develop, strategic partnerships between these different stakeholders will probably need to be formed and this cannot happen successfully unless each stakeholder understands the different perspectives of each of the other stakeholders.

Conceptualizing the scene

The accessibility literature is littered with talk of tools: tools for authoring accessible e-learning, tools for evaluating the accessibility of e-learning and tools for auditing the accessibility of e-learning related services. A central premise of this book is that in additional to developing these practical tools we need to develop conceptual tools. Conceptual tools such as metaphors, models, frameworks and theories are important in that they can help us to understand and evaluate current accessibility practices as well as to develop and improve future accessibility practices. These tools however need to take into account: the range of stakeholders and the interaction between them; the context in which these stakeholders are operating and the interaction between the stakeholders and the context.

Chapters 11 to 13 will explore a range of existing conceptual tools that might help us to understand accessible e-learning practices from an institutional, community and individual level. Chapter 14 will seek to distill out, from an analysis of the existing conceptual tools, proposals for new conceptual tools that might offer different ways of thinking about developing accessible e-learning practices for the future.

A personal perspective

Accessibility is not a neutral, techno-rational field. All the players in accessible e-learning have their own perspectives and their own stories to tell. What we learn from these perspectives and stories is important for the development of practice. For example, I recently attended an international e-learning conference and was pleased to see that I was not the only one presenting on web accessibility issues. It was with great anticipation therefore, that I attended a talk on how a particular higher education institution had attempted to address the accessibility of its main web pages. I was quickly disappointed however. The presenter turned out to be a student, who had been given the sole responsibility of transforming the institutional web pages as part of her 'student project'. It quickly emerged that the student knew very little about accessibility. Her sole point of reference throughout the whole talk was a Wiki Encyclopaedia definition of accessibility! She was not aware of any of the classic accessibility tools such as Bobby, and was naive about the practicalities of accessible design. The student's presentation left me with mixed emotions:

- I was angry with the institution at which the student was studying for appearing to think that it could delegate its responsibilities for accessibility to a student;
- I was frustrated with the student's lecturers and supervisors for appearing not to have adequately prepared the student for her accessibility project;
- I was shocked that the conference programme committee had 'let through' such a weak paper that was based on limited knowledge and awareness of current research and practice;
- I was disappointed in myself for being so desperate to find 'the magic solutions' to accessibility that I did not scrutinize the conference abstract more carefully before deciding to attend the presentation;
- I was proud of the conference delegates who supported the student through her presentation by sharing what they knew about accessibility and offering references, resources and tips.

My experience at this conference gave me a powerful lesson. I learnt that in the field of e-learning there is, in some areas, a lack of knowledge of specific accessibility tools, methods and approaches and that there is a lack of scrutiny and criticality regarding the accessibility research and practice that is currently disseminated. I also learnt that despite a lack of knowledge and criticality there is an acute awareness that accessibility issues need to be addressed and a willingness of those who have some accessibility expertise to share it with those who do not.

In seeking to develop accessible e-learning practice, we cannot rely on finding 'magic fairies' with magic solutions. I did not find a magic fairy at my conference and as as author of this book I cannot sprinkle 'accessibility dust' over all those who read it and conjure up accessible e-learning from nothing. What I hope I can do through this book is help all those involved in accessible e-learning to see how they can take ownership of the process and practice of delivering accessible e-learning and gain some understanding of how to develop their practice in the future.

Part I

Contextualizing the scene

Chapter 2

Disability and higher education

> I had to rely on goodwill and be grateful for being able to learn whereas
> everybody else was entitled to learn straight away, and it was a disadvantage,
> and I wasn't encouraged to make noise about it or ask for any help.
>
> (ALERT 2005: 10)

Introduction

One of the key levers that could be used to promote or force changes in the
way disabled students are viewed or treated in higher education is the fact that
the numbers of disabled students in higher education are increasing. For
example, in the UK, figures from the Higher Education Statistical Agency
(HESA) suggest that the numbers of disabled undergraduate students has
increased between 1995 and 2000. In the year 2000/1 almost 5 per cent
(26,000) of UK undergraduates self-assessed themselves as having a disability. In 2000/1 dyslexia was the most commonly declared disability (35 per
cent), with unseen disabilities (e.g. epilepsy, diabetes, asthma) coming next at
26 per cent. Students who were deaf or had a hearing impairment accounted
for 7 per cent, and a similar percentage had multiple disabilities (HESA
2002). Hurst and Smerdon (2000) note that according to the US 1995–96
National Postsecondary Student Aid Study roughly 6 per cent of all undergraduates reported having a disability. Among 1995–96 undergraduates with
a disability, approximately 29 per cent reported having a learning disability
(e.g. dyslexia), and 23 per cent reported an orthopedic impairment. About 16
per cent of students with disabilities reported having a hearing impairment;
16 per cent a vision impairment, and 3 per cent a speech impairment.

However, the figures in the UK are considered by many to be an under-
statement for at least three reasons. First, there is no obligation for students
to report a disability; second, only disabilities which might necessitate extra
support for their studies, accommodation or daily living are recorded; and
third, HESA statistics depend on institutional recording procedures, which
vary in their tracking of students who declare disabilities during their course.

Hence, the actual number of disabled students in UK higher education may be closer to 10 per cent (Healey *et al.* 2001).

One of the key consequences of the growing numbers of disabled students that are entering higher education is that it has influenced those working within these sectors to address the extent to which they understand the needs of students with disabilities and can provide support that adequately addresses those needs. Educators' understanding of the needs of disabled students and the way they respond to those needs is however mediated by historical, social, cultural and legal definitions of disability. This chapter will explore a range of definitions and understandings of disability and consider the impact they have on disabled students' experiences in higher education.

Defining and understanding disability

Our understanding and attitudes towards disability is reflected in the models, classification systems and legal definitions that we adopt and operationalize.

Models of disability

For many, disability is understood through the models that are operated in educational, health and social welfare settings. Individualistic models of disability are built on the assumption that the problems and difficulties that disabled people experience are a direct result of their individual physical, sensory or intellectual impairments. One key example of this kind of model is the medical model, which views disability in terms of disease processes, abnormality and personal tragedy. With the medical model, disability need arises directly from impairment and the major task of the professional is to adjust the individual to the particular disabling condition.

Another model, which emphasizes the personal tragedy of disability, is the charity model of disability. Ten to 15 years ago, this model was accused of portraying disabled people as helpless, sad and in need of care and protection. Such portrayals were argued to be perpetuating damaging stereotypes and misconceptions. More recently, charities have been using more positive images to portray (and thus define) disability.

Administrative models of disability usually relate to specific areas of life such as education or employment and are used to assess whether or not people are eligible for certain benefits or compensation. The associated definitions of disability are written into legislation with legal implications and are viewed by many to be rigid and dichotomous. The definitions almost always relate to people's impairments rather than their physical or social environments. Health and welfare professions are often required to work within the framework of administrative definitions, but critics of this model argue that disabled people rarely fit into the neat boxes that administrators provide.

The social model of disability, put forward by disability activists, was a move against viewing disabled people as dependent and in need of care (Oliver 1990). Disability was viewed as stemming from the failure of the social and physical environment to take account of disabled people's needs. The problems of disabled people were therefore not seen as within the individual person, but within society. According to the social model, it is not the individual with a disability that needs to be changed, but society. In the early years of the social model, impairment as a concept or experience was rejected for fear of weakening the argument that altering the environment would solve the difficulties that disabled people faced. There is now, however, a growing acceptance by disability activists and those working in related fields such as assistive technology, that acknowledging impairment does not necessarily undermine the social model:

> If we think of a disability in a functional context instead of in the abstract, it becomes easier to overcome. In this context, a disability is not so much an attribute of a person as it is a mismatch between a particular person and a particular environment. When we think of a disability as a personal attribute, it is the person who must be changed. If we put it in a functional context, we have the choice of altering either the person or some feature in the environment. Our choices have been dramatically increased.
>
> (Coombs 2000)

Different models of disability give rise to different models of service provision. Services based on the administrative model, reflect the view that disabled people cannot solve their problems on their own and that they need to be helped through the provision of specialist services. A social model of disability on the other hand, leads to service approaches that focus on barrier removal. Disability activists argue, however, that analysing the social and personal barriers that disabled people face should not be done solely by the professional helper, otherwise there is a risk that administrative control will be re-established over a disabled person. Disabled people therefore need to exercise control over the support systems they use (Finkelstein 1993). Service provision models based on the social model therefore emphasize individual and collective responsibility as opposed to professional help and medical responsibility.

Systems of classification

The influence of the social and medical models of disability can also be seen in the development of classification systems that attempt to distinguish between impairment and disability. One example is the International Classification of Impairment, Disability and Handicap (ICDH), first developed by the World Health Organization in 1980. This classification initially had a very medical focus, where handicap and disability were seen as a problem of the person and caused by disease or trauma:

- impairments are a consequence of disease or disorder;
- disability is a consequence of impairments;
- handicap is a consequence of disabilities.

Social models of disability distinguish between disability and impairment differently, however (Oliver 1990). According to social models, impairment is an individual limitation, while a disability is a socially imposed restriction. Not being able to walk is an impairment but lack of mobility is a disability (a socially created situation).

Influenced by the social model, the World Health Organization (WHO) began to re-develop its classification (initially called ICDH-2, but now called ICF) in the late 1990s. This new classification facilitates a merge between the medical and social model and attempts to include environmental factors. Disability is now seen as:

> an interaction between health conditions and contextual factors where both health and contextual factors may have an influence on the activities a disabled person can perform or the extent to which they can participate in the social world around them (and vice versa).
>
> (WHO 2001)

Disability is therefore understood as the extent to which performance of activities are limited and:

- activity is defined as everything that a person does;
- participation is defined as the interaction of impairments, disabilities and contextual factors and comprises all aspects of human life;
- contextual factors are defined as the complete background to a person's life and living, including external environmental factors and internal personal factors.

The WHO argue that their new classification now operates a universal rather than a minority model of disability where every one may have disability; disability is seen as a continuum rather than dichotomous and is understood as multi-dimensional. This universal model is based on the value of inclusion and rejects the view that disability is a defining feature of a separate minority group of people.

Legal definitions of disability

The move from ICDH to ICF has not necessarily been reflected in discrimination legislation across the world. For example, Lindsay (2004) argues that

Australian law has yet to respond to the challenges posed by the new international approaches to participation and inclusion, such as the WHO International Classification of Functioning. An inspection of the way in which five international disability discrimination laws define disability reveals certain similarities (see Table 2.1). For example, in both the UK and American Disability Discrimination Acts, disability is defined as either a physical or mental impairment that has a substantial effect on a person's ability to carry out their day-to-day activities. There are problems with the legal definitions of disability however, in that they have been argued to be overly medically oriented and not entirely inclusive.

Table 2.1 International legal definitions of disability

Legislation	Definitions of disability
UK Disability Discrimination Act (HMSO 1995)	A physical or mental impairment that has a substantial and long-term adverse affect on (a person's) ability to carry out normal day-to-day activities.
UK Special Educational Needs Discrimination Act (HMSO 2001)	A person has a disability if he or she has a physical or mental impairment, which has a substantial and long-term adverse effect on his or her ability to carry out normal day-to-day activities.
Section 504 of the 1973 Workforce Rehabilitation Act (US Department of Labour 1973a)	A physical or mental impairment that constitutes or results in a substantial impediment to employment; or substantially limits one or more major life activities.
Americans with Disabilities Act 1990 (US Department of Justice 1990)	A physical or mental impairment that substantially limits one or more of the major life activities or: <ul><li>holding a record of a physical or mental impairment</li><li>being regarded (by other employees or employer) as having a physical or mental disability.</li></ul>
Australian Disability Discrimination Act 1992 (Australian Government Attorney-General Department 1992)	Disability, in relation to a person, means: <ul><li>total or partial loss of the person's bodily or mental functions; or</li><li>total or partial loss of a part of the body; or</li><li>the presence in the body of organisms causing disease or illness; or</li><li>the presence in the body of organisms capable of causing disease or illness; or</li><li>the malfunction, malformation or disfigurement of a part of the person's body; or</li><li>a disorder or malfunction that results in the person learning differently from a person without the disorder or malfunction; or</li><li>a disorder, illness or disease that affects a person's thought processes, perception of reality, emotions or judgement or that results in disturbed behaviour.</li></ul>

Medical orientation of legal definitions of disability

In critiquing the UK Disability Discrimination Act (DDA), Roulstone (2003) argues that the legal stipulation that the 'disability' has to be 'substantial' and 'long-term' has been borrowed from the wording of the Chronically Sick and Disabled Persons Acts of 1970 and that the DDA therefore reinforces medical model notions that disability is identified by the extent of bodily or intellectual difference. Roulstone (2003: 122) argues that this is 'symbolic of a new Act being based on dated and disablist epistemologies'. Furthermore, when disabled people make claims of discrimination, many disability discrimination tribunals place significant reliance on medical evidence in determining whether or not an applicant has a disability (Income Data Services 2000).

It is interesting to note that the third part of the American Disability Discrimination Act definition allows for a social construction of disability in accepting that people may be discriminated against based on how others perceive their ability or disability, irrespective of whether perceptions are correct. Leverton, meanwhile, (2002) uses 'case law' to highlight the finding that the perceptions of disability which lay members of a tribunal hold, may influence their decisions.

A further consequence of medically oriented legal definitions of disability is that it can lead to legal hearings and tribunals where complainants are required to assert and catalogue in great detail what they cannot do, in order to try and persuade 'judges' that they are in fact disabled, as the law would understand it. Roulstone (2003: 123) perceives this as a further injustice and argues that it is 'not natural or uplifting for a person to have to dwell publicly upon the minutiae of what they cannot do.'

Exclusion and legal definitions of disability

Definitions which specify that the disability has to have a long term effect can exclude some severe conditions that are not long term (twelve months or more), as can sometimes be the case with some heart attacks or strokes. Furthermore, in using terms such as physical and mental impairment, legislation often goes onto stipulate what conditions or categories fall under these umbrella terms. This can be done quite simplistically or arbitrarily. For example, in commenting on the UK DDA Roulstone (2003: 122) highlights a legal case where a person with schizophrenia was discriminated against because they did not easily fall into a category and instead had to be: 'spliced into the "difficulties with physical coordination" and "memory and concentration" categories.' Roulstone argues that the placing of complex human interactions between impairment and social barriers into legally abstract categories seems questionable.

The impact of definitions and understandings of disability on the student experience

The different definitions and understandings of disability that are reflected in models of disability, classification systems and disability discrimination legislation gives an insight into the way in which educators may be influenced to operationalize definitions of disability in terms of models and approaches to service provision and the impact this might have on students with disabilities. The research and practice literature has certainly provided evidence of both negative attitudes and responses from peers and staff to the fact that disabled students need support and the negative experiences of disabled students when they publicly declare that they need support.

Negative responses from peers, academic and support staff

There is evidence to suggest that disabled students experience negative attitudes from both students and staff (Quick *et al.* 2003). For example, Kowalsky and Fresko (2002), in a study of the impact and role of peer tutoring for disabled college students, reported that while there were clear benefits of the scheme, disabled students reported some difficulties with their peers. In particular students with learning disabilities felt that their peer tutors doubted their need for help or were less willing to help them compared to their visually impaired counterparts. Negative responses from non-disabled peers may perhaps be explained by the fact that for many they will have had very little contact with disabled students in their primary and secondary schools. For example, Taylor and Palfreman-Kay (2000) investigated the relationships between disabled and non-disabled students and used their findings to argue that a lack of contact between disabled and non-disabled children in primary and secondary education is an important factor in relationships between these two groups in tertiary education.

Studies that report the experiences of disabled students in their interactions with academic and support staff, typically report a wide range of responses from highly supportive to highly unhelpful. For example, Holloway (2001) in a study of six students notes that where staff were well briefed or well supported, students reported positively. However, where staff lacked awareness or specific knowledge of the disability and support available, students reported adverse experiences. Holloway also argues that much of the students' discontent was experienced at the departmental level:

> The underlying reasons are, first, that departments perceive disability as a problem affecting individual students and then assume that this only requires an individual response. Secondly, there are no guidelines on practice ... regarding the provision of support disabled students may

need, so each department evolves its own response with resulting inconsistencies, both within and between departments.

(Holloway 2001: 608–609)

Awareness of disability does not necessarily reduce the negative responses of staff. For example, Fuller *et al.* (2004a) in a systematic study of the experience of 593 students in one university notes that there were some instances where lecturers did not make accommodations for the student's disability, where this failure to be flexible or understanding could be the result of not knowing about the disability. However, there were also cases where staff had been unhelpful even when they were aware of the disabled student's presence and needs.

One way to help students to counteract negative attitudes and responses may be to encourage them to advocate for change through collaborative work with staff. For example, Roer-Strier (2002) presents a case study of a project involving social work students with learning disabilities at Hebrew University in Jerusalem. The students were appointed to a committee of teachers, field-work supervisors and administrators and were encouraged to work with the committee and lobby and advocate for their needs. Analysis of interviews with students suggests that the project positively affected the students' perceptions by helping them reframe the social and emotional connotations of their learning disability. Students reported marked social and emotional change, including reduced stress and anxiety levels and increased self-esteem.

Negative experiences of declaring a disability

Disability discrimination legislation differs in the extent to which it may require students to declare their disabilities. For example, UK discrimination legislation and associated codes of practice do not require students to declare their disability. Instead higher education institutions are required to antici-pate need. This is in stark contrast to US legislation where disabled students are responsible for notifying colleges of their disability, requesting academic adjustments and auxiliary aids and providing any necessary evidence of a disability-related need for them (Milani 1996). Irrespective of whether there is a legal requirement to declare a disability, the experience of most disabled students in higher education is that in order to receive support and resources, they need to declare their disability to their tutors, disability officers, etc. Evidence suggests that students have very mixed feelings about this, feelings that include reluctance, discomfort and bemusement.

Reluctance and discomfort in publicly declaring a disability

The evidence from the vast majority of students indicates that moving away from home to university or college is a time when they have to confront their disabilities. Living at home with family and friends, going to a school which they have attended for many years, or coming from a village or locality where they are accepted, their disability has been a private matter. However, in coming to a new place, a new institution, working with people they have never known, disability suddenly becomes a public matter (Borland and James 1999).

Hall and Tinklin (1998) in their study of the experiences of disabled students in Scotland noted that students were very different in the approaches they took to discussing their needs with the institution. Some students were proactive. This was often because they had received some kind of provision at school and knew that they may be entitled to additional support. Some students, however, did not know that they may be entitled to anything or that support was available. Others feared that they would be disadvantaged if they asked for anything or disclosed a disability. Others knew that they could get support but chose not to take it because they wanted to be treated like other students. Even when needs had been discussed, students may still have felt uncomfortable about asking for something, especially if it would affect the whole class. Some of the students chose not to disclose their disabilities in some situations. This was because they believed they may meet with a negative reaction or that they may be disadvantaged in some way.

In a US study, Olney and Brockelman (2003) examined the ways in which university students with apparent and hidden disabilities actively managed how others perceived them. Participants gave a number of practical reasons, similar to those highlighted by Hall and Tinklin (1998), for why they concealed their impairments:

- those with invisible disabilities expressed concern that others would not believe that they had a real disability;
- participants felt that others would see them as less competent;
- they wished to be viewed as consistent and trustworthy;
- they worried that others would see them only as needing help rather than as a peer who can give and take in a relationship.

Regardless of whether the disability was apparent or hidden, the students endeavoured to control the timing and setting of disclosure. It appeared that students with disabilities engaged in an intricate decision-making process about revealing disability information.

The participants in this study shared such information with people to whom they were close, people who might discover the disability, and those from whom they needed accommodations while attempting to keep as much information private as possible.

Depending on the kind of relationship, people chose to reveal little or much information. Olney and Brockelman argue that such behaviour is not so much indicative of a hiding or denying of one's disability as it is of an act of self-determination. They argue:

Regardless of disability label or level of support needed, people with disabilities regularly confront doubts, judgments, and stereotypes. Daily, they engage in a decision making process about the relative advantages and drawbacks of telling others about the disability. They often need to choose between the risk of being stereotyped and the risk of failing to procure appropriate accommodations.

(Olney and Brockelman 2003: 49)

Bemusement that a declaration of disability does not affect change in support

Doyle and Robson (2002) offer advice to academics on how to encourage disabled students to disclose their disability, but there is evidence to suggest that even when students do disclose, their needs are not addressed. For example, Fuller *et al.* (2004 a, b) investigated disabled students' perceptions and experiences of learning and found that students did not appreciate that having declared their impairment, whether on registration or subsequently, that there was no mechanism within the institution for that information to be relayed routinely to their tutors. Consequently there were some instances where lecturers and other students did not understand the disabled student's needs because they were ignorant of the impairment. From the student's perspective this gave rise to frustrating incidences of having to inform individual members of staff about their impairment and ask for adjustments in a climate that could be difficult. There were occasional examples of staff unwillingness to be flexible or understanding, even when a disabled student had made their needs known.

Borland and James (1999) summarize the results of an investigation into the social and learning experiences of students with physical disabilities in a UK university. Students were reportedly troubled by what they perceived to be an 'invisibility' of their disabilities and attributed this to a breakdown in communication with the University. They thought that having notified the institution on their application form that they were disabled, the institution 'knew' and had taken it into account. They worked on the assumption that the institution, knowing of their disabilities, would not offer them a place if it could not provide the necessary support. They were also quite mystified by the fact that their school (academic department) did not appear to know about them or that their personal tutor was unaware that they were disabled. In some cases this was confusing. In other cases it raised questions in the student's mind about their value to the institution. More seriously, some students felt that breakdowns in communication reinforced their disabilities by forcing them to identify themselves as disabled to many different people all of whom were seen as strangers.

Declaring a disability is a complex decision, which raises complex issues regarding disability identity and needing and receiving support. For example,

Lambert (2001) argues that when students complete an enrolment or admissions form and declare their disability, they are making a transition from an individual identity to an institutional identity where they will be labelled and recorded accordingly. Further, Parker (1997) notes that students with epilepsy, asthma, diabetes and arthritis may 'tick a box' to indicate a disability because they think others would see their condition as a disability, although they themselves do not. Dyslexic students, on the other hand, may not be aware that the label 'specific learning difficulties' is used to describe them. The meaning given to the term 'disability' varies considerably depending upon who is defining the term, to whom and for what purpose.

Conclusion

The way we define and understand disability has the potential to have a significant impact on the learning experiences of students with disabilities. In particular it can impact on the e-learning opportunities provided to students with disabilities and on educators' attitudes and responses towards making e-learning accessible for students with disabilities. It can affect whether educators adopt or reject the view that disability is a defining feature of a separate group of people and thus whether they adopt universal or individual approaches to designing learning experiences and whether they adopt mainstream or specialist models of support. Key figures and organizations within the e-learning and higher educational field are therefore seeking to redefine disability in a way that discourages individual practitioners from viewing disability as the problem that needs to be addressed and encourages them to see the barriers to education as the problem that needs to be addressed:

> The term disability has been re-defined as a mismatch between the needs of the learner and the education offered. It is therefore not a personal trait but an artefact of the relationship between the learner and the learning environment or education delivery. Accessibility, given this re-definition, is the ability of the learning environment to adjust to the needs of all learners. Accessibility is determined by the flexibility of the education environment (with respect to presentation, control methods, access modality, and learner supports) and the availability of adequate alternative-but-equivalent content and activities.
>
> (IMS Global Learning Consortium 2004a)

Chapter 3

E-learning, disability and higher education

Technology often fails to deliver results, but in the creation of e-learning environments, we are its driver. If we understand how the barriers to inclusion are being created in the profiligacy of spending on and acceptance of poor and narrow-minded design, then we can challenge our mindsets and apply consideration to the additional needs of disabled students.

(Neumann 2002: 18)

Introduction

E-learning is often used as a unifying term to describe the fields of online learning, web-based training and technology-delivered instruction. Whilst the term e-learning has superceded terms such as educational technology, learning technology or Information and Communications Technology (ICT), these are often incorporated into definitions of e-learning. Definitions of e-learning however, vary in their detail and specificity. Some definitions emphasize a wide range of technologies. For example, e-learning is defined by the UK government's Post-16 E-Learning Strategy Task Force as:

learning with the help of information and communications technology tools. These tools may include the Internet, intranets, wireless networking, PC (personal computer) based technologies, handheld computers, interactive TV and also e-technology to support traditional delivery, for example using electronic whiteboards and video conferencing.

(DfES 2002: 2)

Other definitions emphasize learning resources, including electronic information resources provided by libraries:

E-learning offers students and teachers the opportunity to engage in electronically mediated interaction with each other and with learning materials. Learning resources (print-based, graphical, audio-visual media) are largely made available electronically, either online or via CD ROM. Participants can access designated Websites or conduct their own search of the Internet.

(O'Connor 2000)

Whilst some definitions emphasize the learning process:

E-learning covers a broad range of activities which involve the embedding or adaptation of information technologies within the learning process. These technologies can be diverse as a Web-based Virtual Learning Environment (VLE), use of email or the use of dedicated software.

(Kelly *et al.* 2004)

Although mainstream definitions do not include assistive technologies within their definitions of e-learning, for the purposes of this book it is important to include assistive technologies within the e-learning remit or umbrella. This is because many students with disabilities can only access electronic material using a computer if they have assistive technologies (Banes and Seale 2002; Scherer 2004).

Assistive technology (AT) can be broadly defined as a 'broad range of devices, services, strategies, and practices that are conceived and applied to ameliorate the problems faced by individuals who have disabilities' (Cook and Hussey 1995: 5). There are a number of AT products that are used to obtain access to computer-based information. These products can range from low-tech to high-tech and consist of hardware (a physical piece of equipment such as a scanner) or software (a program that is installed on a computer that will provide a specific feature or expand a specific function). AT products are designed to meet the needs of people with various disabilities, including physical, learning, cognitive and sensory. Examples of ATs that can be used to meet the needs of students with hearing disabilities include digital audio recording of lectures (that may be streamed online) and captioning and subtitles to ensure that information provided in audio format is also provided in a visual medium (Wald 2002). Examples of assistive technologies that can meet the needs of students with visual impairments include screen magnification software and speech output systems consisting of a speech synthesizer and screen reading software (Neumann 2002). Draffan (2002) outlines AT for dyslexic students including speech output systems (text being read back through synthesized speech); spell-checkers and speech recognition software. Henderson (2002) describes the kinds of AT that students with physical disabilities may use including alternative input devices such as switches, head mice or voice and keyboard emulators.

The fact that e-learning can be employed in face-to-face campus settings or at a distance as learners connect from home, work or other public spaces such as libraries (Burgstahler 2002a; Burgstahler *et al.* 2004) gives it a flexibility that is very attractive when thinking about the needs of disabled students who may not wish to be dependent on single location resources or single media. However it is widely acknowledged that e-learning can have both a positive and a negative impact on the learning experience of students with disabilities:

> E-learning can be an enriching and stimulating environment within which learning can take place. While the pedagogy employed within a course or unit must be at the heart of the experience, the technology employed also has an impact, both negative and positive, on the experience for the student.
>
> (Kelly *et al.* 2004)

This chapter will explore the positive and negative impact of e-learning further and consider the impact this has on students with disabilities as well as the implications for future design and provision of e-learning.

The positive impact of e-learning on students with disabilities

The flexibility and adaptability of e-learning means that it has the potential to remove barriers to higher education for disabled students by facilitating access to inclusive and equitable education as well as access to subject specific aspects of the learning experience. One of the key consequences of the removal of barriers to inclusive and equitable education is that e-learning can also promote freedom, independence and individualized learning.

Flexibility and adaptability

E-learning is argued to be flexible and adaptable because it can suit varying learning styles, rates and communication formats and reduce issues of distance, transportation and physical access. In addition, electronic text, unlike printed text, can be read by individuals who are blind, vision impaired, dyslexic and by individuals who cannot hold a book or turn pages (Gay and Harrison 2001). The potential impact of such flexibility is huge:

> The new millennium heralds exciting opportunities to diversify the ways in which we offer education. We can now provide greater flexibility through online access to learning – when, where and how we do it. Breaking the shackles of tradition empowers all learners, including students with disabilities, as their diverse needs are increasingly accommodated in educational programs that are supported by information technology . . . Many people with disabilities have languished at the edge

of mainstream post-secondary education for a long time. They have coped with delays in obtaining timely services and learning materials in accessible formats. They have endured passing rather than higher grades because of low expectations. While e-learning is not a panacea, it has an enormous capacity to honour diversity in learning styles and capabilities if we become more enlightened about its potential uses for all learners. E-learning has the potential to progress people with disabilities from the outer edges of educational opportunity to the leading edge of educational innovation.

(O'Connor 2000)

Access to inclusive and equitable education

The language of e-learning in relation to disability contains powerful metaphors and images. For example, the metaphor of a bridge (Purcell and Grant 2004), gate or door (Klein *et al.* 2003) is often used to emphasize how e-learning can overcome barriers (Coombs 2000), break shackles (O'Connor 2000) and open up opportunities to facilitate inclusive and equitable education. In describing a text-based virtual reality environment called GrassRoots, Parsons (2000) writes:

> When students and adults access GrassRoots as well as all other aspects of their computers by using these advantages, it creates a rich environment where students compete on an equal footing. One might ask if computers continue to level the playing field for students and adults, whether today's 'learning disabilities' might disappear? Might adults who have significant disabilities be merged into the work force without fuss? GrassRoots is one small aspect of the Internet, but it typifies this new exciting trend toward equalization and inclusion.

Other writers also use the metaphor of the level playing field to emphasize the potentially equalizing effect of e-learning (Burgstahler *et al.* 2004; Banks *et al.* 2003; Evans 2002). While EASI (Equal Access to Software and Information) write:

> Just as there are physical barriers to people with disabilities accessing some buildings, there can be barriers to their accessing e-learning classes. Accessible e-learning means courseware and content that is designed to be accessible to the widest possible variety of computer operating systems and specialized applications removing needless barriers for students with disabilities and providing a level playing field to let them work and learn like everyone else.

(EASI n.d.)

Access to the learning experience

In addition to considering how e-learning can generally facilitate access to inclusive and equitable education, some researchers and practitioners have considered how e-learning can facilitate more specific access to learning such as access to subject specific notations and concepts and access to subject specific teaching and learning activities such as laboratory work. For example, Ferreira and Freitas (2004) describe the development of AudioMath, an AT designed to enable visually impaired people to access mathematical expressions contained in online documents. AudioMath can be connected to a text-to-speech engine, providing speech rendering of MathML (coded mathematical expressions of the World Wide web Consortium (W3C)). While Dixon (2004) describes the development of a 'Code Memory Diagram Animation Software Tool' designed to aid dyslexic computer programming students by expressing the temporal aspects of programming concepts. Dixon concludes:

> The software had the same effect for dyslexic students as for other students. However, this effect was to a greater degree. Hence the software acted as an equaliser – raising the performance of both students, but dyslexic students to a greater degree, thus closing the gap.
>
> (Dixon 2004: 7)

Colwell *et al.* (2002) describe the development of a remote experimentation system (the PEARL system), which can extend access to laboratory work for students who are unable to attend a conventional laboratory for a variety of reasons, such as disability, caring responsibilities or part-time study. They argue that the system can reduce the barriers to science for people with disabilities because:

> People with physical impairments may have difficulty with the use of standard laboratory equipment. People with hearing impairment will have difficulty in accessing oral laboratory instruction and communication with peers or tutors. People with learning difficulties may not be able to access written laboratory instruction. For people with visual impairment there may be safety issues associated with moving around a laboratory and manipulation of hazardous materials.
>
> (Colwell *et al.* 2002: 67)

Empowerment, independence and freedom

> Digital technology has the potential of transforming what is possible, particularly for people with disabilities, for whom technologies like the Web offer unprecedented access and empowerment.
>
> (Horton 2002: 1)

A major consequence of the removal of barriers to inclusive and equitable education is that e-learning can also promote freedom, independence and individualized learning for students with disabilities (Bain *et al.* 2002; Theofanos and Redish 2003) as well as empowerment (Schmetzke 2001; Horton 2002):

> Our participants told us over and over how the Internet has opened up a whole new world for them and has given them a sense of independence and freedom.
>
> (Thefanos and Redish 2003: 2)

The negative impact of e-learning on students with disabilities

Whilst there are clearly benefits of e-learning, it can also cause problems or difficulties leading some to describe e-learning as a double-edged sword (Byerley and Chambers 2002: 169; Katseva 2004):

> Technology is a double-edged blade: it can empower or it can disable. Technology empowers when it levels the playing field by rendering disabilities irrelevant in a given context. In this case, it fosters equality. However, technology disables when it is developed without considering accessibility because it marginalizes segments of the population
>
> (Katseva 2004)

Thus, there is a paradox. E-learning (including assistive technologies) can liberate, but it can also confine. E-learning confines and hinders freedom where barriers to equity and accessibility are not addressed and ignored (Schmetzke 2001; McInnery *et al.* 2003; Banks *et al.* 2003):

> Ironically, the very technology that has opened doors to unprecedented access is now at risk of closing them down again. With the evolution of the World Wide web into a complex and glamorous multimedia entity, designers, who are often ignorant of principles of accessible design, are likely to create access barriers that are unsurmountable . . . and that leave people with print disabilities stranded.
>
> (Schmetzke 2001: 36)

These barriers may therefore lead to experiences and feelings of inhibited opportunities (Pilling *et al.* 2004), lost independence and fettered freedom:

> The Internet has the potential to revolutionize disability access to information, but if we're not careful, we can place obstacles along the way that destroy that potential, and which leave people with disabilities just as discouraged and dependent upon others as before.
>
> (Bohman 2003a)

The second digital divide

Students in higher education are not normally considered to be affected by a 'digital divide' (Selwyn 2003; Selwyn and Gorard 2003) because they usually have high access to computers and the Internet (Steyaert 2005). However, for students with disabilities, even if they do have access to computers and the Internet, they may not necessarily have access to accessible e-learning opportunities. These students therefore are still 'have-nots' and may experience what Burgstahler (2002a) describes as the 'second digital divide'.

> But, even some people who are 'haves' with respect to computers and the Internet are still 'have-nots' when it comes to making full use of Internet resources. They are on the wrong side of a 'second digital divide'. This line separates people who can make full use of the technological tools available through their computer systems and the Internet, from those who cannot. This second digital divide is a result of the inaccessible design of many electronic resources.
>
> (Burgstahler 2002a: 420)

To gain an understanding of the impact of this second digital divide, we must understand the experiences of students with disabilities. Whilst students with disabilities face differing experiences when they reach inaccessible sites, a classic example of the barriers faced by disabled students, is that of those faced by students who are blind or visually impaired. For example, a student who is blind could encounter this type of message read to them by their screen reader coming into a 'class' website:

> [image], [image]. . ./syl/info/info.html,. . /wkgps /ctlg.html,. . /asmt/ asmt.html,. . online/crs.html.

It is doubtful that this student could participate in or benefit from such an experience. Rowland (2000) argues that if the web developer made simple accommodations to the site, the student would be able to hear what others see. Cook and Gladhart (2002) explain why the design of web pages can present barriers to students with a range of disabilities. Web pages divided into segments or frames can confuse software programs that translate text to voice. Graphics that have not been labelled with text will be read only as 'image' by the software reading the text on the screen and will deprive students of valuable content. Whilst web pages with a long list of hyperlinks crowded together can confuse a student with visual, cognitive, or motor disabilities. In essence, the second digital divide is caused by poor inaccessible design:

> The curse in the inclusion of computers into education is that frequently computer and software design needlessly creates new barriers to accessing information for students with disabilities. Speech synthesizers with screen reader software can give the blind person spoken output of what is on the computer display. However, the synthesizer can only speak text that is displayed on the screen. The increasing use of graphics leaves the synthesizer speechless. Yes, the newer screen reader software can recognize some standard graphics and connect words to them. If software designers would put text labels with their graphics, access would be simplified. Using redundant features in the original design can provide a better interface for everyone. Some people who are not blind respond better to text and some prefer pictures. Providing both makes the interface better for everyone.
>
> (Coombs 2000)

Conclusion

Although e-learning has great potential to facilitate an equitable learning experience for students with disabilities, that potential is not being fully met. Just as technology on its own is not a panacea, neither is e-learning. The potential of e-learning is highly influenced by its design and its designers. As Seale (2002: 84) argues:

> ... the potential that technologies hold to improve the accessibility and inclusivity of tertiary education for disabled students will be highly influenced by the staff that design, develop, use and support them.

If the staff in higher education do not design, develop and support accessible e-learning materials, then the gap between disabled and non-disabled students will widen and technology will outstrip its usefulness as a tool that can facilitate access to learning, curricula, independence and empowerment.

Chapter 4

Accessibility, e-learning and higher education

Even though talk about accessibility has become commonplace, never in history has there been as much confusion about accessibility as in this day and age. To say the least, the confusion has a lot to do with the meaning of accessibility and taking responsibilities for accessibility facilitation.

(Mirabella *et al.* 2004: 165)

Introduction

In attempting to define and understand accessibility and explore answers to the question 'access by what or whom?' this quote by Tim Berners-Lee, W3C Director and inventor of the World Wide Web is frequently referred to:

The power of the Web is in its universality. Access by everyone regardless of disability is an essential aspect.

Whilst this definition of accessibility is well known, one of the key problems is that it is cited so much that very few people have unpacked what it means and the implications of what it does and does not include. The first thing to notice regarding this definition is that it is quite general, focusing only on access to the web in its broadest sense and specifying just one criteria of accessibility: access by everyone. Other definitions broaden out this definition to be more specific about what they mean by web access and include additional criteria such as:

- Access by any technology (e.g. computer system, browser or specialized technology): Caldwell *et al.* 2004; Pearson and Koppi 2001;
- Access in any environment or location: Chisholm *et al.* 1999; HREOC 2002.

Some definitions also emphasize the positive consequences of designing for accessibility, including inclusion and the removal of barriers:

Accessible e-learning means courseware and content that is designed to be accessible to the widest possible variety of computer operating systems and specialized applications removing needless barriers for students with disabilities and providing a level playing field to let them work and learn like everyone else.

(EASI n.d.)

Other definitions hint at the need for flexibility, suggesting that accessibility is also about designing for future as well as current needs:

The overall goal is to create Web content that is perceivable, operable and understandable by the broadest possible range of users and compatible with a wide range of assistive technologies, now and in the future.

(Caldwell *et al.* 2004)

Accessibility in a general sense is therefore about removing barriers to participation and engagement in the online experiences and the degree to which someone can access an online resource regardless of their disability, technology or environment.

In addition to exploring answers to the question 'access by what or whom?' higher education practitioners have been challenged to address two more related questions:

- What aspects of e-learning need to be made accessible?
- What can help me make these aspects of e-learning accessible?

In attempting to answer the first question this chapter will explore those aspects of e-learning which have gained the most attention in accessibility research and practice literature. In attempting to answer the second question this chapter will explore the extent to which accessibility guidelines, standards and legislation are helping practitioners to make e-learning accessible.

What aspects of e-learning need to be accessible?

E-learning accessibility researchers and practitioners are considering every aspect of e-learning including web collaboration technologies (Koivunen 2004); mobile learning technologies such as personal digital assistants (Michael May 2003; Lagace 2004; Thompson 2004a) and ubiquitous computing (Vanderheiden 1997; Koivunen 2003). However most attention is currently focused on websites, courseware, library resources and the content contained within them.

Courseware

The term courseware is generally used to mean any software or application that contains instructional modules that deliver a collection of learning activities focused on a specific topic and includes: Virtual Learning Environments; Managed Learning Environments and Learning Management Systems. Courseware use is so prevalent in higher education that it has led some to conclude that it is probably the best place to start in terms of improving the accessibility of online learning experiences (Gay *et al.* 1999). A number of studies have explored the accessibility of courseware environments and although they have not been able to produce a league table of which environments are more accessible than others, they have highlighted a number of accessibility issues/problems, which vendors and others have started to address:

- absence of consistent and clear functions related to items within the courseware (Luke 2002);
- difficulties in navigating to and from the pages or links which are launched from the central courseware (Stiles 2001);
- lack of, or unclear, help messages (Luke 2002, Stiles 2001).

Current courseware systems are very teacher-centric, but moves towards electronic portfolio systems where there is a greater level of learner authoring of material as well as learner collaboration and participation is likely to raise a different set of accessibility issues that need to be thought through (Heath 2005). For example, complex accessibility issues are likely to arise when a document within an e-portfolio system needs to be edited at different times, by different people, all of whom have different access requirements.

Library resources (electronic reserves and digital collections)

Evidence suggests that the accessibility of library resources is an issue that needs to be addressed. For example, Horwath (2002) evaluated the accessibility of four proprietary online databases and found that the way they were designed made them difficult for disabled students to use. Poor design features included lack of explanatory text on screen to provide directions to users and use of frames. McCord *et al.* (2002) present the results of an assessment of eight web-based databases including: PubMed, OVID and Medline. They note that whilst images, tables, frames, forms, animations, graphics, colours and fonts make indexes easy to read and navigate they also serve as barriers for users with vision and mobility disabilities. Their accessibility assessment found that none of the databases were completely accessible to users of adaptive software tools. Schmetzke (2001, 2002a) conducted a review of 24 studies, which investigated the accessibility of websites, including ten library websites. He concluded that the average accessibility in the various library data sets ranges between 19 per cent and 75 per cent.

Text documents

The Portable Document Format (PDF) has become the standard for documents used and transferred on the Internet because it provides an electronic visual representation of paper documents. However, advocates for the blind and partially sighted argue that in some circumstances PDF files are either partially or completely unreadable to the visually impaired using assistive technology and that alternative, accessible formats must always accompany PDF files (Sajka and Roeder 2002; Konicek *et al.* 2003; Keegan 2004; Guarino-Reid and Pisocky 2005).

The main reason why PDF documents created using early versions of Adobe Acrobat (e.g. version 4.0 or below) were inaccessible to screen reader users is that in the process of producing the document and converting it to a PDF file, the underlying information on the structure of the document was not made explicit or 'tagged'. When Adobe released a plug-in for version 4.0 of Acrobat Reader, it enabled 'tagged' PDF files to be created from 'untagged' PDF files. A tagged PDF file has the page content contained in a logical read order; word boundaries explicitly identified and font encoding mapped to a standard font encoding. For Acrobat Reader Version 5.0, accessibility was integrated into the product without the need for a plug-in. However, Downie (2004) notes that files prepared with older versions could still not be read by screen readers and that the default setting for version 5.0 was not to allow access by screen readers.

Reid *et al.* (2005) describe how Adobe have engaged AccessWorld Solutions (AWS), the consulting division of the American Foundation for the Blind to assist in the development of Acrobat software for disabled users. The resulting features of the new generation of Acrobat software include an accessibility Wizard that assists in configuring Acrobat preferences for disabled users and a built in read-out-loud functionality that provides a text-to-speech feedback on systems without AT installed. Downie (2004) notes that under the right circumstances, PDFs are now largely accessible and can offer some advantages over other formats. However, this does largely depend on the PDF being properly constructed in the first instance.

Presentation applications

Presentation applications such as PowerPoint can be used within a lecture or seminar and they can also be exported to the web. Accessibility commentators usually focus on web-based PowerPoint but many of their design advice tips could also apply to lecture based use. Banks *et al.* (2005) note that when PowerPoint is exported to the web, 'the end result is an accessibility nightmare'. The basic problem in making PowerPoint presentations accessible, stems from the ability to add non-text elements such as images, audio narration, animation and video, which cause problems for people with disabilities. Banks *et al.* offer two strategies to improve accessibility. First, create an alternative text outline of the slides to export to the web or second, use a robust exporting tool such as Office Accessibility Wizard, PP2HTML Open Office or eTeach. Bleach and Zavoli (2005) offer some guidelines on making PowerPoint presentations accessible to people who are blind, including describing graphics and using sound transitions.

Multimedia

When considering the accessibility of multimedia, commentators focus on the need to provide captions and transcriptions for visual and auditory media (e.g. streamed audio and video) as well as making proprietary applications such as Flash and Java more accessible.

Captions allow web audio and video to be both perceivable to those who do not have access to audio and understandable to a wider audience (Smith 2005). Though captioning is primarily intended for those who cannot receive the benefit of audio, it has been found to greatly help those who can hear the audio, those who may not be fluent in the language in which the audio is presented, or those who may have learning/cognitive impairments. The process of capturing on-demand web multimedia is relatively straight forward and typically involves: acquiring a text version of any 'relevant' spoken content; converting text into a form understood by the media technology; generating synchronization information; and presenting the media and the captions to the user. With live or real-time multimedia, the process is a little more complicated as either a stenographer or speech recognition system is involved in acquiring the text version.

Two projects in the US are currently involved in developing tools to assist in the captioning process. WebAIM is developing a real-time, Web-based captioning program that easily and cost effectively allows live audio and video broadcasts on the web to be fully accessible to people who are deaf or hard of hearing. The National Centre for Accessible Media has played a major role in providing tools (e.g. MAGpie) to assist in synchronizing the streaming of video, audio, text captions and audio video description. Whilst in the UK, The Skills for Access Project (Stratford and Sloan 2005) has developed a website that contains a comprehensive guide to creating accessible multimedia for e-learning.

Early versions of Flash were considered to be relatively inaccessible, but more recent versions are considered to have improved considerably (Klein and Thompson 2005). Klein and Thompson outline two key advantages of Flash that mitigate some of its disadvantages. First caption files created for other players such as QuickTime or Windows Media Player can also be used with the Flash Player, saving development time. Second, additonal features such as text size and background colour can be configured in the caption file. Jordan (2005) argues that although developing accessible Flash content is challenging, it is an achievable goal.

Java applets are frequently used to add multimedia effects and interactivity to web pages. This has caused accessibility problems in that assistive technologies have not always been able to access or read these applets. Stiles (2001) notes that the common use of the Java programming language by software developers poses many problems for disabled users unless good practice is ensured by both VLE vendors and the producers of assistive software and hardware. O'Gribin (2004) outlines how accessibility of the Java platform has been increased by the development of four key applications including the Java Access Bridge which enables a single assistive technology to function effectively within the operating system 'world' and the Java 'world'. These utilities have enabled software vendors to improve accessibility by providing interfaces in non-traditional modalities and building new assistive technologies (Stiles 2001).

Guidelines for producing accessible e-learning

The most well known and perhaps influential accessibility guidelines are those developed by the Web Accessibility Initiative (WAI) of the World Wide Web Consortium (W3C). It is important to recognize however that other guidelines have been developed, many of which are more specific or local in their outlook compared to the generic, global nature of guidelines developed by the WAI.

The Web Content Accessibility Guidelines

The WAI has issued a number of guidelines including version 1 of the 'Web Content Accessibility Guidelines' (WCAG-1), the 'User Agent Accessibility Guidelines' and the 'Authoring Tool Accessibility Guidelines'. The most influential of these guidelines has been the WCAG-1.

Using the 'Unified Web Site Accessibility Guidelines' from the Trace Research and Development Centre, the WAI produced the first version of Web Content Authoring Guidelines in 1999 (Chisholm *et al.* 1999) The fourteen guidelines are underpinned by two central themes:

- ensuring graceful transformation (guidelines 1 to 11);
- making content understandable and navigable (guidelines 12 to 14).

A list of checkpoints is provided that explains how the guidelines apply to typical content development scenarios. The checkpoint definitions in each guideline explain how the guideline applies in typical content development scenarios. Each checkpoint also has a priority level assigned, based on the checkpoint's impact on accessibility:

- Priority One: A web content developer must satisfy this checkpoint. Otherwise, one or more groups will find it impossible to access information in the document. Satisfying this checkpoint is a basic requirement for some groups to be able to use web documents.
- Priority Two: A web content developer should satisfy this checkpoint. Otherwise, one or more groups will find it difficult to access information in the document. Satisfying this checkpoint will remove significant barriers to accessing web documents.
- Priority Three: A web content developer may address this checkpoint. Otherwise, one or more groups will find it somewhat difficult to access information in the document. Satisfying this checkpoint will improve access to web documents.

The guidleines also define 'levels of conformance', where at conformance level 'A': all priority one checkpoints are satisfied; at conformance level 'AA': all priority one and two checkpoints are satisfied and at conformance level 'AAA': all priority one, two, and three checkpoints are satisfied.

The WAI is now working on version 2 of their Web Content Guidelines (WCAG-2). The editors of this second version argue that the aim of the second version is the same as the first, that is to: explain how to make web content accessible to people with disabilities and to define target levels of accessibility (Caldwell *et al.* 2004). Incorporating feedback from WCAG-1, the working draft of version 2 attempts to apply guidelines to a wider range of technologies and to use wording that may be understood by a more varied audience. In order to facilitate understanding of the guidelines and to help people focus in on just the parts they need, the guidelines are presented as a set of interrelated documents. There are, therefore, three layers to the guidelines information: overview of design principles, guidelines and success criteria; technology-specific checklists and technology-specific application information. Success criteria for every guideline are categorized into three levels and the conformance requirements are similar to version 1.

Chisholm and Brewer (2005) argue that WCAG-2 differs from WCAG-1 by introducing a new priority scheme, defining testable success criteria, removing technology-specific information from the guidelines, providing testable information in checklists, techniques and test suites, and providing an overview of materials to orient users to the suite of documents. Slatin (2005) notes that because technology specific information is not in the guidelines themselves, the techniques documents and checklists that accompany WCAG-2 will play a vital role in helping web developers and others interpret and implement what is required for conformance. While WCAG-2 is abstract, the techniques documents that deal with specific technologies (HTML, CSS,

Scripting, SMIL, etc.) are highly detailed and particular. WebAim (n.d.a) argue that WCAG-2 focuses less heavily on the techniques for accomplishing accessibility and more on the principles of accessibility, therefore making it more flexible and encouraging developers to think through the process conceptually.

Guidelines for more specific purposes

The WCAG-1 have had a huge impact on the design process, particularly in relation to setting the benchmarks or perceived standards that designers should aspire to. However, a major criticism of the WCAG-1 is that they are too generic (particularly in relation to technologies). Therefore, despite the impact of the WCAG-1, other guidelines have been developed since their first publication. These guidelines appear to be attempting to be more: organization or company specific; service specific; disability specific; media specific or technology specific. Despite the supposed specificity of these guidelines, many refer explicitly to the WCAG-1. Some even include a guideline that states that designers must use the WCAG-1.

Organization or company specific guidelines

Several high profile organizations and companies have developed their own guidelines. For example, The Australian Capital Territory has developed a set of guidelines, which was endorsed by the Chief Minister's Office (Chief Ministers Department 2004). All seven government departments and forty or so agencies are bound by its mandatory or recommended requirements. The guidelines state that they must:

* maximize the accessibility of information and services;
* support all users irrespective of their physical limitations;
* provide a text-based version of the website;
* provide non-English versions of information and services;
* comply with the Web Content Accessibility Guidelines.

BBC New Media has stated its commitment to making its output as accessible as possible to all audiences in order to fulfil its public service mandate and to meet its requirements under the Disability Discrimination Act. To reinforce this, they have developed standards and guidelines to support accessibility. The guidelines are divided into five sections including: content production/coding; technical and design. Interestingly the guidelines state that the technical guidelines are 'in addition to WAI-1' (Hassell 2005). IBM also has a web accessibility checklist, consisting of 26 checkpoints, accompanied by rationale, techniques and testing. Whilst these guidelines do not explicitly reference WCAG-1, there is substantial overlap (IBM 2004).

Service specific guidelines

One particular service area that appears to have felt the need to produce more specific guidelines that match the service context is education. For example, Guenaga *et al.* (2004) argue that accessibility guidelines do not cover all the needs of accessible e-learning. As guidelines, they are very general and try to cover as many contexts, usages and target users as possible, so when they have to be applied to a concrete context such as education, it is difficult to find the way to do it.

Local examples of education specific guidelines include The Chancellor's Office of California Community Colleges (1999) access guidelines for distance educators working with students with disabilities and the Australian Vice Chancellor's Committee's (2004) 'Guidelines on information access for students with print disabilities'. The Californian guidelines consider a range of delivery media including print, audio and video conferencing as well as the web. In outlining recommendations for web design in distance education, the guidelines simply point designers to the WCAG-1. The Australian guidelines 'are presented as advice on good practice, with the aim of assisting individual institutions to meet the needs of students with print disabilities through strategies and arrangements which are appropriate to their local circumstances'.

A more global set of guidelines designed to cover education is that produced by the IMS Global Learning Consortium (IMS 2004b). The Consortium recognize that other guidelines exist but argue that they are offering specific guidelines for areas that these guidelines do not cover (e.g. specific guidelines for subjects such as Maths and Music). Interestingly, some of the advisors for the WCAG-1 are also advisors for the IMS Guidelines. The IMS guidelines are underpinned by six accessibility principles, the majority of which are implicit within the WCAG-1. Barstow (2003) considers that these guidelines provide a comprehensive overview of problems and harmonizing this work with other international accessibility standards initiatives is important.

Disability specific guidelines

The most common disability specific guidelines to be developed are those for dyslexia (Lockley 2001; Blankfield *et al.* 2002; Rainger 2003; Powell *et al.* 2004). Other disability specific guidelines include those developed for people who are ageing (Becker 2004). Powell *et al.* 2004 analysed both generic and dyslexia specific guidelines and drew out twelve recurrent themes, which they distilled into guidelines for designing online resources for dyslexic students, including:

- allow the user to control the font sizes and styles, and colours of the background and text;

- avoid strongly coloured or patterned backgrounds, as these can effectively obscure the text;
- use white space judiciously so that the text does not appear cluttered;
- use front-loaded hyperlink sentences, which provide a brief description of where a link will lead and why it is there.

Media specific guidelines

Most guidelines, whether generic (e.g. WCAG-1) or more specific (e.g. IMS Global Learning Consortium) include advice for dealing with particular media (e.g. text, images, etc.). However, some organizations such as TechDis in the UK (TechDis 2004) have chosen to distil out from these guidelines media specific advice on dealing with text, images, diagrams, graphs, audio, video, animation, content navigation and proprietary file formats. The advantage of such guidelines is that they are simple and user-friendly. The disadvantage of such guidelines is that they may be seen as less authoritative than those produced by larger organizations such as WAI (although it has to be said that the advice contained in both do not vary dramatically).

Technology specific guidelines

A major concern with the WCAG-1 was that they were very generic or abstract in relation to specific technologies or applications. This has required those interested in specific technologies to consider the extent to which the WCAG-1 covers the technologies in which they are interested, but more importantly, offers techniques specifically targeted at them. For example, Koivunen (2004) considers that while existing WAI guidelines are a good starting point for collaboration technologies, more targeted advice and techniques are needed.

Examples of technology specific guidelines include guidelines produced for designers of online courses such as WebCT (Pearson and Koppi 2001) and guidelines to facilitate access to web pages for users of alternative and augmentative communication aids (Nicolle et al. 2004; Poulson and Nicolle 2004).

Guidelines confusion

This review of accessibility guidelines has revealed a plethora of guidelines, and whilst some of them are clearly more influential than others, there is for some people a clear need for the community to come to a consensus and converge on one all-encompassing set of guidelines that are both commonsense and based on definitive research (Rowland 2004).

Given the impact and influence of guidelines such as WCAG-1, some have questioned how the guidelines have been derived and what their evidence base is. The WAI does have a well defined process for building consensus and obtaining comments from a range of stakeholders regarding the appropriateness and workability of their guidelines. However, there are some who consider that this process or approach is not as formal (and perhaps by inference rigorous) as those used by standards agencies such as the International Standards Organization (Reed *et al.* 2004). Akoumianakis and Stephanidis (1999), meanwhile, argue that accessibility guidelines are not experimentally valid and that there is a need for the development and maintenance of 'experienced-based accessibility guidelines as an organizational repository of evolutionary design wisdom'. Kelly *et al.* (2005), in a critique of the Web Content Accessibility Guidelines, also address concerns regarding the extent to which the guidelines are based on 'real world experiences'. The organization, service, disability, media and technology specific guidelines described in this chapter could perhaps be viewed as examples of more 'real world' or 'experienced-based' guidelines.

To add to the debate and confusion over which guidelines should be used and whether they have any validity, many are interpreting the WCAG as standards that are somehow enforceable. For example, Sampson-Wild and Burmeister (2001: 127) note that 'Though national standards exist . . . the dominant standards in the area of accessibility for the disabled have been and continue to be set by the international World Wide Web Consortium.' Many organizations and governments are using the WCAG-1 as a benchmark by which to judge levels of acceptable accessibility, but accessibility standards separate from the WCAG-1 do exist, and it is worth exploring these further.

Accessibility specifications and standards

Heath (2003) suggests that learning technology standards fall into two camps. Those that standardize existing practices and those that enable new practices. He considers that accessibility standards will fall into the second camp in that they will enable technology to be used in ways that can improve participation and lessen social exclusion. A number of accessibility standards exist or are in the process of being formulated. For example:

- The International Organisation for Standardisation Technical Specification for software accessibility of human computer interfaces (Gulliksen and Harker 2004);
- The Instructional Materials Accessibility Act of 2002 (IMAA) requires the US Department of Education to develop Instructional Materials Accessibility Standards that will define standards for electronic textbooks (Waddell 2004);
- The Disability Rights Commission has commissioned the British Standards Institute to produce a Publicly Available Specification (PAS). Entitled 'PAS 78: Guide to good practice in designing accessible websites', the

PAS will describe the standards to which websites should conform but will not be designed to replace any existing guidance, such as that developed by the WAI.

There are however two prominent accessibility standards that are specific to e-learning and education: the IMS Global Learning Consortium Standards and the Learning Federation Accessibility Specification for Content Development.

IMS Global Learning Consortium specifications and standards

The IMS Global Learning Consortium has two accessibility related specifications:

- IMS ACCMD: AccessForAll Meta-data (IMS 2004a);
- IMS ACCLIP: Accessibility for Learner Information Package (IMS 2003).

AccessForAll Meta-data

The AccessForAll Meta-data specification is intended to make it possible to identify resources that match a user's stated preferences or needs. These preferences or needs would be declared using the IMS Access for Learner Information Package specification. The needs and preferences addressed include the need or preference for alternative presentations of resources, as well as methods of controlling resources, equivalents to the resources themselves and enhancements or supports required by the user. The specification provides a common language for identifying and describing the primary or default resource and equivalent alternatives for that resource.

Accessibility for Learner Information Package

The Accessibility for Learner Information Package defines two new sub-schemas for the IMS Learning Information Package that define a means whereby accessibility preferences and learner accommodations can be specified. A learning system built according to the Accessibility for Learner Information Package specification will allow users with disabilities as well as users with situational challenges, such as a noisy environment to customize and personalize settings if the standard settings of a learning system are not ideal for them. Some of the preferences that might be chosen by learners include:

- Display: e.g. learners can indicate that they would prefer materials in a format that can be read by a screen reader;

- Control: e.g. learners can save settings for voice recognition, onscreen keyboards, or other input devices;
- Content: e.g. learners can choose to 'read' a video (through captioning) rather than or in addition to hearing it.

Rothberg *et al.* (2005) provide a useful overview of new learning tools that are using the IMS specifications to provide flexible interfaces and to automatically deliver appropriate content for each learner. In the summer of 2005 the IMS specifications were put forward to the International Standards Organization (ISO) and a first public draft of the standard: 'Individualized Adaptability and Accessibility in E-Learning Education and Training', which builds on these IMS specifications, was made available for comment. The ISO is also working with the International Electrotechnical Commission (IEC) to produce a multi-part standard that provides a common framework to describe and specify learner needs and preferences on the one hand and a corresponding description of the learning resources on the other hand so that individual learner preferences and needs can be matched with the appropriate user interface, tools and learning resources.

The Learning Federation Accessibility Specification for Content Development

The Learning Federation (2003) Accessibility Specification for Content Development describes accessibility principles, requirements and guidelines for creating accessible online curriculum content for the Learning Federation (an initiative of state and federal governments of Australia and New Zealand).

The accessibility specification is part of the initiative's suite of quality assurance specifications. These specifications are all embedded within the larger context of educational soundness. Educational soundness relates to providing online curriculum content in appropriate interactive multimedia formats to meet pedagogical aims. Educational soundness is the major design principle underlying the development of online curriculum content by the initiative.

The accessibility specification will be used to assess whether online curriculum content conforms to the: principles of legislative compliance; appropriate learning object design; access device independence; flexibility of operation and presentation; communication of accessibility information with content and equitable user system requirements. The Learning Federation has also defined four high-level accessibility user profiles for: vision impairment; hearing impairment; physical impairment and cognitive impairment. These accessibility profiles are high-level categorizations of groups of learners that are used within content design and development to guide appropriate learning object design. The profiles are used during content development in two ways:

- to determine whether a learning design can support a particular accessibility profile, or whether an equivalent or alternative realization is required;
- to indicate the accessibility of content to the profiled group of users via metadata.

Additionally, design requirements and guidelines for supporting these profiles are under development.

A common standard or benchmark?

This review of accessibility specifications and standards has revealed that in addition to the plethora of guidelines, there is a plethora of standards. The resulting confusion has led many to conclude that commonality and convergence is required. Whilst there are slow-moving, but determined efforts to deliver a common standard, the influence and impact of such efforts will be affected in part by how individuals and nations choose to interpret standards and guidelines. As Russell (2003: 244) argues:

> In order to create true accessibility across the Internet a common standard needs to be employed. The WCAG are the nearest approximation of such a standard but individual nations have added to or manipulated these guidelines with the result of modifying the definition of 'accessibility'.

One key factor that may influence how guidelines and standards are interpreted is the way that different national laws choose to interpret them.

Legislation

Legislation in a number of countries has influenced the accessibility design practices of both education and non-education organizations. In some cases there is evidence that legislation in one country (e.g. US) is influencing the work of practitioners in other countries (e.g. Witt and McDermott 2002).

United States legislation

In the United States there are three piece of legislation that could have an impact on whether an online site or service is accessible:

- Americans with Disabilities Act of 1990 (US Department of Justice 1990);
- Section 504 of 1973 Rehabilitation Act (US Department of Labour 1973a);
- Section 508 of the 1973 Rehabilitation Act, as amended by the Workforce Investment Act of 1998 (US Department of Labour 1973b).

The Americans with Disabilities Act (ADA) was created to provide individuals with disabilities the right to obtain an equal education and equal access to all programs. It was also designed to limit barriers that prevent individuals with disabilities from accessing opportunities that are available to people without disabilities. As a result of this act, organizations, public agencies and educational institutions that receive federal funds are required to make available information accessible.

Section 504 of the Rehabilitation Act was designed so that any individual with a disability cannot be denied access because of their disability to any educational activities that receive federal funding. Section 504 also stipulates that programs which receive federal assistance be free of barriers and provide reasonable accommodations, such as the use of assistive technologies.

Section 508 requires federal agencies to purchase electronic and information technology that is accessible to employees with disabilities, and to the extent that those agencies provide information technology to the public, it too shall be accessible by persons with disabilities. Section 508 was originally included in an amendment to the Rehabilitation Act in 1986, with the requirement that the federal government provide accessible technology to employees and to the public. But the 1986 version provided no guidance for determining accessibility of information technology and there were no enforcement procedures. The 1998 amendment addressed both these issues.

Section 508 required that an 'Access Board' establish standards for accessibility. To do that the Board set up the Electronic and Information Technology Access Advisory Committee (EITAAC) in October of 1998. The EITAAC was composed of representatives from industry, academics, government and disability advocacy organizations. The group proposed standards for accessible electronic and information technology that finally became the heart of the Section 508 enforcement in June of 2001.

Both the ADA and Section 504 apply directly to higher education institutions in that they are prohibited from discriminating against individuals with disabilities (Banks et al. 2003; Johnson et al. 2003). There is a difference of opinion however, about whether Section 508 applies to higher education or not. Johnson et al. (2003) argue that Section 508 does not apply to higher education. However, individual institutions of higher education may have chosen to adopt some or all of the Section 508 standards. Furthermore, Johnson and Ruppert (2002) note that some institutions of higher education believe they must comply with Section 508 (e.g. University of Wisconsin, Maddison) whilst others do not.

Canadian legislation

In Canada there is no specific accessibility legislation relating to online sites and services. Organizations must, however, adhere to a number of government-wide statutes, policies and standards when providing services and information online. These include the Access to Information Act, the Communications Policy for the Government of Canada and the Use of Electronic Networks Policy. However, in Canada, federal websites must comply with the Treasury Board Secretariat's Common Look and Feel (CLF) guidelines, which were first approved in 2000. The CLF guidelines are based on the checkpoints contained with the WCAG-1 and require that Level 2 priorities be met. Within Canada the CLF guidelines are now commonly perceived as and referred to as standards (O'Grady and Harrison 2003).

Australian legislation

In Australia, Section 24 of the Disability Discrimination Act 1992 (DDA) makes it unlawful for those providing goods or services to discriminate against another person on the grounds of their disability. The Act empowers the Australian Human Rights and Equal Opportunity Commission (HREOC) to issue advisory notes or guidelines, in order to assist organizations to discharge their responsibilities under the Act. Whilst the Act does not specifically mention online services or websites, HREOC (2002) stress that the provision of information and online services through the web is a service covered by the DDA.

In interpreting the guidance from HREOC, Arch and Burmeister (2003) consider that while in Australia it may not be illegal to have an inaccessible website, it is illegal to discriminate; thus an inaccessible website may not be discriminatory if alternative, equivalent, access to the information or service is provided.

The Ministerial Council on Education, Employment, Training and Youth Affairs has been working since the mid-1990s towards 'Disability Standards for Education', which interpret the DDA for the education sector. The Standards were tabled in March 2005 and are expected to come into effect shortly after. The effect of the standards will be to give students with disabilities the same right to education and training opportunities as students without disabilities. This includes the right to comparable access to services and facilities and the right to participate in education and training. No specific mention is made, however, of standards for the provision of online learning.

European Union legislation

Individual countries within the European Union such as Portugal (Abecasis and Fernandes 2002) and the United Kingdom (Wilder 2002) have developed discrimination legislation that is having some impact on accessibility practices. On a larger scale the European Union has launched initiatives that may impact on the practices of its member countries in the future (Ball 2002; Waddell and Hardy 2004). For example, the European Commission has examined the application of legislation in member states to Internet accessibility and concluded that the current patchwork of member states' laws was weak (European Commission 2002). It recommended developing specific legislation at both European and national levels. More recently, in 2005, the European Commission also launched a public consultation on how best to make computers, mobile phones and websites accessible to the widest number of people, including the disabled and the elderly. One of its suggestions is to pass new legislation. The documents note that several EU member states already have e-accessibility related laws, and that there are indications that harmonizing the relevant technical requirements across the EU could help to make these laws a more powerful driver for change, while at the same time promoting interoperability and preventing market fragmentation.

UK legislation

The two key pieces of legislation in the UK that may be applied to accessibility are the Disability Discrimination Act (DDA) (1995) and the Special Educational Needs and Disability Act (SENDA) (2001). The Disability Discrimination Act (1995) was introduced to end the discrimination that many disabled people face. The main focus of the Act was the employment of disabled people and their access to goods and services. However, the Act did affect higher education institutions to the extent that in their capacity as 'service providers' they had to make reasonable adjustments in the way they provided their services to make them accessible to disabled people. There are also provisions in the Act that state that 'access to and use of means of communication' and 'access to and use of information services' are both examples of services that would be covered.

The 2001 Special Educational Needs and Disability Act was brought in as an amendment to the 1995 DDA and is being implemented as Part Four of that Act. From 1 September 2002, the Act made it an offence for educational institutions to discriminate against a disabled person by treating him or her less favourably than others for a reason relating to their disability. Discrimination will be considered to have occurred if a disabled person is treated less favourably for a reason relating to their disability than a non-disabled person to whom that reason does not apply or if there is a failure to make 'reasonable adjustments without which the disabled person is placed at a substantial disadvantage'.

In 2002, the Disability Rights Commission (DRC 2002) published a new, revised Code of Practice which provided detailed advice on the way the DDA law should work. It also provided practical examples and tips. Whilst the DDA does not make any explicit reference to e-learning or web accessibility, the Code of Practice makes express reference in two key areas. First, in listing the services covered by the Act, the DRC includes:

- distance learning;
- independent learning opportunities such as e-learning;
- learning equipment and materials such as laboratory equipment, computer facilities, class handouts, etc;
- libraries, learning centres and information centres and their resources;
- information and communication technology and resources.

Second, the DRC offers two e-learning examples of reasonable adjustment including: producing all teaching handouts in electronic form thus ensuring that they can easily be converted into large print or put into other alternative formats and introducing new procedures to ensure that all notes put on the intranet meet established guidelines to ensure there is no conflict with specialist technologies.

Legislation and standards

Some of the legislation relating to accessibility has felt it necessary to establish accessibility standards (internal benchmarks), while others have been content to refer to accessibility standards that exist outside of the legislation (external benchmarks).

Internal benchmarks

Section 508 in the US is the most prominent legislation to create its own standards or benchmarks. Section 508 required that the Access Board establish standards for accessibility. With the help of an advisory committee the Board proposed standards for accessible electronic and information technology, which have been at the heart of the enforcement of Section 508 since June 2001. Eleven of the 16 Section 508 standards are drawn directly from WCAG-1. Five of the 508 standards do not appear in the WCAG-1 checkpoints and require a higher level of access or give more specific requirements. On the other hand, there are four Priority 1 WCAG-1 checkpoints that were not adopted by the Access Board.

Paolucci (2004) argues that the emergence of this new standard, while welcome in one sense, also establishes a potentially confusing alternative. Certainly, the WAI has found it necessary to produce a document that maps the relationship between the two evolving 'standards' and shows how and where they are similar and where they are different.

External benchmarks

Jahankhani et al. (2002) highlight the fact that neither the UK legislation nor the DRC code of practice actually define what an accessible website is or give guidance on creating one. This means that an external benchmark must be found. Wilder (2002), McCarthy (2001) and others point to the WCAG-1 as a suitable benchmark, but as yet this has not been tested in the UK courts.

The Australian DDA also does not specify standards for web accessibility. Instead, it empowers the HREOC to give guidance on standards. HREOC's advisory note concerning Section 24 of the DDA endorses WCAG–1 as the standard for web accessibility in Australia (HREOC 2002). In addition to these guidelines, HREOC points designers and authors to a range of tools and resources to choose from in meeting accessibility goals including the Ausinfo Guidelines for Commonwealth Information Published in Electronic Formats. Arch and Burmeister (2003) comment on how the international guidelines and standards have taken precedence over the national guidelines and contrasts this to the US, which has developed local accessibility regulations (Section 508).

The European Committee for Standardization has been working towards a European quality kite mark for web content accessibility and consultation workshops have been held to define the certification process. Whilst it appears (but is by no means certain) that WCAG will be used as the benchmark, what is currently uncertain is for which version (1 or 2) the quality mark will be awarded. Evidence from initial consultations suggested some confusion and lack of clarity, but the work was nevertheless completed by March 2006.

What is the impact of accessibility guidelines and standards on current e-learning in higher education?

Despite (or perhaps because of) the wide array of accessibility guidelines and standards that exist, there does not appear to be a marked improvement in the accessibility of online material. In fact there is some evidence to suggest that the accessibility of public websites have worsened over time. For example, Hackett *et al.* (2004) used the Internet Archive's 'Wayback Machine' to retrospectively analyse a random sample of 240 archived websites from 1997–2002 for accessibility. Using a 'web accessibility barrier' formula, results showed that random websites had become progressively inaccessible through the years, whilst the complexity of the websites had increased.

The relative inaccessibility of website and online services of non-educational institutions such as government departments and commercial companies is well documented (Duchateau *et al.* 2002; Lazar *et al.* 2003; Lemon and Wilcock 2003; Opitz *et al.* 2003; Ritchie and Blanck 2003; SciVisum 2004; DRC 2004). A similar story appears to exist for higher educational institutions. Kurniawan (2000) investigated the accessibility of web information resources for students with disabilities of 120 academic sites from UK, US, Australia and Canada. He found 48 per cent of sites were inaccessible but that UK and US websites were more accessible than Australian and Canadian sites. Table 4.1 presents a summary of a number of studies that have surveyed the accessibility of academic institutions websites and their main findings. Although accessibility levels vary, there are trends in terms of the most common accessibility errors: in particular providing text equivalents. Whilst this is a common error that renders sites inaccessible according to evaluation tools such as Bobby (see chapter 7), it is an error that is relatively quick and easy to fix (Spindler 2004; Flowers *et al.* 2001).

Conclusions

All the accessibility guidelines, standards and legislation outlined in this chapter have been developed with the aim of changing practice. In some cases the aim has been to force practice to change through conformance and compliance. Yet the evidence suggests that practice is not changing. There are a number of possible reasons why practice is not changing, including:

- confusion over which guideline and/or standard to adopt;
- confusion over the difference between guidelines and standards;
- difficulties in interpreting and applying guidelines and standards.

The current strong push towards global standardization is in part an attempt to relieve some of the confusion and difficulties. But standardization will not solve what I believe is at the heart of the problem: the tension between flexibility and rigidity. One of the main reasons why current guidelines and standards are not an overwhelming success is that they are frequently 'sold' as providing a black-and-white checklist of things to do that will guarantee accessibility. The reality is often different. What practitioners are finding is that such checklists cannot always be followed rigidly. Frequently, practitioners are required to make judgements based on the local contexts in which they are working and the results of those judgements introduce a flexibility and adaptability into accessibility practices. Such flexibility and adaptability may be interpreted as a divergence from the 'norm' that standards and guidelines require. However, students with disabilities are a widely divergent group and it does not appear logical that there will be a 'one right way' to meet the e-learning needs of such a diverse group of people.

Accessibility related legislation is useful because it requires us to address the needs of disabled students. Accessibility guidelines are useful because they provide recommendations of good practice. Accessibility standards are useful because they offer a set of benchmarks or rules against which to judge our practice. What would also be useful to practitioners however is access to detailed accounts of how other practitioners have interpreted the legislation, guidelines and standards and the different judgements they have made regarding the implementation of these.

Table 4.1 Overview of the results of web accessibility surveys in higher education

Study	Country	Number and type of sites	Level of reported accessibility	Common accessibility problems
Sams and Yates-Mercer (2000)	UK	Web sites of 10 University lecturers	Half of sites failed meet WCAG Priority Level 1	Lack of alternative text descriptions to images
Sloan *at al.* (2002)	UK	11 University sites	Overall level of accessibility of the subject sites was reasonable	Failure to provide equivalent alternatives to graphical information Inconsistent and inefficient navigational systems
Kelly (2002a)	UK	162 University Home Pages (entry points)	4 University entry points had no errors at WCAG Level 1 or 2; 70 entry points had no Priority 1 errors	'In a number of cases, pages which appear to have a high degree of accessibility are, in fact, inaccessible.'
Witt and McDermott (2004)	UK	80 University sites that claimed that claimed Bobby Priority 1 compliance	Only 58; 75% of these sites meet the relevant criteria for WCAG Priority 1 compliance	'There is a misunderstanding of the requirements necessary to create accessible websites.'
Patterson and Ellis 2002	Australia	42 University websites	The majority 'lacked basic site characteristics'	Consistency of navigation
Alexander 2003a	Australia	45 tertiary education sites	98% failed to meet the most basic (WCAG 'A') standards for Web accessibility	Lack of text equivalents
Lamshed *at al.* (2003)	Australia	65 TAFE websites (vocational and educational training)	80% of the websites failed to meet WCAG Priority Level 1. Nearly all sites failed to meet Priority Levels 2 and 3	Lack of site maps Poor navigation structures Non-compatibility with browsers such as Lynx Problems when images switched off

Flowers et al. (2001)	US	253 community college home pages	Only 23% were determined to be 'accessible'	Not providing alternative text for all images, image map hot spots and applets
Flowers et al. (2002)	US	120 Counselling Education Programs	81.7% of home pages had 'accessibility problems'	Not providing alternative text for all images and hot-spots
Schmetzke (2002a)	US	Library home pages of 56 universities	53% were Bobby approved compared to 59% in 2000	Images and image map hotspots without alternative text
Spindler (2004)	US	188 home pages of college and university libraries	79/188 found to be 'accessible'	Failure to provide alternative text for at least some of the images

Part 2

Surveying the scene

Chapter 5

Accessing e-learning

The student's perspective

> I think the dyspraxia does make a big difference in terms of how easy it is to use something that appears complex. Just logging onto the VLE . . . the first few times you use it, it is a particularly daunting experience . . . when different stuff is posted in different places all the time, that is a big hindrance. But I think that's a hindrance that would apply to anybody, but having dyspraxia just makes it particularly difficult.
>
> (ALERT 2005: 8)

Introduction

From a disabled student's perspective, the issues that are probably important to them in relation to e-learning are:

* Will the e-learning tools and environments I am expected to use as part of my studies be accessible to me?
* Will lecturers, support staff and others respond positively to my needs in relation to facilitating my access to e-learning?

In order to demonstrate why the answers these questions are important to students with disabilities this chapter will explore and describe the disabled student's experience of e-learning, using both primary and secondary sources of evidence. The primary sources of evidence will be personal accounts (narratives) of higher education as it relates to e-learning, computing and technology. The secondary sources of evidence will be research studies that have surveyed the needs and experiences of students with disabilities.

Personal accounts of disabled students' experience of e-learning that are published in academically recognized journals and books, are extremely rare. One example is an article published by Julie Perks in the *British Journal of Educational Technology* (Perks 2003). Julie, a dyslexic student at Staffordshire University, describes in her own words, her experiences of using voice recognition software called 'Dragon Naturally Speaking' in her exams:

'All caps', I told the machine, and dictated the question I had chosen. I gazed fixedly at the screen in front of me, the peppermint green background normally serves to pin the shimmering letters of words in place and hold them flat. But I had never tried to look at a computer screen in an exam before and could barely make out one word from another amidst the sort of three-dimensional distortions that might in Gestalt terms be described as exaggerated figure ground reversals. Gradually I read the words I had dictated by catching a part of the word or a whole word at their optimum point of discernability like a series of snap shots, or like trying to record the exact shape of a wave without the aid of a camera, one wave then the next and so on until a picture had been built up. The picture looked good. I had the title for my first essay and as far as I could tell the Dragon had written exactly what I had dictated.

(Perks 2003: 103)

The majority of personal accounts that exist in the academic domain are usually in the form of case examples or case studies, produced by publicly funded teaching and learning developments. Examples include:

- The ALERT (Accessibility in Learning Environments and Related Technologies) project: <http://www.dur.ac.uk/alert/>;
- The DART (Disabilities Academic Resource Tool) project: <http://dart.lboro.ac.uk/case.html>;
- The Skills for Access project: <http://www.skillsforaccess.org.uk/>.

These accounts are highly edited and de-contextualized so they vary in the extent to which they are written in the voice of the student and the extent to which personal issues such as feelings, thoughts and attitudes concerning a particular experience are addressed. They are however, written in a style and language to which academics are used:

Dave values on-line resources in two specific ways. They support his preparation for lectures through research and also specific disability support websites help him come to terms with his disability. Paper serves the simple objective of retaining information in an accessible format. His condition has compromised his ability to remember and recall factual information. Thus bullet point summary handouts are a great help to him.

(Dave, DART Project Case Study)

Some personal accounts of disabled students' experiences of learning are available in non-academic domains such as websites owned by public service organisations:

- SKILL: National Bureau for Students with Disabilities: <http://www.skill.org.uk/info/case_studies/index.asp>.
- OUCH: BBC Disability Magazine: <http://www.bbc.co.uk/ouch/lifefiles/student/>.

These accounts are less mediated or edited and tend to focus on student life in general. Although e-learning is not a central focus of these accounts, they can give a useful insight into how computing and technology impacts on everyday student life:

> Then in the afternoon, I had a surprise awaiting me in the computing lab. Unfortunately, it wasn't all that pleasant. It seems that today's practical isn't programming, but involves running an electronic circuit simulation. This particular software turned out to be inaccessible to any kind of screen reading software I cared to try with it, and so I missed out on that. However, the underlying learning objective is merely to become familiar with the construction of truth tables (kind of like logic construction diagrams), so I'm going to try and suss it out through looking at the PowerPoint slides the lecturer has given me.
>
> (Darren, BBC Ouch Diary Entry)

This chapter will use both primary and secondary sources of evidence to identify and report on the positive and negative experiences of e-learning from the perspective of students with disabilities studying in higher education.

Positive experiences of e-learning

Evidence from both primary and secondary sources suggest that, for students with disabilities, the positive experiences of e-learning fall into three categories:

- use and availability of generic technology;
- use and availability of specialist technology;
- provision of electronic or non-electronic 'alternatives'.

Use and availability of generic technology

Students with disabilities value the ability to be able to use and benefit from generic technologies such as campus computers, network access in student accommodation, laptops and email.

Campus computers

> I was very impressed with the support structure at the university for a number of reasons. Firstly, the fact that all the computers on campus are

networked which makes studying much more accessible for someone with my disability as they all have screen-reading software installed on them. Furthermore, in certain laboratories Braille translation software, as well as scanning facilities, are connected to the computers.

(Andy, SKILL Case Study)

Network access in student accommodation

(With the VLE) when the library shuts I can still be in my room and I can check my emails and things in the comfort of where I've got like, a back support and things. I've got a special kneeling chair that gives my back a break and I can't use that in a library facility so it's really easy to have (the VLE) straight into your room, being able to contact people straight from your bedroom.

(ALERT student 1)

Laptops

My equipment came today! Almost everything arrived, and the delivery men were either on time or early! It's brilliant! I am still waiting for the disk drive for my laptop (I am getting an external drive of some type, so that it cuts down on the weight of the laptop I am actually carrying around). My room was a sea of brown cardboard boxes! I feel all set up now, and it was such a lovely feeling to be able to return the Alphasmart to Disability Services! I'm sure they'll be glad to be seeing less of me!. . . Laptop has got a lot of use today. The battery seems to last about four hours, which was perfect for today, but I guess it means I will need to use a combination of techniques on days like Thursdays, when I have seven hours timetabled.

(Ruth, BBC Ouch Diary Entry)

Email

The Information Technology Department, in conjunction with many other administration and disability bodies, also provides a high level of support in terms of course information. Students of modern languages have much of their semester's work pre-prepared and e-mailed to them during Fresher's Week. This is mainly due to much of the material being difficult to scan using the latest version of Kurzweil 1000 – scanning software widely used by visually impaired students on campus. For other subjects, students are given photocopied material to scan, or electronic versions of documents where possible . . . With regards to admission and feedback on assignments I use e-mail. I find this is a lot easier than printing work off and handing in the wrong assignment by mistake. All my tutors are more than happy to receive work in this way. This is particularly impressive as nearly all faculties have an anonymous marking scheme, which I am glad my particular departments are flexible about.

(Andy, SKILL)

The value disabled students place on being able to access generic technology is influenced by the extent to which it enhances their independence, facilitates their learning needs and enables them to use their additional specialist technology. The accounts from students are also useful in terms of demonstrating that students with disabilities do not necessarily rely solely on 'home' specialist equipment. For some students however 'home equipment' is an important part of their technology use. In a survey of students with disabilities attending post-secondary settings throughout Australia Leung *et al.* (1999) found that whilst 25 per cent of students used a campus computer daily and that campus computers were used weekly during the academic year by 20 per cent of students, daily use of campus computers was significantly lower for students who had home computers. They concluded that since a little less than half of student respondents used a campus computer daily or weekly, usage by students who have accessible equipment at home becomes an important aspect of the use of technology.

Use and availability of specialist technology

Findings from a study by Fichten *et al.* (2000) indicate that the overwhelming majority of students with disabilities use computers and the Internet, but 41 per cent need some type of specialist technology or adaptation to use computers effectively. Wimberley *et al.* (2004) conducted a study to identify barriers encountered by students with learning disabilities when attempting to access education-based information technology. Student comments clearly indicated that assistive technology had removed barriers for them that had impeded their academic success. Fichten *et al.* (1999) evaluated the views and opinions of both students with disabilities and of Disabled Student Services Officers concerning the use of computers in post-secondary education. Asuncion *et al.* (2002) reported on findings on computer technology needs and concerns of 725 Canadian college and university students with a wide range of disabilities. Both studies report two main reasons for what they perceived to be an important trend in cross-use or multiple use of assistive technologies:

- many students have more than one disability and therefore require technologies that can adapt to a range of needs;
- students find that they can benefit from technologies that were not specifically designed for their own disabilities. For example, screen readers are not only used by those who are blind, but by those who have a learning disability such as dyslexia.

Examples of specialist technologies include text enlargement tools, screen readers and note-taking machines.

Text enlargement tools

The specialised equipment and advice available at the college was very useful. I started to use Zoom text and CCTV and this enabled me to learn word processing and other computer applications. My next challenge was to take on a work placement and I worked towards this with help from the careers adviser attached to Edstart. I was lucky enough to be placed with Ethicon, one of the partner companies in the programme, and part of the Johnson & Johnson organisation. I worked in sales and marketing and was involved in several projects. Zoom text and CCTV were made available by the college and I was able to practice my new skills in a real office. My duties included word processing, faxing, photocopying, joining in meetings and being part of the launch of exciting new products. I never felt alone on the placement, as I knew I had the full support of the staff at college.

(Sharon, SKILL)

Screen readers

Any paper resources have to be provided in an electronic format to be of any use to Chris. Interestingly, Chris comments that online resources are not usually as helpful as one would imagine. The problem is that the prevalence of graphics on home pages hinders the use of screen readers – a text-only version is what is needed to overcome the difficulty but if the designer of the web page has not included this option, the resource is lost. Chris praises the help he has received from the specialist Faculty Librarian who has arranged easier access to certain web resources using two particular applications known as Jaws and Kurtzweil which both take the text shown on screen and read it out aloud by means of an electronic voice. Chris comments that the voice is rather artificial, more 'dalek' than human, but it is something that 'one gets used to'.

(Chris, DART)

Note taking machines

All week I have been typing notes on my Alphasmart in lectures, and I had been starting to worry that I actually had rather a lot of information on this little machine, so I decided the time had come to pay another visit to disability services. To take the information off the Alphasmart you plug its lead into the keyboard port on the back of a PC. Unfortunately it doesn't seem to work with my PC, so I have to go and bother them every time I want to transfer notes onto a floppy disk. There were 13 pages of notes when I finished! I was going to keep a paper copy of all my notes, because I don't trust computers in the slightest, but maybe I will just keep a back-up! It will cost me a fortune in paper and ink otherwise!

(Ruth, BBC Ouch)

A range of studies have identified the need to support and train students in their use of specialist technologies as well as the use of computers generally (Hall and Tinklin 1998; Grott 1999; Leung *et al.* 1999; Riemer-Reiss and Wacker 1999; Roer-Stier 2002; Goodman *et al.* 2002). Roer-Strier (2002) and Grott (1999) focus on how peer support can enable students with disabilities to improve their confidence and competence levels with regards to technology use. Roer-Strier (2002) reports on efforts at Hebrew University to support the technology needs of students with learning disabilities. On the basis of student needs identified through a first-year evaluation, the school opened a special computer course for students with learning disabilities, aimed at utilizing specialist computer technology. The course earned much positive commentary at the end of year feedback session. Students reported that the course improved their personal abilities and gave them a sense of partnership with other students with learning disabilities, which reduced their feelings of social isolation. Peer support was found to be one of the most beneficial aspects of this venture. Grott (1999) describes the START project where teams of disabled students met to problem-solve around their academic and off-campus issues of living with a disability. The project was designed to help students address their non-academic (as well as academically-related) obstacles to success. Graduate students studying assistive technology participated in the teams when needed, helping to research and implement possible assistive technology solutions. An 'Assistive Technology and Resource Lab' was available for trying out different computer-based software and hardware and researching other available lower-tech products. The focus throughout was on soliciting ideas and input from all the team members while developing each student's ability to advocate for themselves and direct the problem solving process. Project staff trained and supervised the peer mentors, monitored team sessions, and ran the Lab.

Leung *et al.* (1999) surveyed students with disabilities attending post-secondary settings throughout Australia and found that some students expressed difficulty in using software or computers due to fear or nerves and lack of sufficient training. Students also identified a range of assistive technologies they considered useful to them including technologically complex devices which required training. However, students also suggested that they found useful some devices that were much simpler and much less expensive. Riemer-Reiss and Wacker (1999) conducted a study of assistive technology use and abandonment in Canada. Fifty-three college students with various disabilities participated in a survey on assistive technology device use and abandonment across the domains of home, school, recreation, leisure, hearing, vision and mobility. Results showed that a total of 51 devices were abandoned across all domains. School was the domain with the highest rate of use and the second highest rate of abandonment. Riemer-Reiss and Wacker argue that such abandonment of assistive devices demonstrates a waste of functional abilities and a disadvantage to college students with disabilities. Without assistive technology, many students with disabilities miss opportunities and options beneficial to success in college. Riemer-Reiss and Wacker conclude that the abandonment rates demonstrate the necessity of providing appropriate support, training and resources. In a study by Goodman *et al.* (2002), 14 college students with disabilities identified factors that influenced them to adopt or reject assistive technology. One of the conclusions emanating from this study was that more follow up and support in the way of assisting the students to secure funding and more training for the more expensive and not readily available technologies may have enhanced the adoption rate for the students in the study.

There is certainly evidence to suggest that students value the support and training they receive from university staff:

> I feel the support I have received from the staff there (and from the tutors in the Education Department) has made a lot of difference. I have been taught how to get the most out of the specialist computer equipment provided through the Disabled Students' Allowances and, more importantly, how to self-correct my work so that I have been able to do without this sort of support on placement. I feel that I have come on in leaps and bounds on this course. My academic tutors have commented on the improvement and I have received distinctions for all my written work. I am also a much better organised student and have not needed to ask for any deadline extensions.
>
> (Kelly, SKILL)

However some researchers feel that the suppliers of specialist equipment should also play a role in providing training and support because 'training and technical support should be considered as a part of the responsibility a company has to its clients' (Asuncion *et al.* 2002: 186).

Provision of electronic or non electronic 'alternatives'

For many disabled students, the need to request 'alternatives' to the standard way of doing things is a fact of life, whether it involves requesting alternatives to the standard lecture material or alternatives to the standard learning activity.

Providing alternative formats for lecture materials

For many students with disabilities their learning experience is enhanced if lecture notes can be provided in alternative formats. Typically this involves providing a text alternative for 'spoken' lecture notes, but it may also involve other alternatives such as providing a text-only format for multimedia (e.g. PowerPoint) presentations.

> The VLE is there if I need extra notes or I've missed notes or something or sometimes if we've got a guest speaker, they'll talk but they won't have copies of their notes there and then, but they get put on the VLE . . . in that way it helps cos then it adds to my notes . . . and you can listen in the lecture then, rather than having to scribble down all the slides.
>
> (ALERT Student 6)

> The lady who took the sociology lecture literally read straight off the paper for an hour with little hesitation and flicked through the slides very fast. Making it very tricky for everyone to take notes. As I am hearing impaired I did my best and later found a copy of her lecture notes online which I read through and annotated. Most of the lectures have summaries online, which are brilliant for me – and 90% have hand-outs at the lectures.
>
> (Kirsty, BBC Ouch)

Blankfield and Martin (2002) evaluated a six week access to higher education course, with twelve students with disabilities and found that the publishing of lecture notes or PowerPoint presentations onto the computer network in advance of lectures was perceived to be particularly helpful to all of the participants, including those without learning difficulties. Having these documents before the lecture meant that the students could make more meaningful notes, which they considered aided their learning and understanding. The late publication of lecture materials was found to be particularly unhelpful. In considering the needs of dyslexic students, Rainger (2003) argues that users with dyslexia may have a slow reading speed and so take longer than normal to read through the large amounts of text that can be contained within a web page. By providing a printable alternative to the web page the user can read the page offline, in their own time. Students may also find it easier to revise from the printed page, due to the kinaesthetic learning effect of having the pages at hand.

Providing alternatives to online teaching, learning and assessment

For many academic staff the provision of accessible learning experiences is understood solely in terms of providing online alternatives to offline materials or activities. There may be times however, when the provision of alternatives involves providing offline alternatives to online materials and activities:

> One exam that could have been a total nightmare but wasn't (thanks to the imagination and thoughtfulness of my neurology lecturer) was 'Movement Analysis'. The standard version of this exam is done on a computer with a tiny little video clip of someone walking. Totally inaccessible to me, I think you'll agree! Well, for this spectacular show of equal opportunities, myself and the other visually impaired student on my course were whisked away to the delights of a Brum hospital for an alternative and more accessible version of the exam where we got our hands on some real patients.
>
> (Sara, BBC Ouch)

The fact that disabled students often have to request one-off, special alternative arrangements has led many to argue for an inclusive or universal approach to curriculum design that avoids the necessity to provide alternatives (see chapter 6).

Negative experiences of e-learning

Evidence from both primary and secondary sources suggest that, for students with disabilities, the negative experiences of e-learning fall into three categories:

- accessibility and availability of generic technology;
- accessibility and availability of specialist technology;
- bureaucracy of systems for assessing and providing specialist technologies.

Accessibility and availability of generic technology

Students with disabilities report frustrations at the inaccessibility of computer systems; online resources and e-learning activities.

Inaccessible computer systems

> None of my DSA-funded access equipment has arrived, and so at the moment I'm being supported by a human note-taker in all my lectures. After a coffee, I had to go back to the Computer Science building for some meetings with various tutors about my access needs. It seems that all the computer systems I am expected to use on the course are currently inaccessible. For those who know, it's XWindows, Gnome and Java programming. I did my best to suggest solutions, but it's looking like I'll

have to use an assistant to read the screen out to me. We ended the meeting with me agreeing to go off and research accessibility to their systems.

(Darren, BBC Ouch)

Darren is not alone in his frustration with the effort that is required of him, simply to find a computer that he can access. In a survey of disabled students' experiences in one university, Fuller *et al.* (2004a) found that 17 per cent of disabled students reported barriers to using the publicly available computing facilities, particularly those students with multiple or mental health disabilities. Reasons given were predominantly to do with the nature of the equipment and where it was located. Students considered computer availability and quality to be poor, with some areas lacking the software (for example, speech recognition) or other equipment (such as anti-glare screens), which would facilitate their use. Others considered the location of the computing facilities to be noisy and hot.

Inaccessible online resources

I think each one has a different layout of the order of the buttons and what actually is there so I sit there for ages just looking, thinking which one do I want.

(ALERT 2005: 14)

Max explains that his condition does not really affect his use of library resources but he feels a greater need for patience in using on-line resources. If he is up against a time limit and cannot find a key piece of information, he becomes very frustrated, loses his confidence and becomes increasingly anxious.

(Max, DART)

The quote from Max is an interesting one, because Max experiences mental health difficulties, and inaccessibility of online resources is normally associated with disabilities such as visual impairment and dyslexia. Nevertheless the inaccessibility of online resources for visually impaired students should not be underestimated. For example, in a study of the information seeking behaviour of 20 sighted and 20 visually impaired people, Craven (2003a) found that visually impaired users spend more time searching or browsing the web, with times varying considerably depending on the design of the site. Overall, visually impaired users have to spend more time navigating around each page, especially if, for example, the page contains a lot of information or has many links. Observations revealed that people with more experience with the assistive technology they were using were more successful with the task. Craven concluded:

Although awareness of web accessibility is increasing, visually impaired users are still faced with huge problems when trying to navigate around some web-sites. As one visually impaired user commented: 'Sighted people just go click, click, click and there's the answer . . . while I'm still looking for the first bloody link.'

Lewis *et al.* (2004) investigated how individuals with different types of disabilities use the web and found a similar success rate for participants with a learning disability and participants with no identified disability. Participants with visual impairments however, had more difficulty completing tasks successfully and took longer than the other two groups.

Inaccessible e-learning activities

In a study, of dyslexic students' experiences of using the Virtual Learning Environment, WebCT, Blankfield *et al.* (2002) reported that tutors generally showed no awareness of WebCT issues for dyslexic students. Although accessing material online and using discussion forums could create problems for dyslexic learners, they experienced a 'sink or swim' attitude from tutors. This lack of awareness can cause students to lose faith and trust in their tutors or the system:

> The first assessed piece of coursework for this module is to create a PowerPoint presentation of rock samples, including animations. Bit of an issue. It turns out that the first time the tutor knew I was on the course was when I went up to him at the end of our introductory lecture to explain my difficulties. Well, we'll see if I can do this or not . . . My faith in their module allocation system having evaporated, I returned to my room to seek out information about the complementary Solar System course I am to take. The course materials are on the intranet thankfully, but I had thought this module would be about basic mathematical principles. But no, that would be far too simple. Instead, the module assignments are based on highly graphical software only available in the Physics computing lab. All four assignments seem to involve this software. Oh dear.
>
> (Darren, BBC Ouch)

Accessibility and availability of specialist technology

Students with disabilities can have negative experiences when there is either a lack of specialist equipment, or the specialist equipment that is available is outdated or incompatible.

Lack of specialist equipment on campus

> Have begun to get extremely frustrated at the lack of facilities available to me. Due to the non-existence of computer software and CCTV equipment in the libraries, I was unable to do the research required for one of my lectures. It was a little embarrassing, to say the least. I felt like I was making excuses, even though I know I genuinely couldn't do what was being asked of me due to lack of accessible resources. It was a group learning session, so when I told them of my woeful problems the lovely lecturer said (in his most patronising voice), 'we'll forgive Sara today, seeing as she has extra problems!' I DON'T LIKE BEING PATRONISED!!
>
> (Sara, BBC Ouch)

> It's very frustrating. I have several books on my shelf now which would really help me with my history strand tomorrow . . . and yet I can't read any of them due to lack of readers and/or scanning equipment. . . . Not looking forward to today's Nationalism seminar because I don't have any of the reading materials in an accessible format. Even went looking online for something relevant that I would be able to read but no luck.
>
> (Darren, BBC Ouch)

The lack of availability of specialist equipment can lead disabled students to question their value and importance to a higher education institution as well as the motives of responsible staff. For example, Leung *et al.* (1999) reported how some disabled students attributed lack of specialist equipment to either staff ignorance, staff agendas or politics and policies between departments.

Incompatible or outdated campus based specialist equipment

> I knew I had e-mail waiting for me, but the internet connection was still down. I decided to go to the Library to access it. . . . It turned out that they have a very old version of the 'Supernova' screenreader on the network, so I couldn't access my mail there either. Being as there is a webmail version of EMail, I called my Dad back home, got him to log on to my mail and read it to me down the phone.
>
> (Darren, BBC Ouch)

Leung *et al.* (1999) also found in their survey that difficulties with computers were linked to outdated equipment and lack of flexibility. In some cases, computers couldn't accommodate the software required as well as providing Internet and word processing access. Internet access was also a problem for students using newer equipment that had relevant software but no Internet access. Goodman *et al.* (2002: 90) also comment on the unreliability of equipment and argue that efforts must be made to upgrade computer access technology to coordinate better with upgrades in operating systems and hardware in a timely manner.

Bureaucracy of systems for assessing and providing specialist technologies

I've arrived at university with no access equipment whatsoever, so studying is going to be a little tricky. This is an NHS-funded course and my equipment isn't coming from the usual Disabled Students Allowance (DSA). Every time I called up or sought info I was given a different story. Information was hard to come by and I didn't get my access assessment until two weeks before I started at uni . . . I was assessed as needing: a laptop with enlargement software, a scanner to help me read texts, a portable CCTV camera for my laptop, a minidisc to record lectures and a printer. However, on day one I'm starting with my Dad's old laptop, which has no screen enlargement software (nightmare!) and I've got a little dictaphone thing that I suppose could be of some use. I'm extremely annoyed about this and don't expect to get anything through until after Christmas now. I'm hoping that they'll OK funding for assistants to help me take notes and read to me, or else I'll really be stuffed. Fingers crossed.

(Sara, BBC Ouch)

I have yet to receive a penny of my equipment allowance, even though the equipment was ordered well over two weeks ago. I also only began reading in my third week of academic study, when other students had had the opportunity to begin their study weeks before even arriving at university. . . . While any support is better than no support, and although a disabled student has to accept that no support will ever be entirely perfect, there is clearly a long way to go before the best possible access to a degree course becomes a reality for everyone.

(Darren, BBC Ouch)

In the UK, full-time disabled students in receipt of a maintenance award are also entitled to access an additional allowance called the 'Disabled Students Allowance' (DSA), which covers 'disability-related costs' such as assistive technology and personal assistance. However, as the student case studies illustrate, the operation of the DSA is not always successful. Frustrations with bureaucratic systems are also reported in the US. For example, the results of their survey lead Goodman *et al.* (2002) to argue that students can become bitter at systems that they perceive have failed them.

Conclusions

The evidence presented in this chapter of the disabled student's experience of e-learning provides a detailed picture of opportunities that have been both provided and denied. This supports the arguments made in chapter 3 about e-learning being a 'double-edged' sword and in chapter 4 about the need to bridge the gap between students and their learning experiences through the development of accessible e-learning. The stakeholders in higher education have an important role to play in helping to bridge that gap. Lecturers, for example, can have a role to play in providing alternative learning formats and experiences. Learning technologists have a role to play in developing accessible online resources. Student stupport services have a role to play in helping students to access and use specialist technologies. Staff developers have a role to play in helping academic staff identify and respond to the e-learning needs of disabled students. Finally, senior managers have a role to play in resourcing the provision of up-to-date, compatible and accessible generic and specialist technologies.

Whilst the personal accounts presented in this chapter help us to see some similarities in the experiences of disabled students, it is important to remember that students with disabilities are not a homogenous group and there will be just as many differences as there are similarities. Each student has an individual need, which they will express in their own individual way:

> JAWS [a popular screen reading software] I found to be extremely irritating as I was presented with a voice describing the screen. Because of my hearing problems I found that I was constantly re-doing my action to make sure I had heard properly. In the end I abandoned it due to the fact I was increasingly getting behind in my work.
>
> Zoomtext [a screen magnification software] I found again to be an irritant due to the over increased size on screen display, and being too large meant difficulties in orientation and constant moving of the screen to find out where in relation I am to anywhere! I adapted Word to compensate for this.
>
> (John, Skills for Access Case Study)

Chapter 6

Planning and developing accessible e-learning experiences

The lecturer's perspective

> My MSc involved modules from three different departments; two of these departments used e-learning sites. One of these departments is an example of good practice. Each lecturer ensured that their e-learning pages met basic accessibility criteria, such as having links meaningfully named. They also ensured that where PowerPoint or PDF was used I was provided with an alternative, either as ASCII text, HTML or as a Word document. One person went beyond this basic level of accessibility and provided me with well thought-out text descriptions of all the diagrams used (and there were many for this particular module). He discussed my needs with me so that he understood what I needed and what I did not need. This provided me with unprecedented access to learning materials, which enabled me to participate fully in the module and achieve good results without my having to struggle to access information.
>
> (Liz, Skills for Access Case Study)

Introduction

From a lecturer's perspective the issues that are important to them in relation to accessibility and e-learning are probably:

- How can I ensure that the online materials I expect my students to access as part of their studies are accessible?
- What is my particular role and responsibility in ensuring the accessibility of e-learning material that my students are using?

These questions assume that lecturers are approaching accessibility from a positive point of view. There are those, however, who accuse lecturers of being resistant to accessibility and having a negative attitude about their own responsibilities for facilitating accessibility. There is evidence, for example, of student requests for accommodations (e.g. provision of lecture notes) being met with suspicion, indifference and resistance (Shelvin *et al.* 2004). Some have put such resistance down to unwillingness to having established practices challenged (Corbett 2001: 120). For some academics the pressure to change practices, can certainly feel like a challenge to the traditional sense of 'academic freedom'. Johnson *et al.* (2003), for example, note how 'faculty members' may feel that they are under no obligation to design a website using accessibility guidelines any more than they would be required to teach using a particular methodology or give a certain type of examination. However, in the US and other countries, it is unlikely that academic freedom will be accepted as a reasonable defence in legal cases and court decisions. Legislation requires courts to look for reasonable adjustment and effective communication of information. Before we write off academics as arrogant or ignorant, it is important to understand why they may feel defensive about required changes. Disability legislation is the most recent in a long line of mandates that has required academics to submit themselves and their practices to judgement and quality assurance measurements. And, as Corbett (2001) notes, this has lead to great disillusionment at the bureaucracy of endless measurement that leaves academics 'found wanting'.

In addition, to resistance and negative attitudes, there is also evidence that many academics have little awareness of accessibility issues (usually taken to mean WAI Content Accessibility Guidelines) or of how disability (general and specific) impacts on the learning experiences of students. For example, Dix (2001: 6), a lecturer in Human Computer Interaction describes a teaching incident whereby he was unaware of the needs of autistic students, until a student with Asperger's Syndrome told him of the difficulties they had had understanding one of his examples in a lecture. Sams and Yates-Mercer (2000) conducted a UK survey of 148 lecturers and their awareness of the web Content Accessibility Guidelines and web accessibility in general and concluded that the general awareness of accessibility issues among lecturers who use the web for teaching and learning materials is poor. Results included the facts that:

- 35 had followed accessibility tips and guidelines but only four of these referred to WCAG or W3C guidelines;
- nine had validated their website with a web accessibility validation tool;
- 50 had not received any training in web content design;
- 23 did not know whether any disabled students were taking their course.

Many universities attempt to meet their responsibilities by providing awareness training for academics. One of the dangers of this approach is that it can be interpreted as attempting to push 'the responsibility for compliance to the level of the individual academic' (Kraithman and Bennet 2004). It may also ignore the context in which academics work. For example, in many institutions, academics are mandated to use specific courseware, which means that they have little control over the accessibility of the system itself (Johnson and Ruppert 2002: 442). The most they can have control over is the content that they place in the system (word documents, PDF and PowerPoint files, etc.). In this respect, guidelines for making courseware accessible, such as those offered by ALERT (2005) and Blankfield *et al.* (2002) may be of help to academics, in that they offer simple achievable and relevant advice such as:

- 'Chunk' text appropriately: avoid long paragraphs (that are too intense to read) and long pages (where it is too easy to lose track).
- Space lists of links: include full line spacing between links to make them easy to read. Links contained within text should not cause problems if they are distinct (e.g. in a different colour) from text.
- Use meaningful subject headings and straightforward language in posts to highlight importance of ideas over format of response.
- Make sure all documents are available in a flexible format that students can customize to their needs.

However, what frequently happens is that academics are advised to consult the Web Content Accessibility Guidelines as their first port of call. Given that experienced learning technologists have admitted that they have found the guidelines difficult to interpret and apply (Witt and McDermott 2002) such advice would appear to be unhelpful. Whilst academics do have a responsibility to address accessibility issues when they are using e-learning, one of the main reasons that many academics have found this difficult is that accessibility has been introduced and framed as a technical problem requiring a technical solution. All the talk of accessibility guidelines and standards (see chapter 3) and validation and repair tools (see chapter 7) has lead many academics to conclude that accessibility is the responsibility of technicians, learning technologists and others. Accessibility has not been framed as a pedagogical or teaching issue requiring pedagogical responses and solutions (Mirabella *et al.* 2004).

In addressing accessibility from a lecturer's perspective this chapter will explore the pedagogical issues involved in planning and delivering accessible e-learning experiences, with a particular focus on how lecturers teach and what they teach.

Addressing accessibility in terms of how lecturers teach

Stefani (2000) argues that in order to develop an accessible curriculum for all students, academics need to be supported and encouraged to critically reflect on all aspects of course design and delivery. Such reflection may be facilitated by the recognition that practitioners have identified three different approaches to accessible curriculum design: inclusive design, universal instructional design and holistic design.

Inclusive design

Inclusive design involves designing curricula that aim to include students with disabilities from the outset. In other words, the inclusion of students with disabilities is a forethought rather than an afterthought. Ho (2004) argues that inclusive methods can make classes more accessible to students with various learning skills, thereby creating an environment that is conducive to learning for a wide range of students, regardless of their backgrounds and circumstances. For example, putting course materials online allows students who are blind to use a screen reader or to download the text to be brailed but may also benefit students who have difficulty participating in class because of language or cultural barriers to contribution. Such flexibility acknowledges the fact that using a single teaching or assessment method can disadvantage various groups of students who do not fit a narrowly defined and perhaps arbitrarily chosen paradigm. What many educators consider to be the best or most effective practice in the classroom often only fits or benefits students of certain learning styles or backgrounds. Inclusive pedagogical designs that explore multiple teaching and assessment measures recognize that there are different legitimate ways for students to meet various defined course objectives.

Ormerod (2002), from a School of Construction and Property Management, presents a case study, which he argues illustrates the potential of e-learning in encouraging disabled students to participate in programmes. Ormerod actively designed a distance learning programme in 'Inclusive Design' with disabled students in mind. The programme was used as a pilot prior to dissemination throughout the university and beyond to encourage the design of further accessible distance learning programmes. Ormerod argues that it is also impacting on other lecturers by raising awareness of access issues and arguing that time can be saved by ensuring that students with disabilities are included at the beginning rather than having to make adaptations later.

Universal instructional design

Universal instructional design (UID) is an adaptation of the broader principals of universal design developed by the Center for Universal Design at North Carolina State University. Universal design principles describe how objects, such as doorways or machines, can be designed to allow access to all users. There are seven key principles of universal design:

- Equitable use: the design is useful and marketable to people with diverse abilities.
- Flexibility in use: the design accommodates a wide range of individual preferences and abilities.

- Simple and intuitive: use of the design is easy to understand, regardless of the user's experience, knowledge, language skills or current concentration level.
- Perceptible information: the design communicates necessary information effectively to the user, regardless of existing conditions or the user's sensory abilities.
- Tolerance for error: the design minimizes hazards and the adverse consequences of accidental or unintended actions.
- Low physical effort: the design can be used efficiently and comfortably and with a minimum of fatigue.
- Size and space for approach and use: appropriate size and space is provided for approach, reach, manipulation and use regardless of user's body size, posture or mobility.

The principles of universal design have been applied to the design of accessible e-learning resources and materials (see chapter 7) as well as design of instructional materials and activities. Universal instructional design is therefore the design of instructional materials and activities that make the learning goals achievable by individuals with wide differences in their abilities (Burgstahler 2002b). Thus, universal design for learning is achieved through flexible materials and learning activities that include students with differing abilities.

Scott *et al.* (2003) argue that universal instructional design does not necessarily imply a new approach to teaching, but rather a proactive consideration of student diversity that is incorporated into instruction and planning. Applying the principles of universal design to higher education teaching may provide tools for addressing disability access and other legitimate student needs in a proactive way that preserves the integrity of the course while promoting learning for a broader range of students. According to Scott *et al.* (2003) the underlying assumptions of this approach to curriculum design are:

- The role of the lecturer is to teach all students in the classroom as effectively as possible without compromising academic standards and expectations.
- An integrative approach is preferable to multiple separate solutions. This encapsulates a significant paradigm shift in instruction from making exceptions for different learners to anticipation and planning for student diversity as the norm.

Burgstahler (2002b) suggests that using text-based, asynchronous resources (instead of synchronous) such as electronic mail, bulletin boards, and listserv distribution lists is as an example of universal instructional design as she argues they generally erect no special barriers for students with disabilities. Other examples of the principle of equitable use include allowing several options for student presentations. These options include the use of a computer, handouts, an over-head projector or role-playing. This way, students with diverse abilities have equal opportunities to show that they have mastered the required content. An example of the principle of flexibility in use would be the inclusion of more than one form of presentation material by lecturers. For example, instructors can easily include both PowerPoint presentations and handouts in their lectures. This can help students who learn better through visual materials, and can help all students stay on track with the lesson.

There are several attractions of the universal instructional design approach to designing an accessible curriculum including:

- it is inclusive of student needs and facilitates student-centred learning (Scott *et al.* 2003);
- students without disabilities also benefit (Burgstahler 2002b; McEwan *et al.* 2003);
- it has the potential to transform broad teaching practices (Pliner and Johnson 2004).

Some also consider that the universal instructional design approach can empower academics in terms of enabling them to feel that they are still in control of their teaching:

> In the rapidly changing environment of college classrooms, faculty need support for responding to student diversity while maintaining their autonomy as the architects and designers of their courses. Viewing the principles as a versatile framework rather than a rigid checklist is compatible with the varying degrees of faculty professional development in the area of instruction.
>
> (Scott *et al.* 2003: 47)

The main criticism of the universal instructional design approach is that is perceived to encourage a 'one size fits all' approach. For example, Kelly *et al.* (2004) argue that rather than aiming to provide an e-learning resource which is accessible to everyone there can be advantages in providing resources which are tailored for the student's particular needs. However, proponents of the UID approach counter such arguments with the defence that the seven principles of UID highlight the need for a varied and flexible approach to teaching, exactly because no single method can support or provide appropriate challenges for all students. Multiple methods and materials provide a sufficiently broad base, which enable all students to learn (Pliner and Johnson 2004). Even with the most effective and 'comprehensive implementation of the principles of UID, individual accommodations will continue to constitute good teaching practice' (Ouellett 2004: 140).

Holistic design

Practitioners have slightly different interpretations of what holistic design means in terms of designing accessible curricula. For example, for Schenker and Scadden (2002), holistic design means starting with the pedagogy first, in their case the pedagogy of collaborative learning, and then addressing accessibility as it relates to collaborative learning. For Kelly *et al.* (2004) holistic design means providing accessible learning experiences, and not necessarily accessible e-learning experiences. They express concern that the current accessibility paradigm places emphasis on total online access, or if materials cannot be made accessible, then providing an equivalent online experience. Kelly *et al.* argue that this can be damaging to the educational experience of attending an institution, ignoring the fact that institutions and their staff deploy a range of learning methods, some of which will suit all students; others will not: 'There is a need to recognize that, just as IT has been used to provide accessible simulations of inaccessible real world learning, so too can accessible real world learning resources be used as a replacement for e-learning resources which may be inaccessible.'

Examples of providing physical equivalents for e-learning include:

- using a physical representation of a molecule for a visually impaired student who will find a 3D visualization of a molecule contained within an e-learning environment inaccessible (Kelly *et al.* 2004);
- using real patients to assess a physiotherapy student's ability to analyse gait because their visual impairment would mean that they would find a video-streamed clip on a computer inaccessible (see chapter 5).

Examples of providing virtual equivalents for physical learning include:

- using 3G phone technologies, videos and simulations to provide students with mobility impairments fieldwork learning experiences that they would otherwise find diffiuclt to obtain due to the inaccessibility of fieldwork locations (Kelly *et al.* 2004; Gardiner and Anwar 2001);
- using video cameras, streaming media technology and collaboration tools to provide students with disabilities who are studying science the opportunity to experience experimentation and laboratory work (Colwell *et al.* 2002).

Proactive and flexible design

With three espoused approaches to accessible curriculum design, it would not be surprising if academics were frightened off because they felt it was too dificult to wade through the minefield of apparently opposing approaches. The arguments about the strengths and weaknesses of the universal instructional design approach can be particularly distracting. However it is important to recognize that all three approaches: inclusive, universal instructional design and holistic, have two key principles in common: the importance of being proactive and the importance of being flexible. Being proactive involves thinking about the needs of students with disabilities at the beginning of the design (or re-design) process rather than making a multitude of adaptations once the course is up and running. Being flexible involves thinking of appropriate ways to offer equivalent and alternative access to the curriculum for students with a disability, which may or may not involve e-learning. Where equivalent access involves providing students with a disability with content identical to that used by a non-disabled user, but in a different modality, and alternative access involves providing students with a disability with a different learning activity to non-disabled students, which achieves the same learning outcomes as the activity undertaken by non-disabled students.

Addressing accessibility in terms of what lecturers teach

As well as addressing how lecturers teach, there is a growing agreement that there is a need to address accessibility in terms of what lecturers teach. For example, for those undergraduate and postgraduate courses that focus on design and development of technological products there is probably a need to include accessibility and related design issues into the curriculum. Such courses might include:

- information and communication technologies (Nicolle and Darzentas 2003);
- computer science or information systems (Keller *et al.* 2000);
- web design and development (Ludi 2002; Lazar 2003; Ortner *et al.* 2004);
- art and design (Gheerawo *et al.* 2004);
- human–computer interaction (McEwan *et al.* 2003);
- engineering design (Piket-May and Avery 2001).

Oravec (2002) argues that students' professional training often focuses on narrow technical considerations that exclude accessibility concerns which can make them ill-equipped to understand the importance of accessibility approaches once qualified and in employment. Oravec believes that the grassroots support of the youngest members of technical professionals (e.g. students) is required if accessibility initiatives are going to be successful. He also sees students as potential agents of change, arguing:

To be effective instruments of change, students must be empowered to present their employers with articulate arguments for accessible design.

They also must be equipped with the technological expertise to design accessible software and websites. Often students are 'ahead of the curve' of their new employers on many technical issues and accessible matters are no exception. Students may thus face considerable hurdles in supporting accessible design, and can need assistance in voicing their concerns

(Oravec 2002: 455)

If we as educators agree that design and engineering students have the potential to be agents of change and that accessibility needs to be incorporated into undergraduate and postgraduate curricula, there probably needs to be some agreement as to what core skills and abilities these students need and what teaching and learning activities need to be incorporated into the curriculum in order to enable students to gain and demonstrate these skills and abilities. Nicolle and Darzentas (2003) describe an EU project called ICDnet, which is attempting to identify core knowledge and skills for 'Design for All' (universal design) model curricula. Workshops with academic and industry experts have produced a taxonomy of knowledge and skills:

- awareness of 'Design for All';
- understanding of ethical, legal and commercial considerations;
- interpersonal skills for teamwork;
- knowledge on how to make content (documents and multimedia) accessible;
- knowledge about accessible interaction: input and output including assistive technologies;
- new paradigms of interaction;
- user-centred design;
- application domains and research.

There is nothing surprising in this taxonomy, but curriculum designers will be challenged to develop new and different teaching and learning activities that enable students to learn and demonstrate the interpersonal skills required to work with disabled users and understand their needs. Oravec (2002) argues that in addition to technical skills, students will need to understand managerial processes as well as the discourse and practice of organizational change. Whilst he is probably right, curriculum developers will need to be careful in how they address such skills, so that the curriculum does not appear too diluted to students and accreditors who may be concerned if there does not appear to be enough 'design' in the course.

Different approaches to including accessibility into the curriculum

The response to calls for the inclusion of accessibility into curricula, is patchy at the moment. Most general design and engineering courses do not appear to be specifically addressing accessibility issues. For example, Emerson *et al.* (2003) present the results of a survey of mechanical engineering courses in the US, in which they were attempting to ascertain the extent to which universal design and accessibility were incorporated into the programmes of study. They found that of the ten universities and 12 colleges that responded to the survey, about half the respondents were not familiar with the terms 'universal design', 'inclusive design', or 'designing for accessibility'. No institution sampled had a programme in universal design or a person on faculty who specialized in universal design. However, there was evidence that ergonomics and human factors were included in the curriculum of the majority of programmes. Emerson *et al.* (2003) conclude that there seems to be no mechanism in place to ensure that the next generation of product designer will be more aware of the 'human side' of product design.

There is evidence however that more specialist courses are beginning to address accessibility within the curriculum in a number of different ways:

- integrating accessibility into the whole curriculum;
- practical projects;
- learning partnerships with user groups.

Integrating accessibility into the whole curriculum

Ludi (2002) describes how she covers accessibility in her own teaching. Rather than appending accessibility as a single lecture at the end of the course, the topic is broken into parts and integrated into all web design topics. Rather than mentioning the need for access by the disabled as that of an insignificantly small group, the need to open websites to all potential customers or users is stressed. In addition, accessibility is included in the list of topics for the assignments. Ludi concludes that students do seem to get the message in the short term, although since the course is only for one semester, no information is available as to whether the students continue to add accessibility to their web pages.

Practical projects

Oravec (2002) argues that in order to motivate students to be interested in accessibility, they need to see accessibility as interesting challenges rather than as obstacles or restrictions to design efforts. He offers class projects in using validation and repair tools or reverse engineering of existing sites as examples of how students can be encouraged to develop creative scenarios that involve accessibility and universal design principles. With such encouragement, students may come to accessibility as an interesting technical challenge rather than an obstacle.

Learning partnerships with user groups

Art and design courses have an established history of encouraging their students to work with user groups in order to gain experience of inclusive or universal design approaches. For example, Boess and Lebbon (1998) describe how students studying art and design worked with a group of 'retirees' to design products to meet their bathing needs. While Gheerawo *et al.* (2004) outline how students at the Royal College of Art undertake a year long project in inclusive design where they are given a small research bursary, access to user groups, specialist inclusive design information and workshops in user-centred design. They note how students are attracted by the chance to problem-solve creatively for a 'real life' situation based on user research rather than speculative design.

Other courses are also beginning to incorporate user-centred projects into their curricula. For example, Piket-May and Avery (2001) describe how assistive technology has been introduced into a first year engineering design course. Students work in groups on individual projects where the brief is to design an assistive technology to meet a particular client's need. The clients are real people that the students get to meet and work with. Evidence suggests that the retention rates for students who take this option/module are better than for those who do not; perhaps because these students feel a sense of need and purpose or value in design engineering.

Lazar (2003) describes how students studying his graduate web usability class at Towson University work with non-profit organizations to make their websites more accessible, giving them the experience of working in real-world situations, with real-world challenges and in teams, which mirrors the workplace setting. The projects could be viewed as limited however, in that although students make recommendations to the organizations about the accessible design of their websites, they don't actually do the design work themselves, or implement their recommendations. Some would argue this is real user-centredness, i.e. not doing something for the user, but empowering them to do it themselves, if they wish. This raises an interesting question about what our understanding of user-centred or user-led design is and how we share that understanding with our students. There are different understandings of this concept, closely linked to different epistemologies and models. Approaches that are called 'user-centred design' can range from situations where the designer/developer sets the agenda/problem and ascertains the extent to which users agree with that agenda/problem to situations where the designer/developer enables users to set their own agenda/problem and ascertains the extent to which they can work with users to address the agenda/ problem. For some, the first approach is born out of a medical model approach to disability where disabled people are viewed as recipients of services whilst the second approach is more emancipatory in nature and disabled people are viewed as equal partners in the process.

Design students are likely to need help in distinguishing between such approaches and encouragement to come to their own position about what approach they feel able to adopt and the skills that this will require. This is highlighted by Bennett (2002), who reports on her experiences of attempting to undertake a project on user-led design for her MA in Design Research. She found that a clash of epistemologies led to an uncomfortable and somewhat painful project experience. She reports how her assessors rejected her initial proposal to conduct an emancipatory research design project and guided her to become involved in an established large research project, which she felt was far from emancipatory in its approach. This clash of epistemologies eventually led her to withdraw from the research. Bennett is clearly an articulate student who felt able to stick to her guns about the kind of design approach she wanted to adopt. Designers of new curricula may wish to examine the extent to which they can design programmes that attract and produce more students like Bennett.

Conclusion

By considering accessibility from a lecturer's perspective two key messages have emerged from this chapter:

- It is possible to address accessibility from a pedagogical as well as a technical viewpoint;
- From a lecturer's perspective the key principles of accessible design are proactivity and flexibility.

By being proactive and flexible, lecturers can successfully address accessibility in terms of how and what they teach.

These messages have key implications for future practice. Disability discrimination legislation has the potential to both assist and limit innovation (Davies 2003). However, if the principles of proactive and flexible design can be supported and promoted, then lecturers may be encouraged to see accessibility issues as opportunities to develop innovative, creative practice as opposed to attempts to fetter academic freedom. Working from a pedagogical as opposed to a technical framework may also help staff and educational developers to offer awareness raising and development opportunities to lecturers which are more likely to meet with a positive rather than a negative response. Lecturers will always be perceived as having some degree of responsibility for developing accessible e-learning experiences (Opitz 2002).

But if accessibility can be viewed as a pedagogical as well as a technical issue then it may help lecturers to see how responsibility can be shared between those stakeholders who have a pedagogical perspective (e.g. lecturers, disability support officers, educational developers) and those who hold more technical perspectives (e.g. learning technologists, assistive technologists) and the value of developing strategic partnerships with these stakeholders.

Chapter 7

Designing and developing accessible e-learning resources

The learning technologist's perspective

> The implications seemed almost insurmountable at the time when he went through them. I was so busy preparing for other things that suddenly I realised I hadn't taken accessibility issues very seriously within my job before, and that made me feel very guilty indeed. That it took SENDA to make me think about those people with disabilities and their needs certainly makes me feel horrified now. In the long run however, I think it has been an enormously positive benefit.
>
> (Kirstine Lehaney, ALT Online Newsletter, July 2005)

Introduction

From a learning technologist's perspective, particularly those unfamiliar with disability issues, the pressing e-learning and accessibility questions for them are likely to be:

- How can I design and develop accessible e-learning material?
- What tools are available to help me design and develop accessible e-learning material?

Finding the answers to these questions is important for learning technologists, because they are regarded by many to have a key role to play with regards to increasing the accessibility of e-learning. Despite this, there is evidence to suggest that levels of accessibility awareness and knowledge are low amongst learning technologists. For example, Pulichino (2005) reports on the results of a survey of members of the E-learning Guild in the US regarding accessibility awareness where 54 per cent of respondents reported very limited or no knowledge of Section 508 with respect to accessible websites; 57 per cent of respondents reported very limited or no knowledge of Section 508 with respect to accessible e-learning and only 29 per cent of respondent's organizations were reported to be at least partially compliant with Section 508 guidelines.

As well as evidence that awareness levels may be low, there is also evidence that attitudes to accessibility amongst learning technologists may not be overly positive. For example, Lazar *et al.* (2004) report on a survey, which asked webmasters about their knowledge of web accessibility and their perceptions of when and why websites should or should not be accessible. Most webmasters who responded to the survey supported the concept of web accessibility, but cited roadblocks to accessibility such as lack of time, lack of training, lack of managerial support, lack of client support, inadequate software tools, and confusing accessibility guidelines. However, there were some webmasters who objected to the idea that websites should be accessible, did not like the interference in 'their' web design, and would only make websites accessible if the government forced them to.

Some would infer from such results that the reason why so many web documents are inaccessible is because of the negative attitudes of designers and developers. But there is a lot packed into these attitudes that needs careful unpicking. For example, Sloan and Stratford (2004) suggest that when confronted with the issue of accessibility and legal implications, developers may experience a number of emotions: fear, embarrassment, defensiveness and helplessness. Sloan and Stratford (2004) also suggest that some developers see accessibility as a procedural or bureaucratic exercise invented by people without knowledge of media production or web development, and apparently with nothing better to do than constrain creativity and innovation. They argue that there are two negative outcomes of this way of thinking: de-motivation amongst some developers and an increase in anodyne (accessible but diluted) e-learning resources.

A lot of responsibility is assumed to fall on the shoulders of learning technologists. The majority of articles written in the field of accessibility and education attempt to offer advice or recommendations for future action. Whilst many of these articles do not make it explicit at which stakeholder the advice is aimed, there is an underlying assumption that it is learning technologists who will respond. Furthermore, there are some instances where learning technologists are deemed to be more responsible than others, such as lecturers. For example, Johnson and Ruppert (2002: 442) write that the 'ability of the instructor to create an accessible Web site is limited by the accessibility provided by the LMS engineers'. With relatively low levels of awareness, but high levels of responsibility, many learning technologists are asking the all-embracing question: where on earth do I start?

Many accessibility advocates advise learning technologists to start by looking at accessibility legislation, guidelines, standards and evaluation tools. Using archaeology as a metaphor, it can be argued that accessibility legislation, guidelines, standards and evaluation tools are not the most helpful or informative place to start. The legislation, guidelines, standards and tools are merely archaeological artefacts that have been scattered on the surface of a significant archaeological site. Whilst it is tempting to gather the artefacts that are on the surface and use these to make deductions about the site, we need to dig deeper below the surface of the site in order to understand the history and significance of these artefacts. An important consequence of digging deeper is that learning technologists will also gain a greater understanding of the design approaches that underpin accessibility legislation, guidelines and standards as well as the efficacy of accessibility design, evaluation and repair tools.

In order to demonstrate why it is important to 'dig deeper', this chapter will explore these two areas in more detail. Many learning technologists believe that accessibility was born out of legislation, guidelines and standards. It was not. Accessibility has a longer history of practice and experience, which learning technologists need to be aware of in order to develop their own practice and experience.

Accessibility design approaches

There are three main approaches to designing for accessibility, universal design, usability and user-centred design. All of these approaches have their origins outside of e-learning, in disciplines such as human-computer interaction, assistive technology and art and design. Two other approaches to design also have an influence on designing for accessibility: designing for adaptability and designing with an awareness of assistive technologies. Each of these approaches will be discussed in turn.

Universal design

The universal design approach to designing for accessibility is also known as design for all, barrier free design or inclusive design. The underpinning principle of universal design is that in designing with disability in mind a better product will be developed that also better serves the needs of all users, including those who are not disabled. 'Universal design is the process of creating products (devices, environments, systems, and processes), which are usable by people with the widest possible range of abilities, operating within the widest possible range of situations (environments, conditions, and circumstances)' (Vanderheiden 1996).

Thompson (2005) offers a number of examples that illustrate how universal web design can benefit a range of users. For example, text alternatives for visual content (e.g. providing ALT tags for images) benefits anyone who doesn't have immediate access to graphics. While this group includes people with blindness, it also includes those sighted computer users who surf the web using text-based browsers, users with slow Internet connections who may have disabled the display of graphics, users of handheld computing devices, and users of voice web and web portal systems including car-based systems.

Central to the universal design approach is a commitment that products should not have to be modified or adapted. They should be accessible through easily imposed modifications that are 'right out of the box' (Jacko and Hanson 2002: 1). Products should also be compatible with users' assistive technologies: 'This practice, when applied to the web, results in web content that is accessible to the broadest possible audience, including people with a wide range of abilities and disabilities who access the web using a wide variety of input and output technologies' (Thompson 2005).

Whilst some purists argue that universal design is about designing for everyone, the majority of proponents agree that designing for the majority of people is a more realistic approach (Witt and McDermott 2004; Bohman 2003a). For example, the European Design for All e-Accessibility Network (EdeaN) defines design for all as: 'Design of technology, products and services, which are demonstrably suitable for a majority of the potential users without any modifications' (Stephanidis 2005). While Vanderheiden (1996) argues:

> There are NO universal designs; there are NO universally designed products. Universal design is a process, which yields products (devices, environments, systems, and processes), which are usable by and useful to the widest possible range of people. It is not possible, however, to create a product, which is usable by everyone or under all circumstances.

There are some who feel uncomfortable with the principles of universal design because they appear to relieve educators of the responsibility of addressing individual student needs. For example Kelly *et al.* (2004) argue that since accessibility is primarily about people and not about technologies it is inappropriate to seek a universal solution and that rather than aiming to provide an e-learning resource which is accessible to everyone there can be advantages in providing resources which are tailored to the student's particular needs.

There are also some who warn that no single design is likely to satisfy all different learner needs. The classic example given to support this argument is the perceived conflict between the needs of those who are blind and those who have cognitive disabilities. For example, the dyslexic's desire for effective imagery and short text would appear to contradict the blind user's desire for strong textual narrative with little imagery. However Bohman (2003b) provides a counterbalance to this argument stating that while the visual elements may be unnecessary for those who are blind, they are not harmful to them. As long as alternative text is provided for these visual elements, there is no conflict. Those with cognitive disabilities will be able to view the visual elements, and those who are blind will be able to access the alternative text.

Usability

Brajnik (2000) defines usability as the: 'effectiveness, efficiency and satisfaction with which specified users achieve specified goals in particular environments'.

Effectiveness, efficiency and satisfaction can be achieved by following four main design principles:

- make the site's purpose clear;
- help users find what they need;
- reveal site content;
- use visual design to enhance, not define, interaction design (Nielson 2002).

Many practitioners talk of usability and accessibility in the same breath, as if they were synonymous. For example, Jeffels and Marston (2003) write: 'Using legislation as the stick will hopefully cease to be as important as it currently is; the carrot of usability will hopefully be the real driving force in the production of accessible online materials one day soon.'

There may be good reason for assuming synonymy between accessibility and usability. For example, Arch (2002) points out that many of the checkpoints in the Web Content Accessibility Guidelines are actually general usability requirements and a number of others are equally applicable to sections of the community that are not disabled, such as those who live in rural areas or the technologically disadvantaged. Many proponents also argue that a usability design approach is essential in accessibility because in many cases current accessibility standards do not address making web pages directly usable by people, but rather address making web pages usable by technologies (browsers, assistive devices). However, usability and accessibility are different, as Powlik and Karshmer (2002: 218) forcefully point out: 'To assume accessibility equates to usability is the equivalent of saying that broadcasting equates to effective communication.'

What is the difference between usability and accessibility?

One simple way to understand the difference between usability and accessibility is to see usability as focusing on making applications and websites easy for people to use, whilst accessibility focuses on making them equally easy for everyone to use. Others see the difference as one of objectivity and subjectivity, where accessibility has a specific definition and is about technical guidelines and compliance with official norms. Usability, however, has a broader definition, is resistant to attempts at specification and is about user experience and satisfaction (Iwarsson and Stahl 2003; Craven 2003b; Richards and Hanson 2004).

Whilst usability and accessibility are different, it is clear that they do complement one another. However, it does not follow that if a product is accessible, it also usable. This is because for usability accessibility is necessary, but not sufficient. Whilst for accessibility usability is not necessary, but it is desirable. In a compelling indictment of the use of automatic accessibility checking tools Sloan and Stratford (2004) argue that 'Accessible remains worthless without usable – which depending on the aims of the resource, could imply "valued", 'trustworthy, "worthwhile", "enjoyable", "fun", or many other desirable adjectives.'

Thatcher (2004) provides a pertinent example of a website of one US Federal Agency to demonstrate how accessibility does not equal usability. The site passed most automated accessibility checks, but failed on a usability check. Thatcher notes that the designers used the techniques that they were supposed to use, such as using alt-text on images. However, he concluded that they must have blindly used those techniques without understanding why. Otherwise they would not have provided alt-text on invisible images that have been used purely for spacing, requiring a screen reader to read the text over and over (a total 17 times), when in fact it was information a user did not need to know.

Usability design methods

Usability is essentially about trying to see things from the user's perspective and designing accordingly. Seeing things from the user's perspective can be difficult, as Regan (2004a) acknowledges when discussing Flash design and screen readers. In order to see things from a user's perspective more easily, usability designers may employ user profiles, investigate user preferences or conduct user evaluations (testing). For example, Kunzinger *et al.* (2005) outline how IBM has employed user profiles (personas of users with disabilities) in an attempt to make their products more usable. The personas are described as composite descriptions of users of a product that embody their use of the product, their characteristics, needs and requirements. According to Kunzinger *et al.* these personas engage the empathy of developers for their users and provide a basis for making initial design decisions.

Gappa *et al.* (2004) report how an EU project called IRIS investigated the preferences of people with disabilities with regard to interface design of web applications as well as user requirements of online help and search engines. The results showed that user preferences for information presentation vary a great deal and that solutions would require comprehensive user profiling. Bryant (2005) documents the results of a usability study in which four participants from each of the seven target audiences for the website were asked to undertake tasks from one of seven 'scenarios', one for each target audience. Participants were observed and videotaped while undertaking these tasks.

Paciello (2005) argues that engaging users and applying usability inspection methods are the cornerstones for ensuring universal accessibility. Whilst most of us are now aware of the existence of accessibility statements and logos on websites, Shneiderman and Hochheiser (2001: 367) propose that web designers should also place usability statements on their sites in order to 'inform users and thereby reduce frustration and confusion'.

User centred design

Alexander (2003b) defines user-centred design (UCD) as a development process, which has three core principles:

- Focus on users and their tasks: a structured approach to the collection of data from and about users and their tasks. The involvement of users begins early in the development lifecycle and continues throughout it (user profiling).
- Empirical measurement of usage of the system: the typical approach is to measure aspects of ease of use on even the earliest system concepts and prototypes, and to continue this measurement throughout development (user testing).
- Iterative design: the development process involves repeated cycles of design, test, redesign and retest until the system meets its usability goals and is ready for release.

Jacko and Hanson (2002: 1) argue that user profiling, or understanding the specific characteristics and interaction needs of a particular user or group of users with unique needs and abilities, is necessary to truly understand the different interaction requirements of disparate user populations. This understanding of diverse users' needs will help to increase accessibility.

User centred design in the field of disability and accessibility is attractive because it places people with disabilities at the centre of the design process, a place in which they have not traditionally been. As Luke (2002) notes: 'When developers consider technical and pedagogical accessibility, people with physical and/or learning disabilities are encouraged to become producers of information, not just passive consumers.'

A range of studies have reported to be user or learner centred in their design approach and in doing so have employed a range of techniques:

- user testing (Smith 2002; Alexander 2003b; Gay and Harrison 2001; Theofanos and Redish 2003);
- user profiling (Keller et al. 2001);
- user evaluations (Pearson and Koppi 2001).

However, Bilotta (2005) warns that if accessibility guidelines are translated too literally, there is a risk that unsuccessful sites will be created that ignore the intersection of UCD and the needs and tasks of people with disabilities.

The relationship between universal, usable and user-centred design approaches

For many, there are clear overlaps between the three design approaches. For example Bilotta (2005) claims that accessible web design is nothing more than the logical extension of the principles of both user centered design and universal design. The three approaches are connected in that all three embrace users' needs and preferences. For example, in discussing universal design, Burzagli *et al.* (2004: 240) place an importance on user needs: 'Design for All can constitute a good approach, as in accordance with its principles, it embraces user needs and preferences, devices and contexts of use in a common operative platform.' As does Smith (2002: 52), when discussing a user-centred design approach to developing a VLE interface for dyslexic students: 'This design approach places an emphasis on understanding the needs of the user and it seems to have produced an interface that is appropriate for both dyslexic and non-dyslexic users.'

Perhaps the easiest way to see the connection between the three approaches is to view usability and universal design as specific implementations of user-centred design, where:

- a traditional usability approach employs a quite specific interpretation of who the end-users are;
- a universal design approach employs a broader interpretation of who the end users are, an interpretation that focuses on how the user maps on the target population in terms of functional capability as well as skill and experience (Keates and Clarkson 2003).

Designing for adaptability

Some research studies that report to be designing with accessibility in mind have focused their attention on designing for adaptability. This can mean one of two things:

- allowing the user to configure the application to meet their needs (Owens and Keller 2000; Arditi 2004);
- enabling the application to make adaptations to transform seamlessly in order to meet the needs of the user (Stephanidis *et al.* 1998; Cooper *et al.* 2000; Hanson and Richards 2004; Alexandraki *et al.* 2004).

Both approaches are reliant on detailed user profiles and in that sense there is similarity with usability and user-centred design approaches. Designing applications that make automatic adaptations appears to be a more prevalent design approach at the moment, however. For example Alexandraki *et al.* (2004) describe the 'eAccessibilityEngine', a tool which employs adaptation techniques to automatically render web pages accessible by users with different types of disabilities. Specifically, the 'eAccessibilityEngine' is capable of automatically transforming web pages to attain conformance to Section 508 standards and 'AAA' conformance to Web Content Accessibility Guidelines. The proposed tool is intended for use as a web-based service and can be applied to any existing website. The researchers explain how users are not necessarily aware of the presence of the eAccessibilityEngine. If users do not wish to modify their initial selection of an 'accessibility profile' they need to directly interact with the tool only once. Paciello (2000: 21) describes the move towards such personalization as the 'Third Wave', arguing that: 'This is the essence of true personalization – Web design that ensures accessibility for every user by adapting to the user's preferences'.

Designing with an awareness of assistive technology

Some definitions of accessibility stress access by assistive technologies (Caldwell *et al.* 2004). Accessibility design approaches such as universal design also stress access by assistive technologies (Thompson 2005). Furthermore, accessibility guidelines and standards such as the WCAG-1 stress access by assistive technologies. For example, guideline nine advises designers to use features that enable activation of page elements via a variety of input devices.

There is a strong case therefore for learning technologists needing to have an awareness of assistive technology in order to avoid situations where users of such technologies cannot 'conduct Web transactions because the Web environment does not support access functionality' (Yu 2003: 12). Colwell *et al.* (2002: 75) argue that some guidelines are difficult for developers to apply if they have 'little knowledge of assistive technology or [of] people with disabilities'. While Bilotta (2005) notes that

> Developers faced with the challenge of generating accessible web content, attempt to translate these standards into solutions without clearly understanding the goal of their efforts . . . It remains a rare occurrence that a database developer has any experience or knowledge of an Operating System Reader such as JAWS or other alternate web browsing strategies.

Accessibility tools

Four types of accessibility tool exist at the moment: filter and transformation tools; design and authoring tools; evaluation tools; evaluation and repair tools. Filter and transformational tools assist web users more than developers and either modify a page or supplement an assistive technology or browser. Examples include the BBC Education Text to Speech Internet Enhancer (BETSIE), which creates automatic text-only versions of a website and the

Kit for the Accessibility of the Internet (KAI). Gonzalez *et al.* (2003) describe how KAI can offer a global indicator of accessibility to end users (particularly blind people) at the moment of entering a site as well as filter, repair and restructure the site according to their needs.

Design and authoring tools that currently exist, appear to fall into two categories: multimedia design tools (Linder and Gunderson 2003; Regan 2005a; Kraithman and Bennet 2004) and tools that simulate disability (Tagaki *et al.* 2004; Saito *et al.* 2005). The number of design tools that exist however, are tiny, compared to the array of evaluation, validation and repair tools that have been developed.

Evaluation tools conduct a static analysis of web pages and return a report or rating, whilst repair tools identify problems and recommend improvements (Chisholm and Kasday 2003). Validation tools such as The W3C HTML Validation Service that check HTML and Cascading Style Sheets (CSS) are often included as evaluation tools because validating to a published grammar is considered by some to be the first step towards accessibility (Smith and Bohman 2004).

Evaluation and repair tools

Evaluation tools can be categorized as either general or focused, where general evaluation tools perform tests for a variety of accessibility issues whilst focused tools test for one or a limited aspect of accessibility. Evaluation and repair tools generally focus on evaluating content, although some do evaluate user agents (Gunderson and May 2005). Most tools see accessibility as an absolute, but some look at the degree of accessibility (Hackett *et al.* 2004). Most tools use WCAG–1 or Section 508 as their benchmark, but as guidelines are continually changing one or two are designed to check against the most recent guidelines (Abascal *et al.* 2004). Finally, most of the tools are proprietary.

Standard referenced evaluation tools

There are a range of tools that identify accessibility problems by mostly following the guidelines of Section 508 and WCAG–1. Examples include AccessEnable, LIFT and Bobby. Bobby is the most well known automatic accessibility checking tool. It was originally developed by The Center for Applied Special Technology but is now distributed through WatchFire. Bobby tests online documents against either the WCAG-1 or Section 508 standards. A report is generated that highlights accessibility checks, triggered by document mark-up. Some checks can be identified directly as an error; others are flagged as requiring manual attention. If tested against WCAG-1, the report lists priority one, two and three accessibility user checks in separate sections. Bobby provides links to detailed information as to how to rectify accessibility checkpoints, the reason for the checkpoint and provides accessibility guideline references for both WAI and Section 508 guidelines as appropriate. If all priority one checkpoints raised in the report are dealt with, the report for the revised page should indicate that the page is granted: 'Bobby approved' status.

Whilst Bobby is the most well-known and perhaps most used evaluation tool, it has not been without its problems. For example, some experts have pointed out that Bobby and the Bobby logo can be used inappropriately to indicate that a site is accessible, when in some people's perception it is not (Witt and McDermott 2002; Phipps *et al.* 2002).

> While Bobby will detect a missing text description for an image, it is the developer who is responsible for annotating this image with meaningful text. Frequently, an image has a meaningless or misleading text description though the validation tool output states that the page is accessible.
>
> (Witt and McDermott 2002: 48)

Tools that identify and prioritize problems that need repairing

Many automatic evaluation tools not only indicate where the accessibility problem is, but also give designers directions for conforming to violated guidelines. Although they can also be called repair tools, almost none perform completely automatic corrections. For this reason, it is probably more appropriate to identify them as tools that assist the author in identifying and prioritizing. Although the tools mentioned in the previous section offer designers some help in correcting problems, there are tools that fulfill this goal more efficiently. Examples include A-Prompt and Step 508.

A-Prompt (Accessibility Prompt) was developed by the Adaptive Technology Resource Centre in Canada. A-Prompt first evaluates an HTML web page to identify accessibility, it then provides the web author with a 'fast and easy way' to make the necessary repairs. The tool's evaluation and repair checklist is based on WCAG-1. A-Prompt allows the author to select a file for validation and repair, or select a single HTML element within a file. The tool may be customized to check for different conformance levels. If an accessibility problem is detected, A-Prompt displays the necessary dialogs and guides the user to fix the problem. Many repetitive tasks are automated, such as the addition of ALT-text or the replacement of server-side image maps with client-side image maps. When all potential problems have been resolved, the repaired HTML code is inserted into the document and a new version of the file may be saved to the author's hard drive. After a web page has been checked and repaired by A-Prompt it will be given a WAI Conformance ranking.

Theofanos, *et al.* (2004) and Kirkpatrick and Thatcher (2005) describe a free tool developed by the National Centre for Accessible Media (NCAM), called STEP 508. STEP 508 is a tool for analysing evaluation data from popular web accessibility evaluation tools, such as Watchfire's Bobby and UsableNet's LIFT. STEP does not perform the accessibility evaluation, but examines the results of an evaluation and creates a report, which prioritizes the results based on the severity and repairability of the errors found, as well as on the importance of the pages where errors were identified. When it was originally designed in 2003, it was limited to prioritizations of evaluations where Section 508 standards were the basis for testing. However, in 2005 NCAM developed a new version of this tool with additional importing, exporting and reporting capabilities, and with the ability to test against the WCAG–1. Like its predecessor, the new version allows site administrators to prioritize accessibility errors and quickly generate reports that provide several views of the errors. Errors are prioritized by several factors including ease of repair, page 'importance' (determined by page traffic and other criteria) and impact on users. With a sorted list in hand, repair efforts are focused first on pages and errors that are the best targets for repair. In addition to prioritizing errors, STEP allows for easy comparisons between accessibility evaluation tools, to help site administrators understand how the outputs from the various tools differ.

Validity and reliability of evaluation and repair tools

With so many tools to choose from accessibility designers need to be able to assess their validity and reliability. Brajnik (2001) argues that the testing tools have to be validated in order to be truly useful. A crucial property that needs to be assessed is the validity of the rules that tools operate. A valid rule is correct (never identifies false positives) and complete (never yields false negatives). Brajnik (2001) argues that rule completeness is extremely difficult to assess however, and considers that assessing the correctness of a rule is more viable and can be achieved through one of three methods: comparative experiments, rule inspection and testing, and page tracking.

Page tracking entails the repeated use of an automatic tool. If a site is analysed two or more times, each evaluation generates a set of problems. If, on subsequent evaluations, a problem disappears (due to a change in the underlying web page/website) it is assumed that this maintenance action on the part of the webmaster was prompted by the rule showing the problem. Brajnik argues that this method provides an indirect way to determine the utility of the rule, a property that is closely related to rule correctness. A rule that is useful (i.e. its advice is followed by a webmaster) is, according to Brajnik, also likely to be correct. Interestingly, in another study that examined developers' responses to the results of automated tools, Ivory et al. (2003) found that developers who relied on their own expertise to modify sites, produced sites that yielded some performance improvements. This was not the case for sites produced with evaluation tools. Even though the automated tools identified significantly more potential problems than the designers had identified by themselves, designers made more design changes when they did not use an automated tool.

A common method of testing the reliability of tools is to conduct tests where the results of different tools are compared against each other and sometimes also against a manual evaluation. Studies reveal mixed results. For example in a comparison between Bobby and LIFT in which tool completeness, correctness and specificity were analysed, LIFT was clearly the better performer (Brajnik 2004). Brajnik was able to conclude that:

- LIFT generated less false positives than Bobby;
- LIFT generates less false negatives than Bobby;
- for the six most populated checkpoints LIFT had a number of (automatic and manual) tests that was equal or greater than the corresponding number for Bobby.

Other comparative studies have found it harder to come out with a clear winner:

- Faulkner and Arch (2003) reviewed AccVerify 4.9, Bobby 4.0, InFocus 4.2 and PageScreamer 4.1;
- Lazar et al. (2003) evaluated the reliability of InFocus, A-Prompt and Bobby;
- Diaper and Worman (2003) reports the results of comparing Bobby and A-Prompt.

Lazar et al. concluded from their study that accessibility testing tools are 'flawed and inconsistent'. Whilst, Diaper and Worman (2003) warn that any overhead saved using automatic tools will be spent in interpreting their results:

> There must be a strong temptation for organisations to rely more on accessibility assessment tools than they should because the tools are supposed to encapsulate and apply knowledge about the WCAGs and check points. Accessibility tools have their own knowledge over-heads concerning how to use the tools and, vitally, interpret their outputs. Indeed, it may well be that at present the tools' related knowledge is additional to a sound understanding of the WCAG by the tools' users, i.e. you need to know more to use the tools, not less.

Choosing an evaluation or repair tool

Decisions about which evaluation or repair tool to choose will depend on a number of factors:

- whether the designer wants to focus on general or specific accessibility issues;
- whether the designer wants to test against WCAG–1, Section 508 or both;
- whether the tools are considered to be operating valid rules;
- whether the tools are considered to be reliable;
- whether the websites to be evaluated are small or large (O'Grady and Harrison 2003);
- whether the designer is working as an individual or as part of a larger corporate organisation (Brajnik 2001);
- whether the designer wants usability testing to be an integral part of the test (Brajnik 2000).

O'Grady and Harrison (2003) reviewed A-Prompt, Bobby, InFocus and AccVerify. The review process examined functionality, platform availability, demo version availability and cost. The functional issues examined included the installation process, availability of tech support, standards the product validates and the software's response to a violation of the checkpoint items. Each software tool was compared on a series of practical and functional indicators. O'Grady and Harrison concluded that the best tools for small to medium sites was A-Prompt and Bobby, whilst for large or multiple sites, InFocus and AccVerify were better choices.

However, Brajnik 2001 argues that comparing these tools can be unfair given their different scope, flexibility, power and price. LIFT is targeted to an enterprise-level quality assurance team and costs from $6,000 upwards, whilst Bobby is available for free and is targeted to a single individual wanting to test a relatively limited number of pages free (Watchfire initially did make charges when it took over Bobby but it has recently announced that they will transition the Bobby online service to WebXACT, a free online tool).

Problems with evaluation and repair tools

In addition to problems of reliability, many researchers and practitioners have identified further potential problems with the use of evaluation and repair tools including:

- difficulties with judging the severity of the error (Thompson *et al.* 2003);
- dangers of inducing a false sense of security (Witt and McDermott 2004);
- dangers of encouraging over-reliance (SciVisum 2004);
- difficulties understanding the results and recommendations (Faulkner and Arch 2003; Wattenberg 2004).

These reasons have lead many to conclude that some element of manual testing or human judgement is still needed. For example, Thompson *et al.*

(2003) argue that one shortcoming of the automated tools is their inability to take into account the 'severity' of an identifed accessibility error. For example, if Site A is missing ALT tags on its spacer images, and Site B is missing ALT tags on its menu buttons, both sites are rated identically, when according to Thompson *et al.* Site B clearly has the more serious accessibility problem. They conclude that 'Some of the web-content accessibility check-points cannot be checked successfully by software algorithms alone. There will still be a dependence on the user's ability to exercise human judgment to determine conformance to the guidelines.'

Witt and McDermott (2004: 49) argue that while the tools are useful for issues such as locating missing text alternatives to graphics and checking for untidy HTML coding they cannot evaluate a site for layout consistency, ease of navigation, provision of contextual and orientation information, and use of clear and easy-to-understand language. Therefore:

> developers must also undertake their own audit of the web page and interpret the advice given in order to satisfy themselves that compliance has been achieved. That said, these tools can give web developers a false sense of security. If presented with a Bobby or A-Prompt generated checklist showing that all issues have been addressed, developers may believe they have met the accessibility guidelines. Yet in reality, they may have only adhered to a set of rules and produced an inaccessible website.

SciVisum (2004) tested 111 UK websites that publicly claimed to be compliant with WCAG–1 by displaying the WAI compliance logo on their website. They found that 40 per cent of these failed to meet the checkpoints for which they were claiming compliance. The report concludes:

> The SciVisum study indicates that either self-regulation is not working in practice or that organisations are relying too heavily on automated web-site testing. Semi-automated accessibility testing on Web sites by experienced engineers needs to become a standard practice for UK Web site owners. Only manual tests can help identify areas of improvement, which are impossible to identify with automated checks alone. Unless sites are tested site-wide in this way failure rates amongst those that are claiming to be compliant will continue.
>
> (SciVisum 2004)

Faulkner and Arch (2003) argue that the interpretation of the results from the automated tools requires assessors trained in accessibility techniques with an understanding of the technical and usability issues facing people with disabilities. A thorough understanding of accessibility is also required in order to competently assess the checkpoints that the automated tools cannot check such as consistent navigation, and appropriate writing and presentation style. Wattenberg (2004) acknowledges that while these tools are beneficial, developers do not always have the time or the motivation to understand the complex and often lengthy recommendations that the validation tools produce.

Combining automatic and manual judgement of accessibility

> The first step is to evaluate the current site with a combination of automated tools and focused human testing. Such a combination is necessary because neither approach, by itself, can be considered accurate or reliable enough to catch every type of error.
>
> (Bohman 2003c)

With the growing acceptance that accessibility evaluation cannot rely on automated methods and tools alone, a number of studies have used a combination of different methods to evaluate accessibility (Hinn 1999; McCord *et al.* 2002; Sloan *et al.* 2002; Borchert and Conkas 2003). Hinn (1999) reports on how she used Bobby combined with computer-facilitated focus groups and focused individual interviews to evaluate a virtual learning environment for students with disabilities. In an evaluation of selected web-based health information resources, McCord *et al.* (2002) also used Bobby, but combined this with a manual evaluation of how the resources interacted with screen reader and speech recognition software.

In thinking about the practicalities of using a combined approach a number of issues arise: time and resources required; the number of people who should be involved in manual evaluation; and the level of expertise required of those people involved in manual evaluation.

Time and resources

Diaper and Worman (2003) argue that they don't think most organisations have the resources, and particularly the expertise, to assess thoroughly their website's accessibility in the way that experts such as Sloan *et al.* (2002) have. In evaluating the resources required to conduct an evaluation and redesign exercise, Borchert and Conkas (2003) highlight what they see as the hidden costs of accessibility testing:

> Researching and understanding the principles and techniques of accessibility testing is a hidden cost. Accessing and installing accessibility testing tools and running the tests requires significant time, but it is the analysis of test results, and the formation of technical solutions, specific

to the needs of your own site and service goals that are the most time consuming tasks.

Number of people

In contrast with the team approach adopted by Sloan *et al.* (2002), many evaluation studies are conducted by just one or two people. For example, Axtell and Dixon (2002) manually checked one service (WebVoyage 2000 – an online public access catalogue) for conformance to the Section 508 web accessibility standard. However, the Web Accessibility Initiative (Brewer 2004) appear to favour the use of review teams, arguing that it is the optimum approach for evaluating accessibility of websites because of the advantages that the different perspectives on a review team can bring. They consider that review teams should have expertise in the following areas:

- web mark-up languages and validation tools;
- web content accessibility guidelines and techniques;
- conformance evaluation process for evaluating websites for accessibility;
- use of a variety of evaluation tools for website accessibility;
- use of computer-based assistive technologies and adaptive strategies;
- web design and development.

Level of expertise

Many evaluation studies adopt a 'have-a-go' response to accessibility evaluation. For example, Byerley and Chambers (2002) documented the problems encountered in using screen readers with two web-based abstracting and indexing services. In the initial phase of the study, the researchers (two sighted librarians) tested the database using JAWS and Windoweyes. They performed simple keyword searches, accessed help screens and manipulated search results by marking citations, printing and emailing full text articles. Others adopt the view that because evaluating accessibility and understanding the guidelines and tools is so difficult, the services of an expert accessibility auditor should be adopted (Sloan 2000).

Two studies that report the involvement of experts are those of Sloan *et al.* (2002) and Thompson *et al.* (2003). Sloan *et al.* carried out an accessibility study of 11 websites in the UK Higher Education sector in 1999. They describe the methodology used by an evaluation team of research experts to carry out the audits which included: drawing initial impressions; testing with automatic validation tools; manual evaluation with accessibility; general inspection; viewing with browsers and assistive technologies; and usability evaluation. Thompson, *et al.* (2003) describe how two web accessibility 'experts' manually evaluated the key web pages of 102 public research universities using a five-point rating scale that focused on each site's 'functional accessibility,' i.e., whether all users can accomplish the perceived function of the site. The evaluators' combined results were positively correlated with those obtained by using Bobby on the same sample.

There appears to be an interesting paradox at work here. For some, there is a perception that tools will help to ease the burden and take a 'great load' off the shoulders of designers, developers and authors (Kraithman and Bennet 2005). The reality appears to be different however, in that many tools place a great deal of responsibility on the shoulders of designers, developers and authors in terms of needing to interpret the results that tools produce. This has led some to argue that the use of tools should be accompanied by human judgement, in particular expert human judgement. Thus, it would appear that those considered not to be experts, may not have a role in judging the accessibility of online material at all. This feels like a retrograde step in terms of helping novice learning technologists to feel that they have an important responsibility and contribution to make to the accessibility of online material. In order to avoid disempowering learning technologists we perhaps need to look at developing better tools and/or effective ways of helping learning technologists to gain the skills required to conduct manual judgements of the accessibility of online material.

Conclusions

In order to understand and make the best use of accessibility guidelines, standards and tools learning technologists need to understand and critique the design approaches that underpin accessibility guidelines and standards and appreciate and critique the strengths and weaknesses of using automatic accessibility tools. By increasing their understanding of these issues learning technologists will be in a stronger position to:

- choose which guidelines, standards and tools they will adopt and justify their choice;
- adopt or adapt the processes and methodologies that have been used to design and evaluate online material.

Furthermore, in exploring in more detail the different approaches to accessible design, learning technologists should start to get a clearer sense of alignment between:

- definitions of accessibility;
- approaches to accessible design;
- accessibility guidelines and standards;
- accessibility evaluation tools and methods.

For example, definitions of accessibility that incorporate or stress 'ease of use' (e.g. Disability Rights Commission, 2004) may be operationalized through design approaches that focus on usability. The products of these approaches may then be judged against standards that emphasize usability (e.g. WCAG–1) and evaluated using tools that use these standards as benchmarks.

There are signs that some areas are attempting to move towards a standardization of methods and tools. For example, the Euroaccessibility Consortium launched an initiative in 2003 with W3C to foster European co-operation towards a harmonized methodology for evaluating the accessibility of websites. Snaprud and Aslaksen (2004) highlight the development of a European Internet Accessibility Observatory, which has as one of its aims the benchmarking of websites. Whilst moves towards standardization may be helpful, evidence in this chapter suggests that the science of standardization will need to be counterbalanced by the art of judgement and experience. For example, Witt and McDermott (2002: 49) argue that 'as a result of the range of standards and guidelines, the levels of interpretation and the subjective judgements required in negotiating these, the creation of an accessible solution is very much an art'. A major advantage of viewing accessibility as both an art and a science is that learning technologists will be encouraged to take all dimensions and variables into account and to not to focus solely on the technology (Stratford and Sloan 2005).

Chapter 8

Supporting the use of accessible e-learning

The student support service perspective

There is a risk that the emphasis on provision for disabled students remains too much on providing students with individual support to access an otherwise inaccessible 'mainstream' system, which remains largely unchanged. In this model the emphasis is placed on student support and individual funding through the DSA to provide the necessary assistance, which is seen as 'extra' to what is viewed as 'normal'. From this perspective, individual students are provided with support to get round or over barriers in the institutional environment. The alternative perspective, informed by the social model of disability, would say that it is the environment that needs to change, in order that barriers to disabled students are tackled and removed.

(Tinklin *et al.* 2004: 649)

Introduction

From the perspective of those who work within student support services, the issues that are likely to be important to them in relation to e-learning and accessibility are:

- How can I effectively support disabled students in their use of e-learning?
- How should the support service in which I work be organized in order to effectively support disabled students in their use of e-learning?

Addressing these issues is a particular challenge because institutions organize their services in different ways. Some services are strategically planned; others are created on a more ad-hoc basis (Stefani 2000; Adams and Brown 2000). Some services are organized to reflect particular specialisms; others are not. This chapter will focus on two different kinds of student support as examples of both specialist and generic support provision: assistive technology support services and library support services. The different issues that each service faces will be highlighted along with the implications for service development.

The way assistive technology support services and library support services address the issues that face them is important because assumptions about the models of disability that these services are operating or adopting will be made from the way they approach service organization and development. For example, with the move towards inclusion, many are questioning the extent to which student support services should be a separate service provision and the extent to which it should be integrated into 'mainstream' service provision:

> A move beyond the well-meaning but often ad hoc response made when faced with disabled students is clearly required. It will no longer be appropriate to view this issue as one of adaptation and add-on. In this way, issues of participation cannot remain closed within a student services arena but must become part of the mainstream learning and teaching debate. This is not to denigrate the value of support services and the important role they will continue to play in enabling access to higher education for many disabled students. Rather, it is a recognition that increasingly this role will involve working in partnership with academic staff in considering the students' learning needs, including course design and delivery.
>
> (Adams and Brown 2000: 7)

Assistive technology support services

The planning and organization of assistive technology support services is often focused on issues regarding:

- making specialist equipment (assistive and adaptive technologies) available;
- assessing the assistive technology needs of students;
- providing generic and specific technology skills training for students.

Making specialist equipment available

The importance of providing specialist equipment for students with disabilities is generally accepted (Owens et al. 1999; Alexander 2002). There is some evidence to suggest however that provision of assistive technologies is varied and patchy in colleges and universities (Fichten et al. 2003). For example, Fichten et al. (1999) evaluated the views and opinions of both students with disabilities and of Disabled Student Services Officers in Canada concerning the use of computers in post-secondary education. Results indicated that there was an even split among institutions that kept their adaptive technology in one central location and those that decentralized their equipment. Similarly, about half of all institutions had a loan program, while the rest did not. In general, smaller institutions were less likely to have specialized computer technologies for their students. A related issue concerned hours of availability, with over 80 per cent of institutions indicating weekend and evening access to adapted equipment mainly through sign-in/sign-out procedures. All institutions studied had access to the Internet, but only half had adapted computers with Internet access.

In an Australian study, Leung, *et al.* (1999) found a similar patchiness in service provision. They conducted a survey of students and Disability Liaison Officers (DLOs) regarding technology needs and provision. Most responding DLOs confirmed that there were relatively few computers (e.g. three to ten) currently available, which allowed access for all. Seventy nine per cent of DLOs estimated that there were fewer than ten computers on their campuses with adaptive software or peripherals available in computer laboratories. Computers on one campus with appropriate software and peripherals were not easily accessible because of the general campus environment. Software required by students with disabilities was often not accessible on all computers on campus. The location of accessible equipment with special software and peripherals varied at different institutions from specific resource rooms and library resource rooms to a central lab. The specialized and segregated use of rooms was seen in both a positive and negative light, with one DLO commenting: 'Why should students with disabilities have to study in a different building to the rest of their faculty?'

Specialized equipment rooms versus adapted mainstream campus computers?

Distance education and open learning institutions have attracted a large number of students with disabilities and so have needed to address how these students gain access to specialised equipment that they may need. For example, Downie (2000) describes the 'equipment pool' that The Open Training and Education Network (OTEN) in Australia had established for its students with disabilities. This was not without practical difficulties such as budgetary constraints, demand outstripping supply and lengthy waiting lists. However, Downie considers that the program has also yielded many positives including the fact that some students who would not have otherwise been competitive have been very successful.

Campus-based institutions have also invested in specialist equipment, which is often placed in 'Assistive Technology Centres'. For example, Blankfield and Martin (2002) describe how at Edgehill College of Higher Education in the UK, an Assistive Technology Area is planned to be situated in the Learning Resource Centre, which will be specifically for the use of students with disabilities, specific learning difficulties and mental health needs. This area will contain PCs and a range of assistive software. In addition, an Assistive Technology advisor has been appointed who will be managing the area, providing training, support and advice for students and staff. Jones and Tedd (2003) provide a case study of how three Welsh universities have attempted to cater for the needs of visually impaired students. All three provide specialist areas, but operate them in different ways. For one university, Jones and Tedd report:

> In three of the libraries . . . there is a Green Card Area where suitable equipment for those with special needs is housed. (It was originally called this as students needed to have special green cards to access the equipment – now access is via the student's username and password.)
> (Jones and Tedd 2003: 110)

Whilst at another of the three universities, Jones and Tedd report that specialist equipment has been made available in the Arts and Social Studies Library as part of a large cluster of PCs which is used by all students. When the large monitor workstations are not required by visually impaired students they are available for use by any student. In addition, one Braille embosser is available in a lockable, soundproofed room, as it was feared that the noise generated by the machine would create a disturbance. Funding has also allowed for a full-time 'PC support assistant' trained in the use of the specialist software to be on hand to oversee the day-to-day running of these facilities. In the central library on one campus, Jones and Tedd note that there is a lockable 'Special Resources Room' for the visually impaired, which is looked after by the member of the library staff with special responsibility for disabled students. The examples provided by Jones and Tedd raise interesting issues about the way that specialist technology areas are set up and managed:

- specialist technology is available to just students with disabilities or for all students;
- specialist technology is locked or protected by keys or passwords;
- specialist technology is supervised by specialist staff.

How universities handle each of these issues will influence the extent to which students with disabilities feel labelled as different. For example, having to ask a member of staff to unlock a resource room, or having to use a 'green card' to access resources.

Access to a wireless Local Area Network

Different solutions to the issue of enabling students with disabilities access to specialized equipment do exist. One possible solution, which may become more prominent as universities develop their IT structures and systems, is the provision of wireless Local Area Networks (LAN). Marshall and Cunneen (2001) outline the rationale for setting up a wireless LAN at the Eastern Institute of Technology in New Zealand, which focuses on the observation that students often have their own very customized personal computers (usually laptops) set up with this specialized software and equipment (see Chapter 5) and therefore rather than setting up specialist networked computers on campus which duplicate all these expensive and sometimes restrictive software it would be easier to allow students to use their own laptops to access the campus network. Marshall and Cunneen (2001: 3) report that feedback from students has been 'extremely positive':

> they are now able to use this technology across campus at a number of locations which has proven to be a real bonus at examination time when they can use their own PC and print to local printers without the hassle of setting up a physical connection . . . Students can access library databases using the network card and are now able to access and use computer laboratories flexibly rather than relying on others for data input and support.

Such an approach is attractive because it has the potential to benefit all students, not just those with disabilities.

Assistive technology assessment

Disabled students attending college or university frequently require an assessment of their assistive technology (AT) needs and advice on appropriate equipment. This raises a number of issues: who is involved in the assessments? How are the assessments conducted? What is the outcome of the assessment?

Who is involved in assistive technology assessments?

Students can be assessed for their AT needs by agents within or outside the college or university they are attending. If an assessment is conducted within the college or university it is most likely to be conducted by a disability officer or equivalent. For example, in their Australian survey, Leung *et al.* (1999) found that of those students who were assessed for their technology needs, Disability Liaison Officers were the primary assessors. In some cases, teacher consultants or assistants had the responsibility for assessment of AT for students. Equipment suppliers and vendors were sometimes involved in the assessment process. However, Leung *et al.* consider that the role of DLOs as members of an assessment team is desirable in all cases, as DLOs will be the ongoing contact staff for students with disabilities.

Students may also be assessed for their AT needs by outside organizations. For example, in order to be able to afford specialist equipment, many students in the UK need to apply to their Local Education Authorities for Disabled Students Allowance (DSA). The Authorities often refer them to an approved assessment centre (e.g. Access Centres) who conduct AT assessment and make recommendations to the Authority (and the student). In reflecting on her experience of being a DLO, Sanders (2000) writes of Access Centres:

> These were scattered throughout the country and were generally where a student went in order to be assessed for appropriate equipment. Access Centres had all the latest technology, the staff were aware of funding issues and how much was available to students under the DSA. In my experience, Access Centres were a wonderful resource and did an excellent job of ensuring students were appropriately set up with suitable technology.

Students may find that they are assessed by both their educational institution and an external agency. This may cause problems, particularly where assessments by an institution conflict with recommendations from external agencies. The Southern Higher and Further Education Consortium (2001) consider that this problem could be overcome if institutions offer to organize or undertake DSA related assessments rather than students needing to arrange these independently.

The knowledge and training of university staff who act as AT assessors is a concern to some (Leung *et al.* 1999; Horwath 2002). There is certainly evidence to suggest that assessors within universities are more comfortable assessing for straightforward cases (e.g. dyslexia) compared to more complex physical, sensory or mental health-related difficulties. This has led some to urge assessors not to be afraid to refer students onto more specialist assessors:

> There is a need to increase the availability of affordable individual expert assessment, but this must be complemented by appropriate signposting to such qualified specialist organisations. That implies a requirement for the education of those who have prime responsibility for assessing the more general assistive technology needs of disabled people.
>
> (Horwath 2002: 39)

Irrespective of whether an AT assessment is conducted by the educational institution or not, assessments vary in the extent and manner in which they involve students. For some, students will be seen as at the centre of the process, for others this may be less so. However, there is a strong argument for adopting a student-centred approach to assessment and working hard to understand the difficulties that each individual student encounters in learning and teaching situations (Leung *et al.* 1999; Draffan 2002):

> Institutions can also do a great deal to ensure their policies and practices assist technology in helping removing barriers to learning and participation. However, since only the individual student can decide whether any particular technology is appropriate to meet their particular individual

needs it is important for student and institution to discuss these needs and how they can be best met.

(Wald 2002: 23)

How are AT assessments conducted?

The purpose of an AT assessment is to find AT solutions that will meet a student's needs: finding the best fit (Phillips 2004) or matching the person to the technology (Scherer 2004). The ways in which assessors go about doing this will vary, but it is unlikely that they will consciously adopt a particular AT assessment model. For many their approach will be trial and error:

> This student found writing assignments a frustrating and laborious task. Her strategy was to dictate and then elaborate her ideas to her writer. Together they went over the grammar, spell checking and general organisation of the essay. She wanted more independence within this process. An assessor from AbleTech Hamilton NZ, discussed with her various options of assistive technology that she could work with. Through trial and error, KeyRep, a scanner and screen reader programme proved to be most suitable. Workbridge funded the assessment and equipment. The student works with a note taker in lectures and a reader/writer in test/exams with her exams being split.
>
> (Haines and Molenaar 2000: 17)

One assessment model that was developed specifically for education settings is Scherer's Matching Persons to Technology (MPT) Model and associated assessment process (Scherer 2004). The model focuses not only on student strengths and needs but also their preferences, motivation and readiness, expectations and mood as well as lifestyle factors. This information is then balanced with the characteristics of the environments in which the technology will be used, along with the features and functions of the technology itself. One of the attractions of this model is its student-centred approach and flexibility. This may provide challenges for some however, as Seale (2002: 85) notes:

> one of the implications of this model is that student needs and perceptions of the value of technologies may change over time, thus requiring a flexible approach to assessing and reviewing their needs. This will be a real challenge for institutions, who in their response to the new legislation, may put systems and procedures in place that work against flexibility.

What Scherer's model does prompt AT assessors to address is the environment and circumstances in which the technology be used. This is particularly important when thinking about whether and how students will use their AT within their e-learning environments. For example, Draffan and Rainger (2004) argue:

> It is clear that some of the assessments used to discover various learner preferences or learning styles do not appear to take account of aspects relevant to the various e-learning environments often used within educational establishments. Nor do these tests evaluate the skills required to use additional technologies in order to access the materials.

Draffan and Rainger also note that assessment may take too much account of the disability label or category that a student has been assigned and ignore their learning styles and coping strategies.

What is the outcome of AT assessments?

AT assessors may recommend specific pieces of equipment for a student. But a successful outcome of an AT assessment depends on whether or not the equipment is purchased and whether or not the equipment is used. In countries such as the UK, where there is a Disabled Students Allowance, funding and purchasing of equipment recommended by assessors is less problematic than in countries such as the US. For example, Goodman *et al.* (2002) found in their US study that lack of financial resources was the major reason why recommended equipment and training was not purchased by students with disabilities.

While many AT assessors in higher education are not using formal assessment models or processes they are also not formally measuring the outcomes of AT assessment, particularly whether or not students actually use or benefit from the AT that has been recommended them. Some practitioners have conducted satisfaction surveys. For example, Cobham *et al.* (2001) conducted a UK survey of the satisfaction of 66 disabled students with the AT assessment process. While results revealed that students were largely satisfied, the issue of a lack of initial training in the use of equipment and software was raised. However, measurement probably needs to involve more than a simple satisfaction survey. For example, Leung *et al.* (1999) note that while the majority of students in their survey were satisfied with the assessment process and the skills of their assessor, there was a possibility that these students were reporting satisfaction despite the fact the improvements experienced through the solution might have been 'far from ideal'. Goodman *et al.* (2002) used Scherer's assessment process (Assistive Technology Device Predisposition Assessment) to explore the factors that influenced the adoption or rejection of AT by 14 college students with disabilities. Follow-up interviews with the students after their AT assessments revealed that most of the AT recommended to the students in the class served to enhance performance and that 75 per cent of the students in the study adopted at least one form of recommended AT and were continuing to use it one year after taking the class. It was noted, however, that most of the technology involved was simple (e.g. part of standard accessibility features of mainstream technologies) as opposed to complex specialized systems.

Skills training for students

Those who work in student support services are gradually beginning to realize that students need training and support to use their technological equipment, once it has been recommended and provided (Haines and Molenaar 2000). Downie (2000) argues that it is unreasonable to make equipment available and not provide training on how to use it. There is recognition that students need help with relatively simple things such as how to use the access features of standard technologies (Keller *et al.* 2000) as well as more complex things such as downloading and installing third-party plug-ins (Sajka and Roeder 2002). Students may also need help with AT solutions that are more complex:

> It is worth noting that, although these technologies can for many, enable independent access to the curriculum, the greater the complexity of the solution the more we ask of the user. The brain power involved in deciphering all the information presented on a computer screen, extracting what is pertinent and using it to best advantage, is often taken for granted-add to this the normal workload of studying and meeting deadlines. Only then can we begin to understand the huge cognitive burden placed on the student.
>
> (Henderson 2002: 32)

Library support services

Because libraries house a great deal of print-based material, there has been a lot of focus on making library services particularly accessible to those who are print disabled (e.g. blind or partially sighted). Surveys that explore the preparedness of libraries to make their material accessible, reveal that libraries have made starts, but are by no means there yet. For example, Harris and Oppenheim (2003) conducted a questionnaire survey of 230 further education college libraries in the UK. Results revealed that disability legislation had affected each library differently. Some were better equipped to implement the requirements of the Act due to the resources already in place. Other libraries had more work to do and concerns surrounding training and funding were raised as possible problems that could prevent the successful implementation of the legislation. When specific services that libraries provide such as websites or online databases and catalogues are examined a similar picture of patchy accessibility is painted.

Library websites

In the US, Schmetzke (2001, 2002a,b) has examined the accessibility of college and university websites. He reports that many libraries have not taken proper action to ensure that their web pages are freely accessible to people with print disabilities. Schmetzke (2001) conducted a review of 24 studies, which investigated the accessibility of websites, ten of which included library websites. He was particularly bemused to find that the web pages of library schools were inaccessible.

Craven (2000) reports on a study which tested the accessibility of university library websites in the UK and explored the accessibility awareness of library web page designers. Results revealed that little had improved since 1998. Craven suggests that this is perhaps not surprising, as once a site has been created there may be little motivation to change it very much, apart from general updates. Factors that may hinder accessible design of university library websites were identified as:

- responsibility for the library web pages resting with staff who have institution wide web responsibilities or who manage a number of department pages, which happen to include the library;
- training that focuses on general web authoring with little specific focus on accessibility issues;
- confusing and unhelpful validation tools and services.

A survey of over 50 project websites funded by the JISC's 5/99 digital library programme was carried out in 2002 (Kelly 2002b). The JISC 5/99 digital library programme has funded projects which provide online teaching and learning resources in a range of subject areas. Despite projects having a contractual agreement to support a number of open standards and best practices (which includes WCAG-1) the findings showed that 46 per cent of the project home pages failed to comply with WCAG-1 guidelines, based on the automated detection of errors.

Library databases and catalogues

The graphical nature and complexity of web design means that there is potential for online library databases and catalogue systems to be inaccessible to students with disabilities. A number of studies have evaluated the accessibility of a range of systems (Byerley and Chambers 2002; Horwath 2002; McCord et al. 2002). Horwath (2002) conducted a user evaluation of four online proprietary databases and concluded that the largest factor affecting ease of use and accessibility was the design of the resources. The following design elements made the databases in the study difficult to use:

- illogical placement of links, buttons or edit boxes on the screen;
- inadequate labels on the links, buttons and edit boxes;
- check boxes and 'combo boxes' that are coded in such a way that keyboard rather than mouse input is difficult or impossible;
- lack of explanatory text on screens to provide directions to users;
- use of frames.

McCord *et al.* (2002: 198) evaluated the accessibility of eight databases and concluded that while they were all to some degree accessible to 'persons with disabilities using adaptive software, many accessibility and usability problems remain'.

Librarians are not in a position to design and develop accessible databases and catalogues themselves. Burgstahler argues, however, that they can play a role in judging the accessibility of systems before they are purchased:

> If you cannot locate an accessible product, ask the vendor of [such] an inaccessible product about what steps they have taken to make their products accessible and what plans they have for making future versions of their products accessible. Make it clear that you will consider accessibility in all purchase decisions and that you expect them to solve their accessibility problems in a reasonable length of time.
>
> (Burgstahler 2002a: 428)

Examples of librarians being proactive in seeking and demanding accessible products include Byerley and Chambers (2002: 177) who sent an email questionnaire to suppliers of two library databases used in their library to ask them about accessibility compliance of their products. While Jones and Tedd (2003) report how three universities acquired the Voyager library management system in a purchasing consortium arrangement. In implementing the Voyager system, staff at each library had to make decisions on customizing the interface for students with disabilities. Axtell and Dixon (2002) report on a review of Voyager for persons with visual disabilities and concluded that 'with some effort, it can be successfully navigated by experienced users of assistive technology'. They also provided recommendations both for the supplier, Endeavor, and for libraries using Voyager so that the search interface could be made more easily accessible for visually impaired users.

Conclusion

The two services highlighted in this chapter are different in that all disabled students will need to use library services, whilst not all students will need to use assistive technology support services. The two services are similar however, in that attempting to meet the needs of disabled students prompts both services to address the specialist knowledge and skills that staff working within the services may or may not be required to have. Library staff may lack knowledge regarding accessible design and accessibility compliance, whilst assistive technology staff may lack knowledge regarding assessment models and assessing for complex disabilities. Sustainable solutions to this problem are unlikely to present themselves as long as support for disabled students is seen as a separate activity to mainstream student support activities. Such a view can isolate those who work in specialist service sections, lead to fragmented student support services as well as lead to a model of provision that does little to reduce the barriers to accessibility.

Edwards (2000) argues that an inclusive model of disability services should be adopted whereby disability services are promoted as an expert resource for assisting institutional staff as opposed to a service that support students who are deficient in some way. Adopting a model whereby specialist disability staff are encouraged to support other staff in the institution could pave the way for strategic partnerships to develop whereby:

- assistive technologists are involved in supporting library staff to develop and procure accessible online resources;
- IT and Computing service staff are involved in helping assistive technology staff to support disabled students in their use of specialist and generic technologies;
- assistive technologist staff and disability officers can contribute to accessibility related staff development programmes;
- lecturers can liaise with assistive technologists and disability officers regarding the kinds of e-learning experiences that they are offering in their courses, so that assistive technologists and disability officers can make more informed recomendations to students about the kind of support and specialist technologies they will require in order to engage with the e-learning on offer;
- staff developers can organize development opportunities that promote discussion and information exchange between all the 'service providers' within an instiution;
- disability officers can be involved in embedding accessibility policies and practices into the wider community and ensuring that disability is integrated into an institution's planning and funding programme (Shaw 2003).

Developing effective support services therefore involves more than supporting students, it involves supporting and working with staff across the whole higher education institution.

Chapter 9

Developing accessible
e-learning practice

The staff developer's perspective

> SENDA . . . has charged staff developers with the responsibility of impact-
> ing on the e-learning accessibility practices of their institutions, by inter-
> acting with key stakeholders and working to integrate the individual
> practices of these stakeholders into the practice of their institution as a
> whole.
>
> (Seale 2003a)

Introduction

From a staff developer's perspective the issues that might be important to
them in relation to disability, accessibility and e-learning are:

- How can I help institutional staff raise their awareness of disability and
  accessibility issues?
- What role should I take in helping staff to design, deliver, maintain and
  support accessible e-learning?

In addressing these issues staff developers will be faced with a number of key
challenges. The first of which is the challenge of addressing accessibility
across the whole institution. The argument that accessibility can no longer be
seen as a specialist subject that only a few specialist staff have the expertise
to address and therefore that expertise and responsibility needs to be established across the whole of an institution is gaining ground and support.
For example, O'Connor (2000) argues that if e-learning is going to benefit
students with a disability 'it is crucial that disability expertise is shared and
embedded throughout the institution'. Staff developers therefore have a role
in designing and delivering programmes that provide a wide range of institutional staff with the opportunity to raise their awareness and develop their
skills in the area of e-learning and accessibility.

If staff developers have a role to play in embedding accessibility across
an institution, they will need to consider how to deliver development
opportunities to more than just the converted (Jeffels and Marston 2003) and

how to match these opportunities with the skill level and responsibility of the various staff (Techdis n.d.). This chapter will explore how staff developers can meet the challenges ahead of them by:

- matching development opportunities to the needs of a range of stakeholders;
- adopting a range of delivery methods;
- developing strategic partnerships with key stakeholders.

What are the development needs of staff in relation to e-learning and disability?

The exploration of the perspectives of lecturers, learning technologists and student support services in previous chapters reveals a range of potential development needs, some of which are very specific to a particular stakeholder group and some of which are more generic. For lecturers, the development needs include: disability awareness; curriculum design (e.g. inclusive, universal and holistic design) and e-learning (e.g. accessibility features of standards tools such as WebCT). For learning technologists, the development needs include: disability awareness, accessible design (e.g. universal, usability and user-centred design); guidelines and standards; assistive technologies; choosing appropriate evaluation and repair tools and combining automatic and manual accessibility judgement methods. For those working in student support services, the development needs include: assistive technologies; assessment approaches and management; procurement of accessible systems and e-learning.

Disability awareness

Disability awareness opportunities can be offered in many different ways. However, evidence suggests that lecturers may benefit from quite detailed and specific awareness raising opportunities. For example, Keats (2003) reports the results of a survey of the staff development needs of teaching staff in UK higher education in relation to disabled students: 616 lecturers (mostly from the Open University) completed a questionnaire survey and results revealed that of the 120 respondents who had received disability awareness training, 50 per cent found it to be fairly useful and 45 per cent very useful. The main reason given for not finding the training very useful was because it was too general and did not deal with the needs of particular groups of disabled students. For the 38 per cent of respondents who felt they were not very knowledgeable about the needs of students with disabilities the main areas where it was felt that knowledge needed to be improved were access to resources to support specific types of disabled students (e.g. an information database), how to support students with dyslexia and mental health difficulties and the uses of assistive technology for different groups of disabled students.

Just as lecturers appear to want more specific disability awareness training, so too do support staff. For example, Scott (2001) reports on the activities of the Integrating Disability in Educational Arenas (IDEAs) project which involved auditing the training and development needs of support staff in four Scottish Higher Education Institutions. The audit concentrated on: identifying the general awareness of disability issues; evaluating staff experience of working with students with disabilities; focusing on specific issues for participating departments and conducting a training needs analysis. A total of 574 staff participated in the IDEAs audit across the four institutions, which involved one-to-one interviews, focus groups and questionnaires. Staff indicated a variety of training needs, the majority of which focused on specific as well as general disability awareness, including: communication issues (e.g. dealing with a student who has a speech impediment, a deaf student who is lip reading); disability awareness: the range of disabilities, attitudes, language; dyslexia; mental health difficulties; mobility impairment; unseen disabilities and visual impairment.

Whilst learning technologists may also benefit from disability awareness opportunities, disability advocates such as the Disability Rights Commission argue that it is important that disability awareness opportunities provide learning technologists 'with the techniques to translate that awareness into practice' (DRC 2004).

Assistive technologies

Surveys of the needs of support staff suggest that there is a need for assistive technology (AT) training. For example, results from a survey by Leung *et al.* (1999) that involved Disability Liaison Officers in Australia suggested that there was a specific need for training that enabled the officers to keep abreast of recent AT developments and conduct confident and knowledgeable assessments that dealt with the potential conflicts of interest between the student, university and vendor/supplier. In a more recent survey by Thompson (2004b), which reports on the professional development needs of people supporting assistive technology and information technology accessibility on college campuses in the US, the need to keep up to date with AT was also highlighted, along with the need for advanced AT training (e.g. programming systems).

Disability legislation has meant that many support staff have taken on a key assistive technology assessment role: a complex role, for which frequently they have not been trained and which requires key managerial skills. In discussing the role of managers of specialist assessment centres Waterfield and Hurst (2000) argue that conducting successful assessment activities requires knowledge of the consequences of particular disabilities on learning support needs and specific curriculum requirements, as well as being aware of developments in specialist assessment methods. Therefore, training for this group of staff is of paramount importance if there is to be parity and credibility of provision across the Higher Education sector. According to Waterfield and Hurst, successful management involves:

- defining models of good practice;
- building teams;
- interacting with a complex 'client group' and understanding the cultural dimensions of the 'client group';
- recognizing the implications of different funding arrangements;
- recognizing the appropriateness of developments in specialist assessment methods.

In order to achieve this, Waterfield and Hurst argue not only that training and staff development is required, but that 'focused and specific HE relevant qualifications are necessary'. Staff developers may therefore need to address the extent to which they not only provide their own development programmes for assessors which address key management issues, but also work towards aligning these programmes with internal or external qualification programmes.

E-learning

In considering the need for a greater understanding of the potential and challenges of e-learning, Alexander (2002) focuses on specific e-learning tools and argues that WebCT training programmes for academic staff should include an accessibility component to ensure that staff are aware of the ways in which course materials can be made more, or less, accessible to students with disabilities. Attention should also be drawn to WebCT tools that are likely to cause problems for disabled students. Where academics wish to use these tools in the delivery of subjects, they will need to be encouraged to provide equivalent accessible alternatives for students who cannot access them.

Support staff cannot help disabled students to use their assistive technologies with the e-learning facilities that institutions provide, if they are not aware of how e-learning works. There would therefore seem to be a need to provide support staff with general and specific e-learning training. For example, in discussing issues surrounding the use of WebCT by dyslexic students at the University of East London, Wright and Stephenson (2002) argue:

> Extra hours should be funded for all visiting dyslexia support tutors for training in online learning and WebCT so that support for on-line assignments can be effectively delivered during the normal support

sessions. If it is not possible to fund a special needs IT staff in the special needs resource areas, training should also be given to Learning Resource Centre staff to give support with WebCT as well as other specialist dyslexia software which they can support at present.

Methods for meeting development needs

Three common methods for meeting the accessibility related development needs of institutional staff are: workshops. online resources and courses and a hybrid approach.

Workshops

Workshops are a familiar and popular method for delivering staff development. In the field of e-learning and accessibility, workshops tend to be very specific and specialist in nature. For example, Rosenbaum *et al.* (2002) describe a workshop that focused on user-centred design and argue that entire development teams and their managers should be involved in user-centred design workshops so that there is a forum for asking questions and discussing world views about design and development. Duchateau *et al.* (2002) describe how BrailleNet has set up workshops for web designers in which they learn how to review, repair and design accessible web pages.

Workshops can certainly be a good forum for discussion between different stakeholder groups, provided the discussion triggers are well designed. For example, Waterfield and Hurst (2000) describe activities they have used in staff development programmes using discussion trigger cases studies that are designed to highlight the tendency of teaching staff to focus on the disability rather than the student. Specialist videos or simulations that highlight the experiences of people with disabilities may also be a useful way of triggering discussion about the needs of students with disabilities (Harniss and Amtman 2005; Ball and Roussell 2004).

One disadvantage, however, of running specialist e-learning and accessibility workshops is that staff may see the issues as an add-on or after-thought rather than an integral part of practice. Pearson and Koppi (2003) argue that accessibility issues need to be introduced early enough in a staff development course to encourage and enable inclusive practices to be embraced in a systematic fashion. However, in the UK, the Academic Staff Development in Support of Disabled Students Project (2002) argues that it is possible to weave and integrate references to disability into many 'mainstream' staff development courses.

Although workshops are a commonly used format for delivering staff development, they are not always well received. For example, in reporting on a staff development event at their institution, Jeffels and Marston (2003) noted:

Although the summer staff development training event in 2003 was extremely well attended, there has been a marked drop in attendance at both accessibility workshops and seminars during this academic session. Most events were cancelled and replaced with individual one-to-one sessions with those who had expressed an interest. Feedback on the reasons for this seem to indicate that most staff who have expressed an interest in learning about accessibility have already attended our events and know who to contact if they do have specific questions.

The experience of Jeffels and Marston (2003) suggest that workshops may be a useful way of beginning a general university-wide awareness 'campaign', but that they may need to be followed up with a range of methods that are more specifically targeted (e.g. focusing on specific disabilities such as dyslexia or on departmental practices as opposed to university practices).

Online resources and courses

A common response to the need to provide staff with development opportunities is to point them to online information and resources, the majority of which have been developed by external agencies. There is a certainly a wide range of resources available (see Table 9.1):

- online courses;
- online AT and specialist equipment databases;
- case studies;
- frequently asked questions;
- web links to other sources of information.

However, staff developers need to ensure that there is alignment between the objectives of the staff development programme and the stated strategic objectives or mission of the resource producers. For example, TechDis in the UK is seen as the primary source of information regarding e-learning and accessibility in higher education. It is however, quite vociferous in urging caution about adopting a universal design approach. If other elements of a staff development programme (and other stakeholders involved in delivering the programme) adopt a less cautious approach to universal design, staff may question the integrity of the programme, unless the discussion of such difference is integrated into the programme. Staff who are attempting to develop accessible e-learning material are confused enough by all the guidelines, specifications and tools that exist, so staff development programmes don't need to add to this confusion by recommending resources that appear to contradict what other resources, trainers and developers have said. Having said that, if staff developers carefully investigate the resources that they recommend to staff, they should be able to identify valuable opportunities to promote

Table 9.1 Online accessibility resources and courses

Project/centre	Mission, aims and activities	Resources on offer online
TechDis UK www.techdis.ac.uk	To enhance provision for disabled students and staff in higher, further and specialist education and adult and community learning, through the use of technology.	Case studies Staff development packs Articles Assistive technology Database (see Draffan and Corbett 2001) Guidelines Web links
Skills for Access UK www.skillsforaccess.org.uk/	To provide a comprehensive resource on issues relating to multimedia, e-learning and accessibility, aimed at both novices and experts.	Case studies Articles Web links
ALERT: Accessibility in Learning Environments and Related Technologies UK www.dur.ac.uk/alert/	To identify methods of supporting disabled students to enable them to achieve the pedagogical objectives of their modules through a learning environment.	Case studies Guidelines Web links
EASI US www.rit.edu/~easi/	To serve as a resource by providing information and guidance in the area of access-to-information technologies by individuals with disabilities. EASI disseminates information across a variety of sectors including colleges and universities.	Online training
Web Aim: Web Accessibility in Mind US www.webaim.org/	To expand the potential of the web for people with disabilities by providing knowledge, technical skills, tools and organizational leadership strategies.	Articles Training resources Discussion forum
National Center on Accessible Information Technology in Education (AccessIT) US http://www.washington.edu/accessit/index.php	To increase the access of individuals with disabilities to information technology in educational institutions at all academic levels nationwide.	Online course (See Amtman et al. 2005) Database of articles Case studies Web links

| ATRC: Adaptive Technology Resource Centre Canada http://www.utoronto.ca/atrc/ | To make education accessible to learners with disabilities and thereby enhancing learning for all learners. | Online course Discussion forum Library of papers Workshop handouts Web links |
| WANAU: Web Accessibility Network for Australian Universities Australia www.monash.edu.au/groups/accessibility/ | To raise awareness of the problems encountered by people with disabilities that affect their use of the web. | Online discussion forum |

discussion and debate within their programmes. For example, in describing the philosophy of the Skills for Access Project, Sloan and Stratford (2004) state: 'Ultimately, the philosophy of the Skills for Access project team, and the resource that will be the end result of the project, is to encourage developers to treat multimedia in learning environments as an "enabler" – as an "assistive technology" in its own "right" ' (Sloan and Stratford 2004). Such a statement could provide a useful trigger for a discussion on different understandings of what assistive technology is. Issues that may arise from such a discussion are likely to highlight issues regarding mainstream and specialist equipment (and services) that may draw out interesting conceptions regarding disability and how it is viewed.

Finally, online resources will only appeal to a certain proportion of the staff population. For example, Peacock, *et al.* (2002) used the 'Roundtables' methodology to develop a WebCT staff development module on accessibility legislation. In discussing deployment of the module within their institution, they acknowledged that success may depend on the extent to which 'IT phobic' staff accessed the resource.

A hybrid approach

Online materials are a useful resource for staff development, but there is a general acceptance that on their own they do not change practice. Thus they need to be used in conjunction with other face-to-face methods such as workshops, one-to-one sessions, and seminars:

> Our experience has shown that the materials can be used within a hybrid approach, i.e. one that uses a mixture of technology and traditional methods to deliver learning. The materials are being used as precursors to face-to-face workshops or as back-up materials for staff who may be undergoing a programme of staff development. Also, for the materials to work fully, it is felt that they need to be used in conjunction with other activities. Although the materials allow just-in-time answers, which busy

staff say they often need, there is a limit to the extent to which they can truly change behaviour and understanding on their own.

(Wray 2002)

In describing the development of an online course in accessibility Pearson and Koppi (2003) consider the benefits of the online course over the workshop:

> It also became apparent how much more valuable an online course can be than an ephemeral face-to-face workshop, which disappears without visible trace. The online course can be revisited and re-examined after further learning or application of learning has occurred. Access to essential information, resources and links to available software is easier, more efficient and available wherever the student has access to the computer. Fleeting ideas in a workshop, too soon gone because of the pace, can be explored in the online course in discussions and in student presentations that can remain on the site for all participants to access.

Following an evaluation of the online course, Pearson and Koppi's recommendations would appear to suggest however, that there is value in combining online methods with face-to-face methods. For example, they recommend that an induction session is provided before the online module starts, in order to introduce some of the assistive technologies and checking tools and to allow sufficient time for participants to have practice and experience in their use. Also, more hands-on practice with these technologies during the module activities would improve the experience for all the participants.

Strategies for meeting development needs

Just as the reasons for making e-learning accessible vary (see Chapter 1), so too can the strategies that staff developers adopt in attempting to meet the accessibility development needs of institutional staff. These strategies will reflect the extent to which institutions feel that staff have a choice about what they do regarding accessibility and e-learning and the extent to which responsibility for accessibility is perceived as an individual or institutional responsibility.

The carrot and stick strategy

Staff developers will probably need to decide what strategies or models they are going to adopt when trying to promote accessible e-learning practice. A key element of this decision may involve deciding what form of 'carrot and stick' (Parker 2001: 110) or coercion and encouragement (Seale 2003a) they will need to adopt.

What form the carrot and stick should take varies from commentator to commentator. Most agree that legislation will be a hefty stick (Parker 2001;

Jeffels and Marston 2003). Opinions vary however, on what the carrot may be. For example, Jeffels and Marston believe that usability will be the carrot that drives the production of accessible online materials. Others believe the carrot will be better design for all students. The Disability Rights Commission (2003) suggests a range of strategies for staff development, some of which may be interpreted as quite coercive:

- make it clear in contracts what standard of behaviour or practice is expected;
- make certain aspects of training compulsory;
- involve the vice chancellor, principal or director in inviting people to attend, or for introducing speakers;
- charge training to departmental budgets to encourage their attendance.

Other suggested strategies from the Disability Rights Commission are more collaborative or encouraging in nature:

- provide encouragement and recognition of development in this area through review and/or appraisal processes;
- take training to departments by adding short sessions onto existing departmental meetings
- provide a free lunch;
- target staff who are about to receive a disabled student into their department;
- make sure disability issues are incorporated into all appropriate training, not just disability-specific sessions;
- ask staff what training they would like and tailor development to their needs;
- involve departments in auditing their services and training needs.

Wray (2002) warns of the dangers of adopting an overly coercive or behaviourist approach to staff development. He argues that legislation such as SENDA could lead to some universities introducing a staff development methodology, which focuses on deficits in the skills of the workforce and on 'training' rather than the 'learning'. Resulting policies may lead to compulsory attendance at staff development events in order to avoid the institution being held responsible for individual staff behaviour but Wray suggests that such an approach will not encourage understanding and meaningful learning.

Develop strategic partnerships

Whether the approach adopted is coercive or collaborative, or a mixture of the two, staff developers are likely to need to develop strategic partnerships with a range of internal and external parties in order to:

- develop the content of staff development programmes and ensure it meets all the desired learning needs and outcomes;
- deliver the content of staff development programmes and ensure it is accurate, appropriate and practicable;
- gain credibility for staff development programmes and ensure support and engagement.

In developing strategic partnerships, staff developers may be in a prime position to be agents of change. For example, Phipps (2002: 6) argues:

> In order to engage with the process of systemic change, developers must act in a brokerage role with all the staff providing perspectives that can inform strategic policy and decisions. Staff and educational developers must be the catalysts that get technical, disability and lecturing staff into a dialogue and then act as a rapportuer to the senior management teams, providing contextualized input to all policies in their institution.

Partnerships with disability services

Phipps (2002) also argues that staff and educational developers should also give serious consideration to using non-traditional facilitators such as disability officers for workshops in this field. Evidence from a survey by Parker (2001) would certainly suggest that staff developers would benefit from the specialist knowledge that disability officers have. Parker describes a small survey of staff developers in the UK higher education sector, aimed at exploring current awareness and knowledge of disability access in higher education amongst those responsible for mainstream or non-specialist staff development. Although a majority of the respondents were familiar with the general difficulties encountered by students with disabilities and the strategies required to address these, awareness of disability-specific difficulties and strategies, was less widespread among respondents. Most respondents indicated that there were issues of access to learning and teaching for disabled students for which they needed staff development themselves and six of these mentioned contact or support from staff experienced in disability. Parker concludes: 'The study is a small indicator of current levels of disability awareness amongst mainstream staff developers. It suggests that there is a need for, and interest in, closer liaison between staff in disability services and those providing staff development more generally within the HEIs' (Parker 2001: 111).

An example of staff developers working with the disability officer community is provided by Middling and Bostock (2002), who describe how part of the response to the SENDA legislation at Keele University has been to develop programmes jointly between disability services, staff development teams and departments themselves. They argue that by working with departments and disability services, staff developers have enabled them to develop their approach to inclusion with support, advice and guidance.

Developing strategic partnerships with disability support staff is certainly a powerful strategy, but it does have implications for resources and roles that need to be carefully considered by managers. Whilst there is no doubt that disability support staff will have the motivation and personal commitment to work with staff developers, it is not clear that they will always have the time to commit to such partnerships. Disability support staff are usually fully stretched working with the students, often trying to sort a backlog of student assessments. The roles of both staff developers and disability support staff will also need to be considered carefully so as to avoid a 'them and us' culture whereby central services are seen as enforcing managerialist policies (Wray 2002).

Partnerships with disabled advocates

In their 'Staff development Good Practice' guide the Disability Rights Commission (2003) recommend that disability equality training be delivered by a disabled person in order to 'help to challenge entrenched attitudes'. The involvement of disabled people in staff development programmes would certainly help to deliver less general and more specific awareness raising activities, which is something that a number of staff have indicated that they would value (Scott 2001; Keats 2003).

Staff developers may find it helpful to brief advocates as to whether they wish them to advocate for disabilities generally, or for more specific disabilities such as dyslexia or mental health. The advocate's brief should also be made clear to those who attend staff development programmes. Some advocacy groups such as those working in the fields of dyslexia and visual impairment are very vocal and powerful in their advocacy but a concerning consequence of this, is that some people assume that the arguments and solutions they put forward apply to all disabilities, which may not necessarily be the case.

Disability officers and disability advocates can undoubtedly both do a very good job in explaining why accessibility in e-learning is important. But staff developers will need to work to ensure that they (or others) can also do a good job in explaining how e-learning can be made more accessible. There is nothing more frustrating for staff than being pressed with a 'thou shalt be accessible' message but not being empowered to actually do something about it.

Partnerships with staff

The Disability Rights Commission (2003) also recommend that staff developers work with academic staff by:

- using examples or facilitators from the relevant academic discipline so that it is more relevant and credible;
- involving staff in audits of provision or expertise, so that they become aware of their own development needs.

There is certainly merit in adopting a staff-centred model of staff development. Herrington (2000), for example, proposes an organic model of staff development that involves working with staff to determine the change agenda, shape and make decisions and create ongoing paths of development. Herrington argues that much of the existing staff development provision in relation to disability does not really address how 'hearts and minds' can be changed across an institution. Examples she gives include:

- awareness-raising courses/events which are attended by staff on a voluntary basis;
- staff training sessions on policy and procedures regarding disability;
- disability slots in existing courses;
- training of designated departmental/faculty special needs staff;
- specialised accredited disability courses/modules.

Herrington argues that the organic model of staff development goes further in that it provides a mechanism through which groups of staff can identify their own required levels of awareness. The model includes the following key elements:

- staff should not be told what to do to develop their own services and must 'own' their own changes;
- staff have to feel free to develop their own resourcefulness instead of feeling that they must always do some 'right thing' regarding disability, if only they knew what it was.

Adopting an organic staff development model such as that proposed by Herrington (2000) may help learning and teaching staff to be proactive so that they are not on the 'receiving end' of other people's edicts about what they should and should not do, but, instead, can work with others to meet the challenges head-on and develop appropriate solutions and options of which they are in control and of which they can claim ownership. Such proactivity is considered a key element in accessible and universal design (see chapter 6).

Conclusion

To some extent staff development in relation to accessibility and e-learning is a 'balancing act'. Throughout their work, staff developers are required to consider the extent to which they can balance very specific needs with more general needs; online methods with offline methods as well as coercion with encouragement. The most important balancing act however is that of balancing individual needs with institutional needs.

The needs of institutions in relation to accessibility and e-learning are often reflected in the accessibility policies that institutions adopt (see chapter 10). These policies will vary in the extent to which they 'compel' institutional staff to change their accessibility practices, which may or may not conflict with the extent to which individual staff themselves feel compelled to address accessibility issues. Staff developers will probably need to very strategic in the way they use both institutional and individual development needs to argue for the resources that they will require to work closely with academics at a departmental and individual level and to bring in external expertise when needed.

Staff developers have a great deal of potential to make a positive impact on the accessibility practices of different stakeholders within an institution; they tend, however, not to be targeted by accessibility related literature, projects and campaigns. It is time, however, that their perspectives and needs were taken into account.

Chapter 10

Managing accessible e-learning practice

The senior manager's perspective

> Members of an educational community, business, or agency can all have the best intentions when it comes to creating a web presence that is accessible to those with disabilities. Too often, however, these individuals with good intentions wait for someone to come and help lead them. Change is a difficult path. It is common to be told to acquire new skills because change is going to happen. So you do just that . . . you obtain the skills you were asked . . . you wait for some new policy, some new set of procedures, someone who will support what you were implicitly asked to do . . . yet nothing happens.
>
> (WebAim n.d.)

Introduction

From a senior manager's perspective the issues that might be important to them in relation to e-learning and accessibility are:

- How can I influence my institution's response to accessibility legislation and help to promote and support accessible e-learning practices within my institution?
- What systems are in place already and what systems will need to be developed in order to ensure an effective response to accessibility legislation and the development of accessible e-learning practices within my institution?

Despite the potential impact that addressing these issues could have on an institution, very little accessibility literature and advocacy is aimed at senior managers. Where there are specific briefing papers for senior managers the content usually provides a brief overview of the legislation and then managers are pointed to look at guidelines such as WCAG, just as everyone else is. Whilst senior managers need to be aware of the guidelines, they don't personally need to implement them, but they do need to know how to support their staff to implement them. Accessibility advocates and agencies are therefore probably missing a trick, by not engaging senior managers in a more detailed, focused and proactive way.

The attitude of and towards senior managers is quite interesting. For example, in reporting the results from key informant interviews about disability policy in UK higher education, Wilson *et al.* (2002: 20) report a degree of sympathy with senior managers in terms of the degree of change which disability legislation may require. They quote one academic who they interviewed as saying:

> I mean actually you can't but have sympathy with senior management because what, what has to be communicated is massive, you know. I think if you went through the code of practice that accompanies the DDA part 4. What you are getting is an extremely tall order in terms of institutional change.

In a follow-up paper Tinklin *et al.* (2004) note that their key informants reported only 'a little nervousness' among senior management about the disability discrimination legislation. Managers appeared to find comfort in the perceived get-out clauses and low probability of being taken to court. There is evidence however that some senior managers are being proactive in encouraging changes in practice in response to the legislation. For example, in a survey of library professionals in 230 further education colleges in England, Scotland and Wales, Harris and Oppenheim (2003) found that those libraries who were better equipped to implement the requirements of the legislation had supportive mangers with a positive attitude, as well as previous experience of supporting students with disabilities.

Disability discrimination means that all senior managers are going to commit to accessibility in the sense that they will publicly be seen to acknowledge that their institutions must respond to the legislation and change their practices. But there is commitment and then there is effective commitment. Effective commitment means leading an institution's response to the legislation as opposed to mandating that other junior staff take on the responsibility (Foley 2003a). Leading an institutions' response increases the visibility of accessibility as an issue, makes it easier to dedicate the necessary resources to the issue and makes the monitoring of compliance more of a probability (WebAim n.d.b).

Accessibility implementation therefore needs to be actively managed (Lamshed *et al.* 2003) and is likely to involve:

- ensuring that the accessibility of e-learning material and resources is monitored and audited (see chapter 7);
- ensuring that there is 'joined up' thinking between the different specialist and mainstream learning support services within an institution (see chapter 8);

- ensuring that staff development opportunities are strategically targeted to raise awareness and that staff are able to respond to accessibility requirements (see chapter 9);
- developing and implementing procurement procedures to ensure accessibility of future technology purchases;
- developing and implementing institutional accessibility policies.

This chapter will focus on the latter two issues in more detail. In some respects procurement and policy development are the standard 'bureaucratic' activities that senior managers undertake. But depending on how senior managers approach these activities, they could take on an innovative and creative role that engages the whole institution and changes expectations, culture and practice.

Developing accessibility procurement procedures

One of the key reasonable adjustments that institutions can make in response to disability discrimination legislation is to ensure that all new purchases of learning management systems, courseware and networked equipment is accessible (Rowland 2000; McCarthy 2001). There may be some resistance to this however:

> advocates for accessible computing often report difficulties in getting the central computing organization to commit to the development and procurement of accessible technology. From the outside it can look impossible to get central computing services on a large postsecondary campus to accept accessibility as a priority.
>
> (Burgstahler and Cook 2005)

Therefore, one of the key things that senior managers can do is to insist upon institutional purchases of accessible computing equipment. When hardware, software and associated packages are being sourced and purchased, senior managers could insist that accessibility be one of the criteria by which institutions make their purchasing decisions.

Many key institutional decisions have already been made that will commit institutions to certain equipment for the foreseeable future, for example, the procurement of institution-wide Virtual or Managed Learning Environments (which may or may not be accessible). However, when such systems are upgraded or reviewed, senior managers should be looking to talk to suppliers about maintaining or improving accessibility levels. Senior managers are also in a good position to have a significant impact on the accessibility of new developments in Information Technology and computing. For example, they should review the extent to which a mainstream development such as installing wireless networks would meet the need of disabled students and reduce the necessity for some specialist, segregated services such as specially adapted technology rooms or centres (see chapter 8). They should also ensure that exploration of new systems such as e-portfolio and Personal Development Planning (PDP) systems includes an evaluation of how accessible the proposed systems are.

In North America, toolkits have been developed to assist purchasers in their decision-making. For example, Katseva (2004) describes 'The Accessible Procurement Toolkit' developed by the Assistive Devices Industry Office in Canada. The Toolkit is a reference for individuals who are purchasing equipment or services for the office. It describes features and design principles that must be provided to a vendor to ensure 'universal acceptability' of the product or service. Fain and Bursa (2005) describe how an online tool called The '508 Assistant' supports the design and procurement of accessible electronic and information technology that conforms to the Section 508 standards (see chapter 4). The '508 Assistant' was developed by the Information Technology Technical Assistance and Training Center with the objective of practically supporting decision-making and action-taking. The content and functionality of the '508 Assistant' are organized around three dimensions: user role, product type and Section 508 background information. Both of these tools have not been developed with universities or colleges in mind and it is not clear who would be willing to fund the development of such a toolkit for higher education. We have also seen that tools on their own do not necessarily make life easier (see chapter 7), human judgement and interpretation are often still required.

Manufacturers often make accessibility statements about their products. Whilst it can be helpful to know whether a product is compliant to a certain standard (e.g Section 508), senior managers need to be careful of the very general or vague statements made by some manufacturers and vendors about accessibility. When asking manufacturers and vendors whether a product is accessible, managers need to be sure that all parties are working to the same or similar definition and level of accessibility. What senior managers in higher education would probably benefit from is a standard check-list of accessibility related questions that they should be asking when they are looking to procure new systems. As yet, one does not appear to exist, but the discussions contained within this book may provide a good place to start in terms of generating such a check-list. An overarching question may be: will any individual or group of students be signficantly disadvantged if they are required by their programme or instiution to use the proposed system? More specific questions can probably be drawn directly from guidelines and design principles. For example:

• Will the system allow users to interact with it using their own input/output devices?

- Does the system provide alternatives to auditory and visual content and if not, how much will this disadvantage disabled students?
- To what extent will the system allow users to change settings in order to suit their own specific needs?

The asking and answering of these questions may highlight tensions within the institution with which senior managers will need to deal. For example, Kelly *et al.* (2004) note that IT Service departments usually aim to provide a secure, robust managed environment, which may conflict with the flexibility many end users would like. In considering how to promote the procurement of accessible IT systems, senior managers will also need to educate procurement and university contractors concerning accessibility (Wall and Sarver 2003).

Developing institutional accessibility policies

Many accessibility researchers and advocates urge institutions to develop accessibility policies (Witt and McDermott 2002; Burgstahler 2002a; Johnson *et al.* 2003). For example, in the UK, Phipps *et al.* (2002) argue that accessibility tools need to be accompanied by accessibility policies:

> It is vital that academic institutions recognise that accessibility for electronic information is a major issue and there is no such thing as a 'quick fix'. Tools such as Bobby can be valuable if used correctly but these tools can only be used to an advantage if they form part of an institutional accessibility policy. This policy must be backed up by an understanding of the relevant accessibility issues and how the issues apply to the institution's website.

Advising managers to start by developing an accessibility policy however, is about as unhelpful as advising learning technologists to start with the WAI Guidelines. A successful and meaningful policy is not written overnight by a senior manager, it is written in partnership with key stakeholders and contains details and specificity that leaves all personnel in an institution in no doubt that action is required.

What do we mean by an accessibility policy?

In dictionary terms, policy is generally understood to mean 'a plan of action'. However, in terms of e-learning accessibility, when institutions publicize what they call 'accessibility policies' it is clear that institutions understand the definition and function of an accessibility policy in different ways. For example, Phipps *et al.* (2004) surveyed 163 higher education websites between September and October 2003 and found that only 88 contained some level of public accessibility information. The information contained in them was of varying depth and quality, some were very structured policy documents linked to strategy and staff development, whilst others only made a broad statement about staff being mindful of disabled students' needs.

In the author's own personal and less formal survey of institutional accessibility policies it was found that some institutions produced what appear to be 'mission statements' rather than polices:

> At Cranfield University, we try to ensure that our services, products and facilities are available to all – irrespective of any disability. This applies to our website, too. Our website has been built following expert disability advice. We also welcome feedback (both positive and negative) from our customers.
>
> (http://www.cranfield.ac.uk/prospectus/note.cfm)

While other institutions appeared to interpret 'policy' as meaning guidelines. For example under a 'policy' directory, Oregon State University provides on its website a set of general web accessibility guidelines:

> The universal access to information is a part of the University's ongoing commitment to establishing a barrier free learning community at Oregon State. These guidelines have been established as a part of this commitment, and to meet the ethical and legal obligations that we have under The Americans with Disabilities Act, The Telecommunications Act of 1996, and The Rehabilitation Act of 1973, as amended.
>
> (http://tap.oregonstate.edu/Policy/web.html)

Whilst mission statements and guidelines are a move in the right direction, they will not necessarily ensure or mandate that practice changes. In order to ensure accessibility, policies need to be specific, detailed and directive.

What should be included in an accessibility policy?

Advice from a number of accessibility advocates would suggest that accessibility polices need to:

- define the scope of the policy (Johnson *et al.* 2003; Brewer 2002);
- delineate a specific and official technical standard (Johnson *et al.* 2003; Bohman 2003d; Brewer 2002; Smith and Lyman 2005);
- indicate whether compliance is required (Bohman 2003d);
- indicate a timeline or deadline for compliance (Bohman 2003d; Brewer 2002);
- define a system for evaluating or monitoring compliance (Bohman 2003d; Brewer 2002; Smith and Lyman 2005);

- indicate any consequences for failure to comply with policy (Bohman 2003d).

Define the scope of the policy

> The institution must consider whether the web accessibility policy will apply to all websites hosted on its servers, faculty personal pages, student personal pages, and sites developed on funding through the institution but hosted by another organization.
>
> (Johnson *et al.* 2003)

Many institutions are vague about the scope of their polices. For example, the University of Durham states that 'official University pages' must be made accessible, without defining what is understood by 'official'. It does however make distinctions between new and existing sites and the level of compliance required:

> All official University pages must be written to be as accessible as reasonably possible to users with disabilities, or with old browsing technology. As a minimum standard, all pages are expected to comply in full with the Priority 1 recommendations of the web Accessibility Initiative. All new sites must comply in full with at least the Priority 2 recommendations of the Web Accessibility Initiative. Existing sites should work towards this level of accessibility if possible, but should ensure that this does not delay compliance with the Priority 1 recommendations.
>
> (http://www.dur.ac.uk/its/services/web/accessibility/policy/)

Some institutions appear to define the scope of their policies in relation to priority actions, and which parts of a website should be addressed before others:

> It is important to make substantial progress with all sites and Web material with regards to accessibility. There will be a breakdown of priority areas, which is expected to be based on site traffic, content information and its purpose in the near future. The University's corporate site, is currently being reviewed in order to be made 'Double-A' compliant and in line with the Special Educational Needs Act. This will be the first stage in its constant development with regards to accessibility issues. Campusweb and the ISS Web site are also well on the way to being made compliant, work is expected to be completed before the end of July 2002.
>
> (http://campus.leeds.ac.uk/guidelines/accessibility/priority.htm)

Delineate a specific and official technical standard

Phipps *et al.* (2004) report that of the 88 institutions in their survey that did have some form of information about accessibility on their websites, there was no consistent reference to standards or guidelines:

- 36 referred to WCAG-1;
- 16 referred to accessibility tools including Bobby and LIFT;
- eight referred to SENDA compliance in meeting the requirements of disability discrimination legislation (but no direct reference to web accessibility was made);
- 28 referred to a variety of other standards including US legislation (Section 508) and 'in-house' standards.

Some institutions specify that their websites must meet the priority check points of either the WCAG or Section 508. For example:

> All Monash websites must meet all of the priority 1 checkpoints. In addition, all priority 2 checkpoints should also be met, except for check-point 3.3 that requires layout to be handled by stylesheets. Stylesheets cannot be used for layout because of the difficulties with stylesheet implementation across different browsers, particularly Netscape 4 which is widely used at Monash. The Monash web templates have been authored to achieve compliance with these standards. They also meet some of the checkpoints listed as priority 3 requirements in WCAG.
>
> (http://www.its.monash.edu.au/staff/web/policy/accessibility.html)

Other institutions require their websites to comply to both Section 508 and WCAG standards. For example:

> All CSU Sacramento affiliated Web documents should meet Section 508 guidelines and Priority Levels 1 and 2 of the Web Content Accessibility Guidelines set forth by the World Wide Web Consortium (W3C). Providing text equivalents for graphics and including captions are two elements that enhance accessibility to Web sites.
>
> (http://www.csus.edu/web/accessibility/)

Indicate whether conformance is required

The language of current web accessibility policies are interesting in terms of how strongly they indicate that conformance is required. From the institution's perspective, they can 'encourage' (or discourage), 'recommend' or 'require' that certain actions are taken. From the staff perspective they 'should' or 'must' undertake an action. For the majority of existing accessibility polices, the language (or interpretation of the language) errs on the side of 'recommend' and 'should' as opposed to 'require' and 'must'. For example, the University of North Carolina states in a list of actions (that do not appear to derive from any specific policy):

> All instructors and other owners of course and other official electronic University data (personal web pages are not included) should familiarize themselves with the University's Guidelines for Accessible Electronic Content. They are urged to make new electronic content under Type 1 and Type 2 (where appropriate) of the Electronic Content Chart comply with the University's accessibility standards.
> (http://www.unc.edu/webaccess/implement.html)

Whilst Michigan State University has produced a 'Statement of Encouragement':

> Students, faculty, staff, and organizational units producing content for the World Wide Web are strongly encouraged to apply principles of Web accessibility as set forth by the World Wide Web Consortium wherever possible in the design and implementation, and in the renewal or replacement, of their Web content. Programs and services offered over the World Wide Web that do not meet Web accessibility standards must offer comparable non-Web based programs and services for qualified individuals with disabilities.
> (http://www.msu.edu/webaccess/principles/encourage.html)

Even where the words 'require' and 'must' are used, Bohman (2003d) argues that the documents are rarely seen as authoritative because:

> Despite the fact that 60% of the policies surveyed use words such as 'must' and 'required', the documents rarely seem authoritative. They are often difficult to find on the university Web site, and are often linked from 'resources' sections of Web sites, rather than 'policy' sections. Only half of them (50%) even use the word 'policy' (or similar words) at all. Without this kind of terminology, Web developers are likely to dismiss the policies as unofficial, unbinding, and unimportant.

Indicate a timeline or deadline for compliance

Without a timeline or deadline, web developers may not have the initiative to independently make their content accessible. They can postpone the task indefinitely without fear of consequences (Bohman 2003d). Timelines appear to be rare in existing accessibility policies and may only be made explicit when an institution is under particular external pressure to do so. For example, the University of Kansas Medical Center formulated a list of dated priorities in order to respond to State of Kansas legislation (e.g. see http://www.kumc.edu/webdev/access/access1_2.html).

Define a system for evaluating or monitoring compliance

A large majority of current institutional policies do not define a system for evaluating or monitoring compliance, which means that errors may be introduced and undetected for a long time (Bohman 2003d). Where monitoring is mentioned it appears to be in the context of receiving and providing formative feedback: 'To assist in monitoring, there will be a feedback email address available to web users from the "Comments?" icon on the home page to enable people experiencing specific difficulties with access to our website to contact the Disability Office in the first instance' (http://www.ex.ac.uk/access/#recommendations).

Indicate any consequences for failure to comply

> Without any consequence or enforcement for failure to comply, Web developers may feel that they can opt out of these 'requirements without fear of retribution, reprimand, or consequences of any kind. Universities may wish to convey the idea that it is better for developers to make their Web content accessible simply because it is 'the right thing to do,' and this will be sufficient for some developers, but the absence of consequences is a loophole that the more reluctant developers are likely to seek out and exploit.
>
> (Bohman 2003d)

Very few institutions appear to specify conequences for failure to comply with accessibility polices, where they do the consequence is often simply the removal of the 'offending' material from the instiution's server. Certainly, the consequence is not framed as a punishment or reprimand:

> Computing Services runs campus-wide accessibility checks approximately every six months. Departments or programs not in compliance with Priority 1 Guidelines will receive a warning and will be given two weeks (for online course content) or four weeks (for public-access Internet content) to make the Internet content accessible. After that time, if necessary changes are not made the links to the content may be deactivated, and notification will be sent.
>
> (http://www.ualr.edu/provost/webaccessprocedures.html)

Developing and implementing accessibility policies

A number of practitioners and advocates have proposed various steps towards developing and implementing accessibility policies (Burgstahler 2002a; Brewer and Horton 2002; Hricko 2003; Byrne 2004; Smith and Lyman 2005). Each proposal differs in the number and nature of steps that are included, however they all agree on certain steps:

- involve all stakeholders, including top-level support (Burgstahler 2002a; Smith and Lyman 2005);
- organize an accessibility committee (Smith and Lymann 2005; Hriko 2003; Byrne 2004);
- provide training and technical support (Smith and Lyman 2005; Burgstahler 2002a; Brewer and Horton 2002);
- promote institutional awareness (Burgstahler 2002a; Brewer and Horton 2002);
- evaluate progress towards accessibility (Smith and Lyman 2005; Burgstahler 2002a; Brewer and Horton 2002).

Organizing an accessibility committee

It is vital that this group be comprised of the major stakeholders of your organization. Those chosen should be respected and have the ability to influence change with their colleagues. They must also be able to commit the time necessary to see the process through. This could be a substantial commitment, sometimes lasting for years.

(Smith and Lyman 2005)

Byrne (2004) suggests that in setting up a 'Web Accessibility Policy and Planning Group' the following stakeholders (among others) should be included: management, student representatives, disabled students, administrators, web designers, lecturers and learning support staff.

In thinking about the need for an accessibility committee, managers may need to address:

- the extent to which existing committees can and should undertake the role;
- how other committees may work with the accessibility committee;
- how much power the accessibility committee will have to insist that practice changes.

Kramer (2004) reports on the activities of an 'Assistive Technology Advisory Committee' at CU-Boulder University in US. This committee was formed in 1998 and consisted of: students with disabilities, faculty, representatives from Disability Services, Web Communications and Information Technology Services and the campus computer services department. In addition to advising on assistive technology matters, members of the committee have lobbied for the amendment of inaccessible websites and systems as well as the development of a Web Accessibility Guidelines page. However, Kramer notes that it was the IT Council (along with the Vice Chancellors) who actually sanctioned the development of a Web Access and Resource Page, suggesting that the committee perhaps had little power.

In order for accessible e-learning practice within an instiution to change, a whole range of stakeholders will need to work together to make it happen. Whether these stakeholders form a committee or not it probably does not matter, but what does matter is that stakeholders work together as a team, and adopt a collective responsibility for trying to promote change.

Developing stand-alone or integrated policies

Given that many advocates argue against 'add-on' specialist services that segregate people and issues from the mainstream, there would seem to be merit in considering whether accessibility should be integrated into existing polices or whether existing policies can be applied to e-learning accessibility. Some institutions have integrated accessibility into their existing web policies (e.g. the University of New Hampshire). This does tend to mean however that the accessibility element of the policy is short (usually one paragraph) and very vague in nature. Other institutions would argue that it is possible to address accessibility through existing policies. For example, the University of Washington states that, 'To address the issue of the accessibility of campus websites, some institutions have adopted separate policies about web accessibility. In contrast, the University of Washington is one of the schools that considers its non-discrimination policy adequate for promoting the accessible design of websites on campus' (http://www.washington.edu/accessit/articles?247).

Tinklin *et al.* (2004) argue that ideally policy and provision for disabled students should be embedded into all institutional procedures in all areas of institutional operation. Using this argument, perhaps accessibility should be embedded into a range of policies and strategies including: e-learning strategies; teaching and learning strategies; non-discrimination policies; inclusion policies; widening participation policies and learning resources polices. One advantage, however, of creating a separate accessibility policy (perhaps in conjunction with the setting up of an accessibility committee) is the opportunity which it provides to forge new partnerships, raise awareness and create a culture of inclusion.

Developing policies that change practice

What is perhaps more important than whether or not a separate accessibility policy is created is whether or not the policy changes practice. There is some agreement that having a policy does not guarantee that an institution will make e-learning more accessible (Lakey 2002; Anderson 2004). Anderson (2004) argues that practice will only change if the policy is actively implemented:

> Developing campus Web accessibility policies, guidelines or standards is often thought of as a way to meet legal obligation, however, implementing Web accessibility policies can be a means for creating a campus e-culture of inclusion. While developing a policy has numerous challenges – implementing, supporting and updating a Web accessibility policy is where the rubber hits the road and separates those who succeed in Web accessibility efforts and those who have a policy.
>
> (Anderson 2004)

Conclusions

Whilst the perspective of senior managers has been ignored in a lot of the accessibility research and practice literature, it is clear that they have the potential to play an important role in leading the development of accessible e-learning practice. A role that will involve:

- embedding accessibility across all institutional activities and systems, from procurement to student support services;
- addressing whether and how the development of an institutional accessibility policy will encourage such embedment;
- identifying a team of key stakeholders, across the whole institution (and not just specialist disability services) who are willing and able to work towards embedment.

The promotion and development of accessible e-learning requires changes in individual and institutional practices. This may or may not be a 'tall order' (Wilson *et al.* 2002: 20), but without leadership from managers the task will not get any 'smaller'.

Part 3

Conceptualizing the scene

Chapter 11

Institutional responses to accessibility

Rules, games and politics

There is some evidence to suggest that educational institutions might play games in terms of how they choose to interpret the legal implications of SENDA. These games may involve waiting for a legal precedence to be set or case law to be created which defines what 'reasonable adjustments' institutions should be making. This waiting game may be played out within the context of cultural or institutional resistance.

(Seale 2003b)

Introduction

Disability discrimination and accessibility issues are frequently introduced to higher education institutions as primarily a legal issue (as opposed to an issue of equity, inclusion or social justice). At a higher education institution level, legislation is therefore frequently seen as the main driver for accessibility (Phipps *et al.* 2004) and accessibility is therefore presented as being about compliance with legal rules and the potential enforcement of those rules (McCarthy 2001; Wilder 2002). If we are to develop an understanding of accessibility practice at an institutional level we need a theory, model or framework that can help us explore the extent to which institutional responses to accessibility are influenced by rules and what mediates an institution's response to rules.

One framework that has the potential to be applicable to this area is North's institutional change framework. North is a Nobel prize-winning economic historian who has worked to develop a political-economic framework to explore long-term institutional change. Linked to this work is the search for an explanation for why people make the choices they do, and why ideologies shape the choices people make and direct the way that economies evolve through periods of time. In the early 1990s North published widely on his ideas about institutional change and economic performance (North 1993, 1994a, b). Underpinning North's framework for analysing institutions (he claimed there were too many gaps to call it a theory) were assumptions that choice was subject to constraints, including competition, conflict and friction.

Although North proposed his framework to explain political and economic phenomena it has been applied in an educational context. Konur (2000) has used North's framework to try and explain why disabled students may find it difficult to enforce their rights following the UK Disability Discrimination Act of 1995. The ideas of North and Konur are compelling in that together they challenge us to broaden our conceptualizations beyond the techno-rational imperatives of accessibility (you must do this, because it is right and logical) and to begin to consider the socio-political responses to accessibility; responses which involve games, conflict and power. This chapter will outline the institutional change framework and explore the extent to which it can be applied to e-learning and accessibility in higher education.

The institutional change framework as a potential analysis tool

According to North, Institutions consist of formal rules, informal constraints (norms of behaviour, conventions and self-imposed codes of conduct) and the enforcement characteristics of both. The degree to which there is a similarity or alignment between the objectives of the institutional constraints and the choices individuals make in that institutional setting depends on the effectiveness of enforcement. To work effectively, formal rules must be complemented by informal constraints (conventions, norms of behaviour) that supplement them and reduce enforcement costs. If the formal rules and informal constraints are inconsistent with each other the resulting tension will induce political instability.

Formal rules may change over night, but informal constraints do not. Changes in the formal rules of institutions may come about as a result of legislative changes such as the passage of a new statute, judicial changes stemming from court decisions that alter the common law, or regulatory and constitutional rule changes. The process of change is overwhelmingly incremental because choices made will naturally be in favour of the existing framework. The larger the number of rule changes, the greater the number of losers and hence opposition. North argues that enforcement of rules is carried out by self-imposed codes of conduct (first party), retaliation from a second party or sanctions/coercive enforcement by the state (third party).

If institutions are the rules of the game, North postulates that organizations are the players. They are individuals engaged in purposive activity. The constraints imposed by the institutional framework define the opportunity set and therefore the kinds of organizations that will come into existence. An organization will engage in acquiring skills and knowledge that will enhance its survival possibilities in the context of competition. The kinds of skills and knowledge that will pay off will be a function of the incentive structure inherent in the institutional matrix. The greater the competition amongst organizations, the greater is the incentive to invest in skills and knowledge to enhance the organization's survival opportunities, and hence the greater the rate of institutional change.

North argues that the separation of institutions from organizations is crucial if one is to get a handle on the dynamics of institutional change. Organizations are the initiators of institutional change. Entrepreneurs and members of organizations invest in the skills and knowledge, which lead to revised evaluations of opportunities, which in turn induce alteration of the rules or the gradual revision of informal constraints. The kinds of skills and knowledge perceived to have a high pay-off will of course reflect the incentives embodied in the institutional framework.

Applicability of institutional change framework to e-learning and accessibility

Applying North's framework to disability, e-learning and accessibility in higher education gives rise to some challenging questions about current e-learning accessibility practice; questions which have the potential to shape the future accessibility research and development agenda:

- What are the formal and informal rules of accessibility?
- Is the development of accessibility practices within higher education institutions influenced by the differences between the formal and informal rules of accessibility?
- To what extent are the formal and informal rules regarding accessibility being enforced by first, second and third parties?
- How are the formal and informal rules of accessibility being regulated and enforced within a higher education institution?
- Are institutions seeing accessibility rules as an opportunity to invest in knowledge and skills required to make e-learning accessible?
- What incentive is there for institutions to invest in the knowledge and skills required to make e-learning accessible?

Formal and informal rules of accessibility

Higher education institutions are likely to be influenced by both external and internal formal rules governing accessibility. External formal rules will include legislation, guidelines and standards (see chapter 4). Disability discrimination legislation is relatively stable, but associated accessibility precepts are less stable while organizations wait for case law to clarify certain aspects of the rules (Wilder 2002). To a certain extent there has been relative stability in the rules associated with the WAI guidelines. However, there is increasing instability as people start to develop their own adapted guidelines and question the utility of the new version of the WAI guidelines (see chapter 4). The greatest instability is probably with respect to accessibility standards.

Although the International Standards Organization is consulting widely on a new set of accessibility standards, a whole array of other standards exists.

An example of internal formal accessibility rules that institutions may have is the rules laid down in accessibility policies (see chapter 10). Organizational accessibility policies differ in the 'rules' that they lay down depending on: which specific technical standard they adopt; whether they require or request compliance; whether they indicate a timeline or deadline for compliance; whether they define a system for evaluating or monitoring compliance and whether they indicate any consequences for failure to comply with policy. These rules may also vary in the extent to which they align themselves with external rules such as those contained within the WCAG-1, or Section 508. Organizations will also differ in the extent to which these rules influence actual practice. Some organizations will actively implement the rules, others will simply treat them as overarching principles.

Some general, informal accessibility rules that may or may not influence higher education institutions are those which appear to be repeated a lot in the research and practice literature, and are on the whole now accepted as valid. These include:

- accessibility needs to be addressed at the beginning of the design process and not at the end as an afterthought (Gay *et al.* 1999; Katseva 2004);
- accessibility requires a user-centred approach (Luke 2002; Alexander 2003b);
- accessibility will benefit all students, not just those with disabilities (Jacko and Hanson 2002; Thompson 2005).

More specific informal rules that may affect different stakeholders within an institution may focus on:

- the different approaches to inclusive and holistic curriculum design that lecturers should adopt (see chapter 6);
- the different adaptations of accessibility guidelines that learning technologists should adopt (see chapter 7);
- the different ways in which student support services should be structured (see chapter 8);
- the different strategies and models that staff development services should adopt (see chapter 9);
- the different emphasis that different senior managers place on the flexibility or rigidity of their technology procurement procedures (see chapter 10).

The challenge for institutions, according to North, is to minimize any potential tension and instability caused by a mismatch between formal and informal rules. In terms of accessibility rules, mismatches are likely to occur where some rules are more stable or entrenched than others and where there is a difference in underpinning values (e.g. formal rules that value universal design principles may come into conflict with informal rules that value more individualized, specialised approaches).

Enforcement and regulation of formal and informal rules of accessibility

North argues that rules are enforced by self-imposed codes of conduct (first party), retaliation from a second party or sanctions/coercive enforcement by the state (third party). Evidence for first-party and second-party enforcement of accessibility rules is currently very thin. In the public domain, there is no record of anyone who works in higher education being sacked, demoted or reprimanded for failing to follow accessibility rules (formal or informal). Conversely, practice that does follow the rules is not openly rewarded or celebrated. Most organizations do not yet appear to have a detailed and structured mechanism for auditing compliance with accessibility rules. The nearest an organization appears to get to stating the consequences of non-compliance with accessibility rules is to indicate that inaccessible material will be removed and taken off-line (see chapter 10).

Third-party enforcement of accessibility rules can be shrouded in mystery. For example, in the UK, there are many staff in higher education institutions (particularly, the older, higher-ranked universities) who are convinced that the large high profile disability advocates such as the Disability Rights Commission (DRC) or the Royal National Institute for the Blind (RNIB) are desperate to find a reason to launch a high profile legal case against them. The reality is, that there have been no public law suits or court cases and there is now a suspicion that a lot of wheeling and dealing has taken place behind closed doors:

> Personally I have been told by RNIB staff that they have supported claims against websites that have been settled out of court. I do not have details because the parties involved have not disclosed them.

> I went to Glasgow March this year for a web Accessibility workshop hosted by an International Law Firm. . They did mention the RNIB law suit (They claim it was a success). But nobody could get a word out of them about the detail etc.
>
> ('A List Apart' Discussion Forum:
> http://www.alistapart.com/articles/accessuk)

If this is case, it is particularly unhelpful in terms of clarifying the rules of the accessibility game, particularly as so many people have been waiting for 'case law' to be established in order to see what the rules are with respect to reasonable adjustment, etc. It has also helped to fuel a 'Chinese Whispers' game where people are left second guessing what the rules might be and passing on distorted interpretations of these rules.

Opportunities and incentives

According to North, the greater the competition amongst organizations, the greater is the incentive to invest in skills and knowledge that enhance the organization's survival opportunities, and hence the greater the rate of institutional change. In accessibility and e-learning terms adopting or enforcing accessibility rules does not appear to be about enhancing survival in terms of avoiding prosecutions, bad publicity or fines. It appears to be more to do with capturing an increased share of the potential 'market'. Whilst for many accessibility is a human right (HREOC 2002; Bohman 2003a), a disability rights (DRC 2004) and a civil rights issue (Waddell 1999), justice and rights on their own do not appear to be powerful enough reasons for most organizations to change their practices. An equally (if not, more) powerful reason for many is the potential increase in market share and business as a result of increasing accessibility. Even those who cite accessibility as a 'rights' issue, mention the business case for accessibility in the same breath: 'The full and independent participation by people with disabilities in web-based communication and information delivery makes good business and marketing sense, as well as being consistent with our society's obligations to remove discrimination and promote human rights' (HREOC 2002).

Jacobs (2005) demonstrates how designing with access in mind can increase market-share on a global basis, arguing that good business practice dictates that engineers avoid unintentionally excluding large groups of consumers (including users who have low band width which makes downloading slower and therefore more costly, who have English as a second language, or have not learnt to read) from being able to access and use technology. For non-educational organizations such as Microsoft, the sheer number of disabled people in the population provides a powerful argument for making their products accessible (Haverty 2005; Perkins and Haverty 2005). For educational organizations in competitive markets such as distance education, similar arguments are made (Foley 2003b).

The business case for accessibility rests on the realisation that globally there are millions of disabled people who could be potential 'customers' (SciVisum 2004; Sloan *et al.* 2000) and has lead some to argue for the abandonment of accessibility arguments based on rights and justice. For example, Gulliksen *et al.* (2004: 97) argue for the replacement of accessibility as a concept with that of 'reachability', thus focusing attention on the percentage of a certain population or target group that can be reached by different media.

The tensions between accessibility rules that view accessibility as a social justice issue and those that view accessibility as a business issue may influence the way in which accessibility rules evolve and the extent to which these rules are seen as progressive:

> The push for web accessibility also becomes a strange bedfellow with other interests in the university that wish to optimize instruction, broaden market bases, and minimize expenses. Thus the progressive aspects of web accessibility initiatives and disability advocacy become articulated to elements of market-based and neo-liberal reform within higher education. This confluence of these disparate interests presents some interesting challenges, particularly for those viewing accessibility as a social justice or political issue. The advocacy for accessibility becomes an advocacy for implementation of technology programs that might have other less-progressive implications.
>
> (Foley 2003b)

Expanding the institutional change framework of analysis

Konur (2000) applied the ideas of North to explore the impact of the UK Disability Discrimination Act of 1995 on the civil rights of disabled students. Picking up on North's focus on rules, Konur expands on this and focuses in more detail on rule enforcement within the context of competitive games where conflict and cheating exist. If institutions, organizations and individual players are analogous to rules, teams and players respectively, Konur argues:

> There are many social, political and economic objectives that can be obtained by individuals only through team effort. In essence this game is a co-operative social competition where individuals are prepared to behave both co-operatively and competitively. Cheating is inevitable in such a game. Therefore referees must be hired to resolve conflicts.
>
> (Konur 2000: 1043)

In the context of enforcing civil rights for disabled students, Konur postulates that four teams exist: rule implementation teams; rule enforcement teams; rule advocating teams and rule making teams. Rule implementation teams play the game concerned and constitute the providers and users of disability-related services in higher education. Rule enforcement teams act as referees to detect the rule breakers and to resolve resulting conflicts. In the context of DDA and higher education these teams include: courts, funding councils, quality assurance agencies and disability advocates. Rule advocating team aim to socialize individuals so that they are taught and persuaded to play the rules of the game. In the context of DDA Konur considers that these teams might include the funding councils, the DRC, the government and disability rights advocates. Rule-making teams re-write the rules of the game rather than enforcing and perpetuating existing rules of the game. Within the context of the DDA, Konur considers that these teams might include service users, service providers, the DRC, courts and tribunals, the government and disability rights advocates:

> The rules of social and economic games are not fixed but are subject to constant change. Each successive rule change motivates teams and players to re-evaluate and modify their corporate and personal strategies. In such a game it is necessary to collect a wide range of information regarding the game played to better understand the outcome of the game. These may include the complete set of rules of the game at the beginning of the game; a list of the relevant changes for these rules over time; a list of the four types of organisations involved in the game over time as well as information about their strategies.
>
> (Konur 2000: 1045)

Applicability of Konur's concept of teams to e-learning and accessibility

Konur's notion of teams and games gives rise to some challenging questions about current e-learning accessibility practice; questions which have the potential to shape the future accessibility research and development agenda:

- Can the teams identified by Konur be related to the different accessibility stakeholders within higher education institutions?
- Is there evidence for the existence of rule implementing, rule enforcing, rule advocating and rule making teams in the field of e-learning and accessibility?

Within a higher education institution it would be possible to equate Konur's teams to the six different stakeholders identified in this book:

- rule implementers: lecturers, learning technologists, student support services;
- rule enforcers: senior managers;
- rule advocators: staff developers, student support services;
- rule makers: students.

Within the wider socio-political context in which higher education institutions operate it also possible to identify external teams which might have an influence on institutional practice:

- rule enforcers: legal and advisory organizations;
- rule advocators: accessibility and disability consultants and researchers.

Whilst it is possible to identify different organizations and players that are taking on the role of rule implementers, rule enforcers, rule advocators and rule makers it is necessary to explore how the organizations and players are interpreting these roles.

Learning technologists as rule implementers

If, according to Konur, rule implementation teams play the game concerned, with some degree of opposition depending on how much the different teams feel that they will lose as a result, then learning technologists can be identified as rule implementers. Whilst most learning technologists are engaging with accessibility issues to some extent, there are also those who are resistant to some extent because they:

- see accessibility as a procedural or bureaucratic exercise invented by people without knowledge of media production or web development, and apparently with nothing better to do than constrain creativity and innovation (Sloan and Stratford 2004);
- see accessibility standards as an example of attempts to enforce conformance and a level of homogeneity (Friesman and Cressman 2005).

This can cause tension with other learning technologists who see accessibility legislation as a positive challenge to freedom and creativity (Herrell 2001) or see accessibility as an opportunity to produce creative and appealing material (Bohman 2003d). In striving to retain creative freedom, designers and developers may be striving to retain identities as artists as opposed to engineers. This might put them in conflict with other teams.

Legal and advisory organizations as rule enforcers

If rule enforcement teams act as referees to detect the rule breakers and to resolve resulting conflicts, there appear to be two kinds of rule enforcement organizations that operate outside of higher education institutions, but which may impact on the practice of higher education institution: legal and advisory organizations. Legal organizations (which may include judges, attorney-generals, lawyers, etc.) could be argued to be involved in establishing case law, while advisory teams are more involved in establishing principles, precepts and paradigm cases (which may eventually influence or lead to case law).

Legal organizations and case law

In terms of accessibility, many of us have been waiting for case law to be established in order to gain guidance on how exactly key concepts and principles within law would be interpreted (Wilder 2002). There have, however, actually been very few cases that have gone to court and where individuals or companies have been found guilty of discrimination through the development of inaccessible online material. Therefore case law is very limited and is almost non-existent in relation to higher education.

Where legal teams have attempted to establish case law by bringing cases to trial, judgements have not always been consistent (Kretchmer and Carveth 2003). For example, in the US one federal judge ruled that Southwest Airlines did not have to revamp its website and virtual ticket counters, while another federal judge ruled that the Atlanta, Georgia mass transit agency violated the ADA by constructing a website that was inaccessible for people with visual disabilities. Waddell (2005) and Feingold and Earl (2005) comment on more recent court cases where the New York Attorney General announced settlements with two major travel websites to make the sites more accessible for people with visual disabilities. The websites, Ramada.com and Priceline.com agreed to implement a variety of accessibility standards from the World Wide Web Consortium Web Accessibility Initiative. In this case websites were interpreted as 'places of public accommodation'.

The lack of a large body of case law is leading commentators to draw inferences about what kinds of e-learning projects will be covered by the law (Sloan 2001); whether legislation will penalize applications that are inaccessible to some and enhance accessibility for others (Stratford and Sloan 2004) or whether legislation will define accessibility in terms of total accessibility or optimal accessibility. There are some who are hoping that the legislation is tested sooner rather than later. 'The difficulty that we are faced with though, is precisely that no cases have been brought to court in the UK as yet. Hopefully they will come soon, as the DDA is couched in extremely general terms' (Hudson 2003: 8).

One of the reasons why the legal organizations may appear not to be very successful at enforcing the rules (and establishing case law) is that many courts discourage disability rights litigation efforts that were not preceded by a 'good faith' attempt to engage in discussions prior to the lawsuit being filed (Feingold 2004; Feingold and Earl 2005; Feingold and Creagan 2005). Complainants are therefore required to enter into structured negotiations with offending institutions, which can have positive results in terms of changing an institution's behaviour, but can also have negative results in terms of resulting in private settlements that do not inform the wider public practice.

Advisory organizations and paradigm cases

In the absence of case law, people have looked to what might be called 'paradigm cases' for guidance on how legislation might be interpreted (Dworkin, cited in Roulstone 2003). Paradigm cases are typically cases where agencies (advisory organizations) appointed to provide advisory notes or guidelines on how to interpret or comply with the legislation investigate the complaints of disabled people and work with all parties to find a resolution. In these cases, the advisory teams find themselves clarifying aspects of the law and these clarifications whilst not necessarily legally binding, are treated as if they were case law.

Examples of advisory teams include the Human Rights and Equal Opportunities Commission (HREOC) in Australia, the Official Office of Civil Rights, United States of Department of Education (OCR) and the Disability Rights Commission (DRC) in the UK. HREOC has been involved in perhaps the most influential paradigm case, the Macguire versus Sydney Organising Committee for the Olympic Games (SOCOG) case (Russell 2003). The case centred on the extent to which the website of the Sydney Olympic Games was inaccessible and therefore discriminating against blind and partially sighted people. HREOC found in favour of the claimant and the paradigm case was used by other countries to consider the extent to which the reasoning used to make the judgment, might also be relevant to their legislation. In the mid 1990s the OCR dealt with complaints from students claiming of inaccessible websites and computer technology (Waddell 1998), but these cases are quite old now and are rarely referred to.

Judging the impact of paradigm cases, and therefore the power of the advisory teams who have attempted to enforce the rules, is interesting. For example, early responses to the SOCOG case suggested that the potential impact of this case was considered by many initially to be significant (e.g. Sloan 2001; Arch and Burmeister 2003) with the potential to cause 'shock waves across the on-line community' (Russell 2003: 241). However, these shock-waves appear to be short-lived, leaving Russell to conclude that actually the impact has been less than revolutionary. One reason why the impact of such paradigm cases may be lower than anticipated is the fact that bodies such as HREOC, ORC and DRC do not have the power to enforce compliance with their decisions or require all institutions to respond in a similar manner (Johnson *et al.* 2003; Roulstone 2003). Indeed in the Macguire versus SOCOG case, SOCOG initially refused to comply with the HREOC order (Darcy 2003: 745). The political context which therefore influences accessibility practices is one whereby legislation is passed that focuses on enforcement and compliance, but practitioners are advised to wait until case law has been established in order to gain more in-depth understanding of how exactly the legislation needs to be interpreted and applied. Case law is, however, rarely established and whilst paradigm cases

have been established, they have been established within a context of resolution and settlement, by agencies who may have influence but little or no
power to enforce.

Accessibility consultants, disability advocates and researchers as rule advocators

If rule advocating teams aim to socialise individuals so that they are taught
and persuaded to play the rules of the game, three different organizations
can be identified in the game of accessibility in e-learning: accessibility consultants, disability rights advocates and accessibility researchers. Each of
these organizations appear to differ in the strategies they adopt to advocate
the rules of accessibility.

Many accessibility consultants appear to have adopted a strategy of
publicly 'naming and shaming' those organisations who are judged to have
inaccessible online material (mainly websites). Take for example, a press
release from Ethical Media in March 2004 headed 'Disability organisations
fail to meet challenge on accessibility', which claimed that nearly 60 per cent
of the 50 leading disability websites that it examined, failed to reach basic
compliance (as measured against the WCAG-1). Whilst Ethical Media (2004)
does not name those 60 per cent, inferences can probably be made by looking
at those that are excluded from the list of exemplary sites. Interestingly,
included in the list of exemplary sites is the DRC. However in a survey by
another company, the DRC is sited as an example of bad practice. Kavanagh
(2005) reports on the findings of site monitoring company 'Site Morse' that
report that the DRC and RNIB amongst others, failed automated accessibility tests. This is despite the fact that the DRC won a Visionary Design Award
from the National Library for the Blind and the RNIB is a vocal and proactive advocate for accessible design. Kavanagh reports how these results
have raised controversy about the use of automated tests and the validity of
their results noting:

> The DRC and the RNIB have raised doubts about automated testing –
> an issue taken up by Accessify Forum, which says they do not take
> account of 'real people and real problems'. It points for example, to a
> flaw in Site Morse's top ranking site, run by web design company Red
> Ant, which it says outweighs those in the DRC and RNIB sites.
>
> (Kavanagh 2005: 7)

One result of the 'name and shame' strategy is that it has focused arguments
on how accessibility should be assessed rather than on whether or not the
rules of accessibility should be complied with. The battle lines have been
drawn over how to test whether or not rules have been complied with, rather
than whether or not the rules should be complied with, or how easy the rules

are to comply with. Some organisations such as TechDis in the UK are attempting to mediate in this battle. For example, in a news report on their website on 21 January 2005, TechDis chose to comment on the SiteMorse report:

> Unfortunately the responses from the disability organisations seem to belittle the findings of automated tools and give a much greater emphasis of testing by users. The article itself is poorly written in places and fails to provide a solution to the issues raised. TechDis has been engaged in this debate for some time and has sought to balance the challenges of conducting user evaluations with disabled people with the limitations of automated checking, the difficulties of implementing WAI WCAG guidelines and ambiguities in the guidelines themselves.

Some disability rights advocates have adopted a similar strategy to accessibility consultants in that they commission surveys of accessibility and report on the findings. For example, The DRC (2004) commissioned the Centre for Human Computer Interaction Design at City University, London to survey a large and representative sample of websites used by the British public. Using a combination of automated and manual accessing City University tested the home pages of 1,000 sites for technical compliance with the Guideline Checkpoints of WCAG-1. Results revealed that:

> Most websites (81%) fail to satisfy the most basic Web Accessibility Initiative category. In addition, the results of the evaluations undertaken by disabled users show that they have characteristics that make it very difficult, if not impossible, for people with certain impairments, especially those who are blind, to make use of the services provided.
>
> (DRC 2004: 9)

However, rather than name and shame the 81 per cent of sites that failed the accessibility tests, the DRC chose to go head to head with the WAI over the perceived limitations of its guidelines:

> Nearly half (45%) of the problems encountered by disabled users when attempting to navigate websites cannot be attributed to explicit violations of the Web Accessibility Initiative Checkpoints. Although some of these arise from shortcomings in the assistive technology used, most reflect the limitations of the Checkpoints themselves as a comprehensive interpretation of the intent of the Guidelines. City University, as a contributor to the Web Accessibility Initiative, has drawn conclusions from this evidence about potential improvements to the Guidelines, and these are summarized at Appendix 2.
>
> (DRC 2004: 17)

The WAI hit back with a swift rebuttal:

> To the contrary, W3C/WAI's examination of the DRC data available as of 14 April 2004 shows that 95% of the barriers reported are indeed covered by existing checkpoints in WAI Guidelines. Of the high-frequency problems identified in Table 5 of the DRC Report, 77% are covered by checkpoints of the Web Content Accessibility Guidelines 1.0, while 18% are covered by checkpoints of the User Agent Accessibility Guidelines 1.0. Essentially, the interpretation of the data in the report fails to account for the role of browser and media player accessibility, and the role of interoperability with assistive technologies, in ensuring that people with disabilities can use Web sites effectively.
>
> (WAI 2004)

Advocates such as the DRC and RNIB have a high profile and a degree of influence, but some are questioning the extent to which they are using that profile and influence to fight the right battles. For example, Carey (2005: 25) considers that both the DRC and the RNIB missed a powerful opportunity through the publication of the DRC report to advocate for the enforcement of rights for blind and visually impaired people:

> The significantly worst performers were blind people, but the DRC and RNIB blew a wonderful opportunity to wax indignant. Perhaps that was not surprising, given their relative lassitude on the publication of the Forrester research for Microsoft, which reported that more than half the population have significant problems with its products, again led by those with blindness and visual impairment. Taken together, these two massive pieces of work should have caused a storm; but nothing happened.

Many academic researchers have used the results of their work to advocate for accessibility and for compliance with accessibility legislation (rules). Their advocacy strategies vary, but they do include the 'name and shame game'. For example, Schmetzke (2002b) argued that accessibility research could bring about change by identifying individual institutions with low accessibility ratings: 'those with low accessibility may become motivated to improve their "ranking". No institution likes to stick out negatively in comparative studies.' However, accessibility studies of higher educational institutions do appear to vary in whether they name the institutions or not. If we give a closer inspection of the 11 studies cited in Table 4.1, only five (Sams and Yates-Mercer 2000; Kelly 2002a; Patterson and Ellis 2002; Schmetzke 2002a; Alexander 2003a) name the institutions sampled. The motive for naming these institutions does not necessarily seem to be one of 'shaming'. Not all five explicitly link the institutions to their accessibility scores or results. Some studies simply described aspects of some of the sampled institutions' websites in order to provide case examples.

Students with disabilities as rule-makers

According to Konur, rule-making teams re-write the rules of the game rather than enforcing and perpetuating the existing rules of the game. One potential rule-making team that has a strong vested interest in re-writing the rules of discrimination is that of students with disabilities. Konur uses his game and team metaphor to argue that students are not equal players in the game and therefore do not currently have the power to enforce changes in the rules. Konur (2002) argues that evidence from the case law that exists relating to general (non e-learning and accessibility related) claims of discrimination by students with disabilities against universities suggests that the relationship between student and university is an unequal one, where the university can use its power to weaken the position of the student and successfully defend claims of discrimination.

Individually, students may attempt to re-write accessibility rules by complaining, negotiating or litigating. But there is some evidence to suggest that students with disabilities may find it very difficult to do any of these three things. In terms of complaining, Konur (2002) argues that the administrative conflict-resolution system in higher education has a large number of inefficiencies and variations that makes it very difficult for disabled people to resolve time-dependent issues and gather evidence for their complaints of discrimination. For example Clement-Lorford (2005), a student with dyslexia, complaining about the withdrawal of a 'yellow sticker' system for exam scripts, writes:

> When I asked Students Union how to make a complaint on this matter they directed me to university complaints system which is personal tutor – student representative – head of school – dean of students. However I think this is a disability matter. And I have already involved most of the listed members. I therefore wonder and asking others how to proceed with this matter, also do I have a point. It is very difficult to find other students like me to ask their opinion as Data protection is always thrown up. I am looking to send an all asking email to all students through my university email account, but IT is not being very helpful.

In terms of negotiating, the kind of advocacy and structured negotiations proposed by Feingold and colleagues (Feingold and Earl 2005) assumes an equal relationship between the negotiators. When thinking about e-learning in higher education, and the extent to which disabled students can engage in such structured negotiations, some would argue that disabled students are in a weak position because institutions can use their power and authority to politically neutralize the complaints of students. This is not helped by the fact that disabled students can be unsure of their rights and often do not feel that they have the financial or legal support to threaten litigation if negotiation fails.

Konur argues that we cannot assume that the 'rules of the game' in terms of disability discrimination legislation is to end discrimination, because evidence from case law within higher education and employment would suggest that this is not happening. Konur suggests that in order to devise rules of the game that will end discrimination we need to develop an evidence-based model rather than a 'good practice' model. By this, Konur means that we should move away from just focusing on positive outcomes of disability initiatives (good practice culture) and towards recording everything that is happening, particularly the bad practice (evidence-based culture).

If e-learning accessibility case law does not exist, then evidence of bad practice in relation to e-learning accessibility is also virtually non-existent. Although there are a number of studies that have evaluated the accessibility of university main websites, there is very little public evaluation and dissemination of the student experience in relation to e-learning in its broadest sense (beyond access to websites and VLEs). A small amount of unevaluated evidence exists on learning and teaching project websites (see chapter 5), specialist mailing lists and in the occasional news reports (e.g. Parkin 2001; Tierney 2002):

> I am a first year university student. I am deafblind . . . [A]re there any other deafblind students. . who have been forced by their university to take exams using a reader and dictating . . . [their] answers[?] I was forced to do this. I use an FM system but it was not adequate for the exams because my reader had to speak sooo quietly. I resorted to using print on palm! So got hardly any of the paper done. In the second exam my reader refused to continue because she said it was unfair on her and on me. So I couldn't do the rest. I asked for brailled papers and to word-process my answers but the university said I had to use a reader.
>
> (Parkin 2001)

According to Konur, disabled students need to be allowed to play the 'game' along with all the other players, and until they are they will not be able to influence or re-write the rules of the game. There may be a role for disabled students, in working together to build a comprehensive evidence base of good and bad practice that can be used to re-write the rules of the accessibility game. However, the chances are, that students will need to collaborate with other players (e.g disability advocates) in order to do this.

Conclusions

The institutional change framework as proposed by North and applied by Konur, prompts us to consider the socio-political responses to accessibility and to explore the influence that rules have on an institution and the people that work within that institution. The framework has therefore been useful in helping us to understand the conflict and tension that can exist in current institutional accessible e-learning practices. Tension that is borne out of conflicting rules (North) and a misalignment of the rules by which different 'teams' play (Konur).

There is a limit however to the extent to which the institutional change framework can help us to understand the goals and motivations of institutions and teams. In one sense, the rule making teams (e.g. government and other standards agencies) have changed the rules, through the production of disability discrimination legislation and accessibility standards, etc. But for whatever reason, the rules have not been sufficiently powerful enough to compel the other teams to completely align their activities to these new rules.

Konur does not explore what motivates teams to make, implement, advocate and enforce rules or what goals the teams might share that influences them to align their activities with certain rules.

Applying North's ideas leads us to conclude that organizations will be motivated to engage in acquiring accessibility related skills and knowledge if they consider that this will help them survive or beat off competitors. Therefore, higher education institutions might invest in developing accessible e-learning if in doing so they can avoid hefty financial (and other) penalties imposed by government or funding bodies or attract more fee paying students and help make them more profitable than their rival institutions. Higher education institutions have perhaps changed their practice 'just enough' to avoid externally imposed punishments, that in itself is a survival strategy that North might recognize. There is evidence however, that the 'rule enforcers' appear reluctant or unable to impose significant changes in practice and neither North's nor Konur's work helps us understand why this might be. Furthermore, not all institutions have changed their practice in order to attract more 'business' from disabled students. While some universities are developing a reputation for the work they do in the area of inclusion and accessibility, other universities have simply decided to find other markets to compete for, for example, international students, research grants, or commercialization of research expertise and products. Applying North's framework would therefore lead us to conclude that accessible e learning practice is unlikely to be fully developed across all higher education institutions. It is unclear therefore how we can use North's framework to help us understand how to change the practice of those institutions who have decided not to compete for the disabled student market.

Whilst accessibility rules do influence and mediate accessible e-learning practice, they do not appear to be sufficient to change practice by themselves. The behaviour of institutions, organizations and teams therefore appears to be mediated by more than rules. A conceptual tool is needed that can help us understand what else other than rules might mediate and influence the development of accessible e-learning practice.

Chapter 12

Individual responses to accessibility

Tools, activities and contradictions

> Until we've established a Web design framework that intrinsically promotes accessibility, we have the responsibility to make the best use of the tools that we have, to provide accessibility to as much of our target audience as we can.
>
> (Hull 2004: 41)

Introduction

Chapter 11 attempted to develop our understanding of institutional responses to e-learning accessibility. In this chapter a framework will be sought to develop our understanding of individual responses to e-learning accessibility, particularly how accessibility tools mediate these responses. In the accessibility arena a plethora of tools exist. We have a whole array of guidelines, standards and design and evaluation software applications (see chapter 7). In fact, there are so many tools that practitioners are experiencing some degree of difficulty in choosing which tools to use. For example, in 2002 Witt and McDermott identified 30 site-evaluation tools, ten web page repair tools and over 20 filter and transformation tools. Now, in 2006 there are probably more. Accessibility tools are however, having a varied impact on practice and the activities that practitioners undertake. There is some debate as to whether this is because the tools are faulty or inadequate, or whether it is because the users are faulty and ignorant. For Phipps *et al.* (2005) tools cease to be appropriate or useful when they are overly prescriptive. However, it is not unusual for commentators to rail against the ignorance of practitioners and proclaim that if they only used or consulted the tools properly everything would be sorted. Steyaert (2005) for example, argues:

> A final myth involves the lack of information. When talking to content providers about accessibility, many recognize the need for inclusive websites but refer to a lack of detailed information on how to accomplish this. In the era that google replaced the Encyclopaedia Britannica as the

ultimate source of knowledge, it is hard to envisage somebody maintaining this myth. For those who need more than their favourite search machine, two references should suffice. The Web Accessibility Initiative is the best portal to start finding information about accessibility for generic web applications, while TechDis (UK) and the National Center on Accessible Information Technology in Education (USA) are good places for information on higher education applications.

(Steyaert 2005: 67)

Steyaert is oversimplifying matters and in doing so missing a vital point. Yes practitioners can easily find information on the web that tells them that the WAI Guidelines exist. There are a billion and one portals that provide links to the WAI Guidelines. But there are not a billion and one portals that provide links to detailed information about how to use and implement the guidelines. Tools are clearly not enough to change practice. There would appear to be a need to understand in more detail the relationship between people and tools, and in order to do this we probably need to look more closely at the context in which tools are introduced.

One theory that has the potential to help us develop an understanding of the relationship between practitioners, tools and the context in which there are operating is Activity Theory. Activity Theory is concerned with practice, which involves the mastery of external devices and tools of labour activity (Nardi 1996). Activity Theory may therefore provide a descriptive language with which to look closely at the activity systems in which new tools are introduced (Dobson *et al.* 2004). Activity Theory has been widely used by practitioners and researchers to explore e-learning generally (McAvinia and Oliver 2004; Issroff and Scanlon 2002; Barab *et al.* 2004; Dobson *et al.* 2004) but it has not been used to specifically explore e-learning and accessibility.

Activity Theory is not a predictive theory, so it will not enable us to predict what behaviours or activities might occur in the field of accessible e-learning, but it might be able to offer a useful framework for describing current practice with a view to understanding what is and is not working particularly well. This chapter will outline Activity Theory and explore the extent to which it can be applied to e-learning and accessibility in Higher Education.

Activity theory as a potential tool for analysis

Activity Theory has its roots in psychology, particularly the work of Vygotsky and Leont'ev. However, today it is a multidisciplinary theory and a number of researchers have applied and extended the concepts contained within the theory (Engeström 1987; Nardi 1996; Kuutti 1996). Activity Theory offers a framework and a set of concepts, for describing activity that provide both an individual and social perspective on practice.

The structure of activity

Activity Theory focuses on activity as the basic unit of analysis, where the context is included in the analysis. Activity is therefore the minimal meaningful context for understanding individual actions. In the original Activity Theory there were three components to an activity system: the subject, the object and the tools. Confusion can arise in understanding these terms, because they mean different things to different people and researchers give slightly different examples of what each concept means to them. The 'subject' is variously referred to as learner, actor, participant or human being. The 'object' is referred to as raw materials, conceptual understandings, problem spaces, 'that which is acted upon', task, objective, plan or common idea. While tools are called artefacts, physical objects, concepts or symbols. For the purposes of this chapter, subject will be interpreted as the person undertaking the activity, object will be interpreted as the purpose or objective of the activity and tools will be interpreted as any physical or conceptual tool that the subject may use to help them meet the objective of the activity.

Early Activity Theory concentrated on understanding the relationship between the subject and object. However researchers began to realize that activity could not be fully understood unless the relationship between an individual (subject) and their environment was also considered. Engeström (1987) therefore expanded Activity Theory to include three more components: rules, community and division of labour. Rules cover both explicit and implicit norms, conventions and social relations within a community. Activity Theorists believe that activity systems can be somewhat constrained by the formal (systematic, general, and expected), informal (idiosyncratic adaptation), and technical (mandated and, potentially, written) rules, norms and conventions of a community. The community of a system refers to those individuals, groups, or both, who share the same general objects, and are defined by their division of labour and shared norms and expectations. Division of labour refers to how a community is implicitly or explicitly organized in order to ensure that the objective of the activity is achieved. Divisions of Labour can run horizontally as tasks are spread across members of the community with equal status, and vertically as tasks are distributed up and down divisions of power. In Engeström's (1987) 'systemic model' there are three central mutual relationships:

- the relationship between the subject (person, actor) and the object (purpose, motivation, idea behind) of an activity;
- the relationship between subject and community (those people who share the same objective, purpose, motivation, idea);
- the relationship between community and object.

The level of an activity

Activity Theorists argue that activity occurs at different levels and in doing so they distinguish between activities, actions and operations. An activity is long term, with objects transformed to outcomes through a series of stages. These stages are shorter-term processes or actions, which are themselves building on smaller operations. At each of these levels (activity, action and operation) separate activity systems can be mapped. If we take the activity of building a house, at the action level an activity system could be mapped for 'fixing the roof' or 'transporting bricks by truck'. At the operation level a corresponding activity system could be mapped for 'hammering' or 'changing gears when driving'.

Key concepts within Activity Theory

There are a number of key concepts within Activity Theory that help to shape understanding as to how an activity system works. These are: transformation; motivation and consciousness; mediation; history and development; and contradictions and conflicts.

Transformation

When discussing activity, Activity Theorists are not simply concerned with 'doing' as a disembodied action but are referring to 'doing in order to transform something', with the focus on the contextualized activity of the system as a whole (Engeström 1987; Kuutti 1996). A central concept within Activity Theory is therefore the transformation of an object into an outcome. If the object is to build a house, the outcome will be a completed, habitable house.

Motivation and consciousness

In Activity Theory, an activity is motivated by the need to transform the object into an outcome (meet an objective, complete a task, solve a problem, formulate a plan). Participating in an activity is therefore the performing of conscious actions that have an immediate, defined goal. Nardi (1996) argues that consciousness is not a set of discrete disembodied cognitive acts (decision-making, remembering), rather, consciousness is located in everyday practice: you are what you do. And what you do is firmly and inextricably embedded in the social matrix of which every person is an organic part.

Consciousness is important when thinking about novice and expert behaviour, where skilled performance suggests a mental ease and access to certain cognitive resources specific to experts who have become very good at something. Novices on the other hand consciously labour to perform actions that will later become automatic, requiring little conscious awareness. The less able performance of novices is attributable to their need to focus deliberate attention on task actions while at the same time working with fewer cognitive resources than they will have available later as they gain expertise and experience in their tasks.

Mediation

A central concept in Activity Theory is the concept of mediation. Nardi (1996) argues that mediators connect us organically and intimately to the world; they are not merely filters or channels through which experience is carried, like water in a pipe. In Engestrom's systemic model, three relationships are conceptualized, each of which is mediated. Tools mediate the relationship between subject and object, the relationship between subject and community is mediated by rules, whilst division of labour mediates the relationship between object and community. These mediators can have a powerful impact on the relationships. For example, Kuutti (1996) argues that the reciprocal relationship between the subject and object of an activity is mediated by a tool, into which the historical development of the relationship between the subject and the object is condensed. The tool is at the same time both enabling and limiting; it empowers the subject in the transformation process with the historically collected experience and skill 'crystallized to it', but it might also restrict the interaction to be only from the perspective of that particular tool or instrument, if other potential features of an object remain invisible to the subject.

An individual's (subject's) actions will therefore be affected by three major factors: the tools used, the environment or community they belong to and its explicitly or implicitly expressed rules, and the division of labour within that community.

History and development

According to Activity Theorists activities are not static or rigid entities; they are under continuous change and development (Kuutti 1996). This development is not linear or straightforward but uneven and discontinuous. This means that each activity also has a history of its own. Parts of older phases of activities often stay embedded in them as they develop, and historical analysis of the development is often needed in order to understand the current situation.

Theorists consider that development can occur at all levels of an activity. New operations are formed from previous actions as participant's skills increase. Correspondingly, at the level of actions, the scope of new actions is enlarging and totally new actions are being invented, experimented with and adapted as responses to new situations or possibilities encountered in the process of transforming the object.

Each of the mediators with an activity system may also develop and change. While they may be transformed, they will also carry with them a particular culture, a 'historical residue' of that transformation or development. Finally, the object of an activity may also be questioned and adapted in response to larger changes and other activities.

Contradictions and conflicts

For Activity Theorists activities are not isolated units but are more like nodes in crossing hierarchies and networks, they are influenced by other activities and other changes in their environment. External influences can therefore change some elements of activities, causing imbalances between them. Activity Theory uses the term 'contradiction' to indicate a misfit within elements, between them, between different activities or between different developmental phases of a single activity. Contradictions manifest themselves as problems, ruptures, breakdowns or clashes. Activity Theory sees contradictions as sources of development where activities are virtually always in the process of working through contradictions. Examples of different causes or sources of contradictions include:

- when a subject is participating in connected activities, which have very different objects (Kuutti 1996);
- when a new tool is introduced into a community, which does not have any rules of practice to make effective use of that tool (Issroff and Scanlon 2002);
- when different but connected activities share an object or an artefact but place a very different emphasis upon it (McAvinia and Oliver 2004).

For activity theorists, to 'develop' means to resolve or transform these contradictions (instead of merely shifting them elsewhere), thus resulting in a change in the activity system: the construction of a new object or practice (Barab *et al.* 2004).

Applicability of activity theory to e-learning and accessibility

Applying Activity Theory to disability, e-learning and accessibility gives rise to some interesting questions about current e-learning accessibility practice, questions which have the potential to shape the future accessibility research and development agenda:

- Can the central components of an activity system be mapped onto components within an accessible e-learning system?

- Can novices in an accessible e-learning activity system eventually become experts?
- Are accessible e-learning activities mediated by tools, rules and division of labour?
- Does the activity of accessible e-learning have a history of development and is that history influencing future development?
- Are there contradictions between central components of an accessible e-learning system and can the identification of these contradictions help to develop and progress future practice?

Identifying the components of an accessible e-learning activity system

Activity Theory has some resonance with accessible e-learning in that elements of accessible e-learning practice can be equated to components of an activity system (see Figure 12.1). If the activity is the development of accessible e-learning material, the objective is to enable disabled students to access

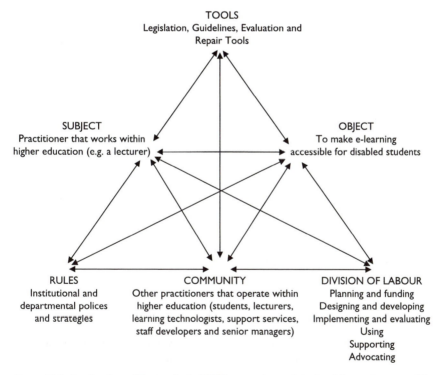

Figure 12.1 Application of Engeström's (1987) systemic model of activity to the accessible e-learning practice of a higher education practitioner.

e-learning and therefore have an equitable learning experience and the outcome will be an accessible 'piece' of e-learning, e.g. a VLE, an online library catalogue system or an e-portfolio system. The subject will be anyone who is responsible for facilitating and supporting the student's learning experience and the community to which they belong will include all the different stakeholder groups identified within this book. The tools that subjects use to carry out this activity will include guidelines such WCAG, standards such as Section 508 and repair and evaluation tools such as LIFT and A-Prompt. The cultural norms, rules and regulations that might govern performance of this activity within an institution could include institutional policies and strategies relating to accessibility. Finally, the stakeholders within a community may need to decide and agree on roles and responsibilities, so that it is clear which stakeholders need to take responsibility for designing, developing, implementing, using and evaluating accessible e-learning, which stakeholders will be responsible for supporting any or all of these actions and which stakeholders will be responsible for advocating for the need for any or all of these actions.

At the activity level, the objective may be to enable disabled students to access e-learning, but at the action level, the objective can become much more specific. For example:

- to build a site that served as a model of accessibility in Macromedia Flash design (Regan 2004b);
- to produce a website which complied with Level AAA (Witt and McDermott 2002);
- to involve dyslexic student volunteers in the testing of a navigation interface for a VLE (Smith 2002);
- to use XML and XSL to separate the interface from the application such that different users can have different interfaces to the system depending on their preferences, needs and the computer equipment they are using (Cooper *et al.* 2000);
- to produce a concise usable guide to the factors which must be taken into account in order to produce accessible online learning materials (Jeffels and Marston 2003);
- to address accessibility issues within a university-based distance learning program in the context of critical benchmarks for success (Burgstahler *et al.* 2004).

Novice and expert behaviour

There is an assumption within Activity Theory that novices in an activity system will eventually become skilled performers, that they will gain the cognitive resources required and that actions and operations will become automatic. Within the accessible e-learning community however, the 'experts' appear to suggest that there are some actions that novices will always find difficult, for example auditing the accessibility of a website:

> Since it is unlikely you will catch all accessibility problems and the learning curve is steep, it may be advisable to commission an expert accessibility audit. In this way, you can receive a comprehensive audit of the subject site, complete with detailed recommendations for upgrading the level of accessibility of the site. Groups who provide such audits include the Digital Media Access Group, based at the University of Dundee, or the RNIB, who also audit web sites for access to the blind.
>
> (Sloan 2000)

The cost of affording experts however, is prohibitive for many institutions (Diaper and Worman 2003), whilst other experts indicate that the skills required are even quite difficult for them to learn (Witt and McDermott 2002). Such considerations lead to some interesting questions:

- Can novices really become experts when even the experts struggle?
- Can the community divide the labour of accessible e-learning to cope with the perceived technical difficulties?

Addressing both issues will require an evaluation of which actions and operations are the most difficult and who is most qualified or capable of undertaking them. Evidence would suggest that auditing e-learning is one of the most difficult actions (Sloan 2000; Witt and McDermott 2002; see also chapter 7). Of the six stakeholders identified within this book, learning technologists might be the most capable within the community to undertake this action, with training and support. Addressing the difficulty levels of the actions and operations required will therefore be an important issue for staff developers in order to pitch whatever they offer at the right level and at the right people (see chapter 9).

Mediation

There is evidence to suggest that accessibility tools, accessibility rules and division of labour can mediate e-learning accessibility activity.

Tools

A number of tools exist that have the potential to mediate individual practice in some way:

- assistive technologies (see chapters 5 and 8);
- generic and specific accessibility guidelines (see chapter 4);
- accessibility standards (see chapter 4);

- instructional design approaches (see chapter 6);
- design, evaluation and repair software applications (see chapter 7);
- user-centred design approaches (see chapter 7);
- assistive technology assessment models (see chapter 8);
- online staff development resources and courses (see chapter 9);
- equipment procurement and service audit tools (see chapter 10).

In some respects the accessible e-learning community is obsessed with tools. The longer e-learning continues to remain largely inaccessible the more tools are produced, particularly software tools that automate tasks previously performed manually (Stein *et al.* 2001; Buck 2004). If the original tools do not appear to be successfully mediating the accessibility activities of practitioners, the answer is probably not to produce more tools, but to help practitioners to learn to use the ones they have. This might involve developing rich descriptions of the tools in use or developing a detailed set of rules of practice to help individual practitioners make effective use of the tools. As Winberg (1999) argues, using a tool (e.g. accessibility guidelines) is not the same as applying a method:

> just using guidelines doesn't qualify as a method at all. What we need is a framework for using these guidelines, if we are to use them at all that is. Perhaps the guidelines should rather be used as a foundation for new methods and as a good way of validating their performance.
>
> (Winberg 1999)

Rules

A number of rule sets exist that could be seen to be mediating accessible e-learning activity:

- the rules contained within legislation, guidelines and standards (see chapter 4);
- the rules contained within institutional policies and strategies (see chapter 10);
- the rules contained within research and practice literature (see chapter 11).

The impact of these rules on individual practice will vary, depending on how much they are questioned. For example:

- the evidence base of the rules that underpin the Web Content Authoring Guidelines has been questioned (see chapter 4);
- the applicability of the rules contained within WCAG to specialised practices have been questioned through the development of a whole array of specialised or specific guidelines (see chapter 4);

- the validity of the rules that evaluation and repair tools apply when auditing accessibility have been examined (see chapter 7);
- the power of the rules contained within legislation and policies have been questioned due to a perceived lack of enforcement of these rules (see chapter 11);
- the potential mismatch and conflict between different sets of rules have been highlighted (see chapter 11).

What Activity Theory particularly gets us to think about is the extent to which the accessible e-learning community has come up with a detailed set of rules of practice to help individual practitioners make effective use of the tools at its disposal. The creation of adapted or specialised accessibility guidelines may indicate the first steps towards producing a detailed set of 'rules of practice', particularly in those cases where the guidelines are derived from detailed research and analysis of user case studies (e.g. ALERT 2005; Pearson and Koppi 2001; Blankfield *et al.* 2002). However, there is little evidence at the moment that the community (however that is defined) as a whole is aware of these exemplars or that it has come to a common agreement that a set of 'rules of practice' is needed.

Division of labour

In thinking about whether the division of labour within a community mediates the practice of an individual it would appear that different communities are dividing labour (in terms of roles and responsibilities) in very different ways:

- some communities place all the emphasis for responsibility onto 'technicians' (learning technologists) and thus ignore the potential role that non-technicians (lecturers) can play (see chapter 6);
- some communities are arguing that learning technologists cannot work in isolation and that they need to be organized into review teams which have a wide range of expertise in order to conduct accessibility evaluations/audits (see chapter 7);
- some are calling for an end to placing the sole responsibility for advocating and promoting accessibility on the shoulders of specialist support services (e.g. disability officers and assistive technology specialists), some are not (see chapters 8 and 13);
- some are recognizing the potential value in staff developers forging strategic partnerships with disability services and disability advocates (see chapter 9);
- a strong case is starting to be built for senior managers to create accessibility teams that cut across the traditional ways in which support services are organized in institutions (see chapter 10).

These different ways of organizing labour mean that stakeholders are given a wide range of roles and responsibilities, some of which fall within their sphere of knowledge and skills, some of which do not.

History and development

According to Activity Theorists activities are not static or rigid entities; they are under continuous change and development. Historical analysis of the development of an activity is therefore sometimes needed in order to understand the current situation. This has particular resonance for accessible e-learning in that novices to the activity frequently assume that accessibility is a new activity that has very little history. For many there is a perception that the history of accessible e-learning only goes as far back as 1999 when the WCAG-1 was developed. This perception is blinding some practitioners to the history that influenced the development of the WCAG-1; a history that includes universal design, usability and user-centred design. It is such blindness that leads some to urge learning technologists to engage in a spot of 'archaeology' (see chapter 7). If we forget the history and don't engage in archaeological digs from time to time, then we render ourselves less capable of being able to deal with perceived conflicts. Conflicts, for example, between usability and accessibility, universal design and accessible design, assistive technology and learning technology. Historical analysis would allow us to determine that the conflicts are less real than we imagined and prevents us from becoming distracted from our objectives (see chapter 7).

If activities have a history, so too do mediators of these activities. The history associated with these mediators may influence the relationship they have with subjects, objects and communities. For example, version one of the WCAG guidelines has a relatively long history in that practitioners have spent the past six to seven years both praising and criticizing them. Some practitioners have gone as far as to adapt these guidelines for their own specific purposes (see chapter 4). The challenge for version two of the guidelines will be the extent to which any residual love or hate of WCAG-1 may prevent practitioners from engaging fully with the newer version.

The evaluation and repair tool, Bobby, has had a history of being well known and ubiquitously used (see chapter 7). Achieving the Bobby stamp of approval (Bobby logo on website) was the goal that many people set themselves. This glorious history became shrouded however, as a new history emerged whereby using Bobby did not guarantee that a site was fully accessible (Seale 2003a; Witt and McDermott 2004). Any new evaluation and repair tools that come out to replace or challenge such tools as Bobby and A-Prompt may first have to overcome or deal with their residual 'baggage' before practitioners become persuaded to use them.

As a mediator, division of labour also has a history in that institutions have been used to making decisions about how to divide labour in order to meet the needs of disabled students. These decisions have tended to divide labour (and thus services) into those who are specialist and those who are main- stream. The history of these decisions is influencing the current decisions communities make about how to integrate disability issues into mainstream e-learning. Communities are having to decide:

- whether to ignore the perceived history of accessibility being a technical activity and encourage stakeholders who may not see themselves as 'technical experts' (e.g. lecturers) to take on some of the responsibilities and tasks (see chapter 6);
- whether student support services should be organized as they have in the past and have separate specialist services such as Assistive Technology Centres, or whether these specialist services should now be integrated into more mainstream services such as libraries, etc. (see chapter 8);
- whether and how specialists should be involved in delivering accessible e-learning related staff development opportunities (see chapter 9);
- whether and how specialists should be involved in forming and serving on accessibility committees (see chapter 10).

Identifying contradictions in the accessible e-learning system

Most people who attempt to apply Activity Theory to their own practice end up producing a diagram similar to the one presented in Figure 12.1. One of the values of using such a diagram is that it offers an easy and simple way to explore the potential contradictions (breakages, weak links) between the central components of the activity system. Figure 12.1 represents an ideal world in which the relationships between the components in the system are in perfect working order. In the real world of accessible e-learning evidence would suggest that not all the relationships are perfect, if they were, then inaccessible e-learning material would not exist, and we know it does!

According to Activity Theory contradiction or conflict may occur between any or all of twelve relationships represented in Figure 12.1. For example there may be contradictions in the relationships between: objects and tools; objects and division of labour; community and division of labour; community and rules; rules and subject; and tools and subject.

Contradiction between the object and the tools

A contradiction could be perceived to exist between the object and tools, if we agree that the tools currently available are weak and not good enough to enable the users to meet the objective of the activity. There is certainly some agreement that some of the tools at the disposal of users have been poorly designed: 'Moreover, in many cases, standards violations are not the fault of individual developers, but of the development tools which are being used, which have also been poorly engineered, and/or released prematurely' (McMullin 2002).

This book has produced some evidence that tools may not be good enough to help users meet the objective of accessible e-learning activities due to:

- difficulties in interpreting accessibility guidelines (Witt and McDermott 2002);
- non specificity of guidelines to service, organisation, disability, media or technology contexts (see chapter 4);
- difficulties in interpreting the results of evaluation and repair tools (see chapter 7);
- poor validity and reliability of evaluation and repair tools (see chapter 7).

The perceived weakness of tools has led some to call for tool developers to do better:

> The world probably does not need yet another tool to analyze Web pages one at a time and give a report. Tools of this nature are already fairly abundant, even if largely inadequate. The next generation of tools requires a deeper commitment on the part of the tool developers to the underlying structure of Web content, the semantic meaning behind it, and the purpose for which it exists: to communicate information to users.
>
> (Bohman and Anderson 2005: 89)

Contradiction between the object and division of labour

A contradiction could be perceived to exist between the object and division of labour if we agree that there is a fragmented division of labour that is pulling the different stakeholders apart and preventing them from working together to meet the objective. In addition to the debate regarding whether accessibility service provision should be divided along specialist or mainstream lines, there also appears to be some disagreement regarding where individual responsibilities for accessibility lie. For some the responsibility lies purely with technical staff (learning technologists). Others consider that assistive technology specialists and disability service providers are 'responsible' for accessibility (Burgstahler and Cook 2005). In other cases, some stakeholders are consisdered to be more responsible than others: 'When using these programs, the ability of the instructor to create an accessible Web site is limited by the accessibility provided by the LMS engineers' (Johnson and Ruppert 2002: 442).

There is also a tension between the need to place responsibility on the shoulders of one particular stakeholder and the acknowledgement that 'partnerships' are required:

Awareness activities and advocacy comes through building strategic
partnerships with those who are responsible for accessibility (disability
service providers), those who make technology decisions (IT planning
and implementation) and a whole host of service providers (housing,
libraries, counseling, financial aid, registration, etc.). These partnerships
will insure that each other's interests are on the table and included
with each decision that involves the Web, accessibility and ultimately an
e-culture of inclusion. Making sure that all stakeholders, including students, staff and instructors with disabilities are represented at all phases
of policy development, implementation and support is a time consuming
process. It is a process that plays off exponentially in terms of buy-in,
support, and long-term success.

(Anderson 2004)

Partnership is an interesting concept, which is generally understood to mean
that people within the partnership have equal power and responsibility. The
accessible e-learning community will need to examine what it understands
by the concept of 'strategic partnerships', and whether they are really going
to work if only one partner (e.g. learning technologist, assistive technology
specialist) is deemed to hold the final responsibility for accessibility.

Contradiction between the community and division of labour

A contradiction could be perceived to exist between community and division
of labour if the rules that the community develop divide labour in such a way
as to mitigate against the objective of the activity being achieved. An example
of where this might potentially happen is the rules that a higher education
institution might embed into its accessibility policy. If the process by which
the policy is created does not involve all relevant parties, and if the outcome
of this process is a policy that is not integrated into the mainstream learning
and teaching activity of the institution then this may set a tone and culture
of segregated specialist services that divides labour unevenly across the community. Any accessibility objective that aspires to inclusion is unlikely to be
achieved if all the relevant stakeholders are excluded. 'Design for all' probably
requires a commitment to 'design by all'.

Contradiction between the community and the rules

A contradiction may be perceived to occur between community and rules
where the community cannot agree on the rules and how they should
be applied. Examples include, if the community does not come up with
consistent rules of practice to enable subjects (individual practitioners) to use
the tools available to them (see chapter 4) in the following situations:

- whilst the community is consistent in pointing practitioners to the WCAG, it is inconsistent in its reference to this tool as a guideline or as standard;
- where sections of the community appear oblivious to the existence of adapted guidelines (rules) for more specific purposes;
- where sections of the community appear oblivious to the existence of standards separate from the WCAG;
- where the community is not working together to help practitioners understand the relationship between the rules contained within legislation, guidelines and standards.

Contradiction between the rules and the subject

A contradiction may be perceived to occur between the rules and the subject where the rules are non-existent, weak or inconsistent and so not good enough to enable the users of the rules (subjects) to meet the objective of the activity. In chapter 10 the rules that might be contained within institutional accessibility policies were considered and there was some evidence to suggest that:

- the rules within institutional accessibility policies often lack detail which means that individuals do not have a detailed 'rule of practice' to guide them in meeting the objective of the activity;
- the rules within institutional accessibility polices rarely compel staff to make e-learning accessible which means that the activity required by the policy may be different to the activity required by the original objective;
- the rules within institutional accessibility policies may contain a level of compulsion that is at odds with the level of compulsion contained within other sets of rules (legislation, guidelines, etc.).

Chapter 11 considered the extent to which the rules contained within accessibility legislation are enforced and who enforces the rules, and certainly there is evidence to suggest that rules will be perceived as weak or confusing if they are not visibly and openly enforced.

Contradiction between the tools and the subject

If the subjects of an activity system are unable to use the tools in the way they were intended, then conflict or contradiction may occur. There is a certainly a lot of evidence to suggest that the subjects of the accessible e-learning activity system have an uneasy relationship with accessibility tools. A relationship that means that in one and the same breath practitioners can criticize the utility of guidelines, standards, evaluation and repair tools and at the same time call for the development of new tools.

Contradiction in any or all of the relationships described in the previous section has the potential to threaten the central relationships between object and community, subject and object and subject and community. For example the conflicts between community and division and labour and community and rules may cause individual subjects to question the extent to which they share the same objectives of the community as well as the extent to which they are able to achieve the objective of the activity.

According to Activity Theory, any or all of the contradictions will prevent accessible e-learning practice from developing and therefore accessible e-learning will not develop or progress unless these contradictions are resolved.

Conclusion

Activity Theory prompts us to consider the socio-cultural responses to accessibility and to explore the influence that tools have on individuals within an 'activity system'. Like North's Institutional Change Framework, Activity Theory also considers the influence of rules as a mediator or activity or practice. However, the main contribution of Activity Theory to accessible e-learning, is that it prompts us to think beyond what's wrong with the rules and the tools and to take into account the wider context, a context which includes community and division of labour. Using Activity Theory it is possible to argue that accessible e-learning activity will therefore not develop unless attention is paid to:

- developing tools around which communities feel able to produce 'rules of practice', enabling subjects to use them effectively;
- developing rules with which communities feel comfortable and can apply consistently, enabling subjects to use them effectively;
- developing roles and responsibilities which communities can apply consistently, enabling subjects to get a clear sense of how the work will be divided amongst community members and what their individual contribution to achieving the objective of the activity needs to be.

Chapter 13

Community responses to accessibility

Enterprises, boundary practices and brokers

> In order to understand why there are so few sites that illustrate great design and great accessibility, web design needs to be understood as a practice of individuals. Sites are built by people, not principles or standards. To state the case in a rather simple way, designers are trained to value the visual presentation. Accessibility advocates are taught to value adherence to standards. Compromising on either front means relinquishing control. In general, this is not something that comes easily within either community of experts.
>
> (Regan 2004b)

Introduction

Chapters 11 and 12 attempted to develop our understanding of how rules and tools mediate the development of individual and institutional accessible e-learning practices. In this chapter a framework will be sought to enhance our understanding of how goals (objectives, motivations) influence the development of accessible e-learning practice, particularly the practice of communities. In the field of accessibility and e-learning, the concept of 'community' is used frequently (see Table 13.1). It is used to refer to both the users and providers of online material, as well as the context in which that material is delivered. Whilst the membership, nature and contexts of the communities identified may differ, it is acknowledged that some of these communities may combine to form a larger 'accessibility community'. For example, Regan (2004b) talks of an accessibility community that consists of different subject experts (e.g. designers and accessibility advocates) each of whom has different and often conflicting perspectives on accessibility. There is also some consensus that the different communities need to work together in some way in order to develop and progress their practice. For example, Coombs (2002) talks about the need for a 'network' of technical and non-technical faculty and staff to provide support for accessible e-learning. While Jeffels and Marston (2003) argue that:

Table 13.1 Scope and nature of references to 'community' within e-learning and accessibility literature

Scope	Nature	Source
Users	Student community	Draffan and Corbett 2001:342
	User communities	Manouselis *et al.* 2002 Ivory *et al.* 2003:212
	Disability community	Schmetzke 2001:40 Ludi 2002 Fichten *et al.* 2003 Folds and Fain 2005
	Internet or web communities	Keller *et al.* 2000 Gay and Harrison 2001 Nevile and Burmeister 2003
Providers	Communities of web developers and designers	Hinn 1999 Lamshed *et al.* 2003 Jeffels and Marston 2003 Hunziker 2004
	Library community	Schmetzke 2001:35
	Academic community	Witt and McDermott 2004:46
	Communities of 'advocacy'	Wattenberg 2004 Regan 2004b
	Education community	Draffan and Corbett 2001:343 Sloan *et al.* 2000:214
	Higher education (post secondary education, college) community	McCarthy 2001 French and Valdes 2002 Michaels *et al.* 2002
Contexts	E-learning community	Kelly *et al.* 2004 Pulichino 2005
	Campus (institutional) community	Fichten *et al.* 2003 Hricko 2003 Johnson *et al.* 2003 Fossey *et al.* 2004
	Global community	Coombs 2002 Waddell and Hardy 2004

For accessibility to really progress, technologists, software developers, hardware manufacturers as well as those developing and using online learning materials have to talk to each other discuss and understand each other's problems. Those at the forefront of developing accessibility guidelines and accessible materials for use in education are the ones who can help to make it all happen.

Central to the notion of different communities connecting and working to understand one another is the belief that in doing so 'practice', as Regan (2004b) calls it, will develop. Members of the different communities that make up the accessible e-learning community are being required to respond to accessibility related legislation. Responding to this legislation requires changes in practice and learning new ways of doing things. Ways that involve interpreting and implementing accessibility guidelines and standards as well as implementing accessibility design and validation tools.

If we are to develop an understanding of accessibility 'practice' we need a theory, model or framework to help us understand how the different stakeholder groups within higher education institutions might form a community and work together to develop accessible e-learning. One theory that has the potential to help us develop such an understanding is Wenger's theory of Communities of Practice (Wenger 1998). Wenger's theory is essentially a social theory of learning. Communities of practice are groups of people who share a common goal, purpose or enterprise. They are often formed outside the boundaries of formal organisational structures and share their own common language, means of communicating and ways of doing things. Learning takes place in a community of practice through active participation in the group and is primarily a social process.

The concept of communities of practice has been widely used by e-learning practitioners and researchers to explore student learning experiences, but it has not been widely used to specifically explore e-learning and accessibility. Seale (2003c, 2004) published a tentative exploration of the applicability of communities of practice to e-learning accessibility. This chapter will expand this exploration by outlining the Communities of Practice Theory and exploring the extent to which it can be applied to e-learning and accessibility in higher education.

Communities of practice as a potential tool for analysis

Central to Wenger's communities of practice theory is the concept of practice, where practice is understood as: giving structure and meaning to what communities do; being a source of coherence for a community and having boundaries and peripheries that may link with other communities.

A practice that gives structure and meaning to what a community does

According to Wenger, practice is about 'meaning as an experience of everyday life'. He argues that what is important about the pursuit of enterprises is the meanings that are produced from these pursuits. Meaning is located in a process he termed 'negotiation of meaning', which involves the interaction of two processes: participation and reification. If participation in communities shapes our experience through membership and active engagement, reification gives form to our experience by producing objects that 'congeal this experience into thingness'.

Reification creates points of focus around which the negotiation of meaning becomes organized. So, for example, reification may produce a range of laws, procedures or tools. The negotiation of meaning therefore, may become focused around using a law to argue a point, using a procedure to know what to do or using a tool to perform an action. Wenger recognized that a very large portion of reification involved in work practices can come from outside communities. In this case, he argues, reification must be re-appropriated into a local process in order to become meaningful.

Wenger talks of the 'the double edge of reification' and states that a good tool can reify an activity so as to amplify its effects while making the activity effortless. A bad tool therefore, can 'ossify activities around its inertness'. Wenger also warns that if reification prevails over participation, if everything is reified but with little opportunity for shared experience and interactive negotiation, then there may not be enough overlap in participation to recover a co-ordinated, generative meaning.

Practice that is a source of coherence

Wenger describes three dimensions by which practice is a source of coherence for a community: mutual engagement, joint enterprise and shared repertoire. In defining mutual engagement Wenger states that practice exists because people are engaged in actions whose meanings they negotiate with one another. What makes a community of practice out of a medley of people is their mutual engagement as they make things happen. Wenger went on to argue that mutual engagement involves not only our competence, but the competence of others. It draws on what we do and know as well as the contributions and knowledge of others.

In defining and discussing the concept of joint enterprise, Wenger introduces the notion of 'indigenous enterprise' and argues that conditions, resources and demands will only shape practice if the community has negotiated that. To exemplify this, Wenger gives an example of a community of practice that has arisen in response to some outside mandate and argues that practice evolves into the communities' own response to that mandate.

According to Wenger, the shared repertoire of a community of practice includes routines, words, tools, ways of doing things, stories, gestures, symbols, genres, actions or concepts that the community has produced or adopted in the course of its existence, and which have become part of its practice.

Practice that has boundaries and peripheries that may link with other communities

According to Wenger, communities of practice cannot be considered independently of other practices. Their various enterprises are closely interconnected, their members and their artefacts are not theirs alone. Communities of Practice are therefore sources of boundary and contexts for creating connections. Wenger presents two kinds of connections: boundary objects and brokering. Boundary objects are defined as artefacts, documents, terms, concepts, and other forms of reification around which communities of practice can organize their interconnections. Brokering is described as the connections provided by people who can introduce elements of one practice into another.

Boundary objects

Wenger notes that the design of artefacts (documents, systems, tools) is often the design of boundary objects. He illustrated this by giving an example of designers of computer systems, who focus on issues of use and often employ the term 'the user' as a generic term with 'mythical proportions'. From this perspective, 'use' is a relation between a user and an artefact. But, that user engages in certain practices and is therefore a member of certain communities of practice. Artefacts can therefore be boundary objects, and designing them might involve designing for participation rather than just use.

Brokers

Wenger argued that when people transfer from one community of practice to another or have multi-membership, they can transfer some element of one practice into another through brokering. Brokers are able to make new connections across communities of practice, enable coordination, and open new possibilities for meaning. According to Wenger, the job of brokering is a complex one. It involves processes of translation, co-ordination and alignment between perspectives. Brokers need to:

• have legitimacy so that they can influence the development of practice;
• be able to link practices by facilitating transaction between them;
• be secure in living on the boundaries of practices.

Boundary practices and constellations

Boundary encounters between members of different communities provide connections and may therefore become part of practice. Maintaining these connections also becomes part of the enterprise.

The term constellation refers to a grouping of stellar objects that are seen as a configuration even though they may not be particularly close to one another, or of the same kind or size. Wenger explains that there are many different reasons why some communities of practice may be seen as forming a constellation. These include having related enterprises, facing similar conditions, having members in common and sharing artefacts.

Applicability of communities of practice to e-learning and accessibility

Applying Wenger's concept of communities of practice to disability, e-learning and accessibility gives rise to some interesting questions about current e-learning accessibility practice, questions which have the potential to shape the future accessibility research and development agenda:

- Does the accessible e-learning community consist of one community of practice or a constellation of practices?
- Is the accessible e-learning community engaged in a pursuit of enterprise through the production of artefacts (reification) and negotiation of the meaning of these artefacts (participation)?
- Is reification prevailing over participation in the accessible e-learning community?
- Is the accessible e-learning community mutually engaged in negotiating meaning, developing joint enterprises and sharing repertoires?
- Is the e-learning accessibility community creating connections with other communities through boundary objects, brokers or boundary practices?

One community of practice or a constellation of practices?

In this book, six stakeholders in accessible e-learning practice have been identified: students, lecturers, learning technologists, student support services, staff developers and senior managers. Each of these stakeholder groups could be viewed as a separate community of practice. But in addition, the stakeholder communities appear to have enough in common to warrant viewing them as a 'constellation' of practices, a constellation of accessible e-learning practices (see Figure 13.1).

All these communities have some role to play in developing accessible e-learning material, and therefore have a related enterprise; all of the communities face similar conditions in that they all operate in the higher education

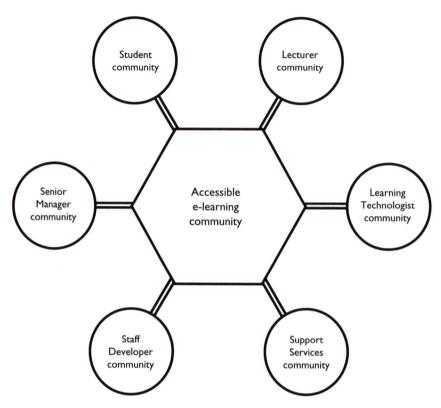

Figure 13.1 A constellation of accessible e-learning practices.

environment; all of them share artefacts such as legislation and guidelines, as evidenced by the references to them in stakeholder literature (see Table 13.2) and each may have members in common (e.g. a disability officer could also be involved in staff development).

   If together, these stakeholder communities form one community of access-ible e-learning practice, it may be helpful to use Wenger's Communities of Practice theory to explore how that community pursues the 'enterprise' of developing accessible e-learning; the extent to which there is a coherent com-munity and how connections might be forged and strengthened between the constellation of practices.

In pursuit of an enterprise

There is a great deal of evidence to suggest that the accessible e-learning community is engaged in reification, thorough the production of a huge array of artefacts:

Table 13.2 The shared accessibility 'artefacts' of the stakeholder communities within higher education

Stakeholders	Web Content Accessibility guidelines	Accessibility related legislation
Lecturers (Academics)	Flowers *et al.* 2001, 2002 Ludi 2002 Blankfield *et al.* 2002 Cook and Gladhart 2002 McCracken 2002 Foley 2003a Johnson *et al.* 2003 Alexander 2003a Powell *et al.* 2004 Ortner *et al.* 2004	Alexander 2002 Oravec 2002 Oravec 2003 Johnson *et al.* 2003 Quick *et al.* 2003 Wall and Sarver 2003 McEwan *et al.* 2003 Powell *et al.* 2004 Bilotta 2005 Kraithman and Bennett 2004
Learning technologists	Arch 2002 Johnson and Ruppert 2002 Kelly 2002a Arch *et al.* 2003 Jeffels and Marston 2003 Mirabella *et al.* 2004 Kelly *et al.* 2004 Witt and McDermott 2004	Kelly 2002a Witt and McDermott 2002 Smith 2002 Jeffels and Marston 2003 Kelly *et al.* 2004
Support services (library, assistive technology, etc.)	Schmetzke 2001 Axtell and Dixon 2002 Borchert and Conkas 2003 O'Grady and Harrison 2003 Burgstahler *et al.* 2004 Spindler 2004	Schmetzke 2001 Bylerley and Chambers 2002 Harrison 2002 Burgstahler 2002 a, b Axtell and Dixon 2002 Fichten *et al.* 2003 Kramer 2004
Staff developers	Bostock 2002	Middling and Bostock 2002 Wray 2002
Senior managers	O'Connor 2000	
Accessibility consultants, advocates, experts	Opitz *et al.* 2003 Thompson *et al.* 2003 Koivunen 2003, 2004 Byrne 2004 Smith and Bohman 2004 Katseva 2004 Kirkpatrick and Thatcher 2005 Chisholm and Brewer 2005 Slatin 2005	McCarthy 2001 Thompson *et al.* 2003 Mark May 2003 Opitz *et al.* 2003

- anti-discrimination legislation such as Section 508 and SENDA (see chapter 4);
- accessibility guidelines such as WCAG Versions 1 and 2 (see chapter 4);
- accessibility specifications and standards such as IMS ACCMD and ACCLIP (see chapter 4);
- accessibility procedures such as universal design approaches; assistive technology assessment processes or staff development strategies (see chapters 6, 7, 8 and 9);
- accessibility design, filter, transformation validation or evaluation tools (see chapter 7);
- accessibility procurement and audit tools (see chapter 10);
- accessibility policies (see chapter 10).

The ultimate artefacts of practice that the e-learning accessibility community might develop, in the pursuit of an accessibility enterprise, would be actual accessible electronic learning materials. However, there appears to be relatively very few of these in existence (see Table 4.1).

It would also appear that in the pursuit of an accessibility enterprise, the negotiation of meaning for the e-learning accessibility community might currently be more focused on reification than participation in terms of:

- understanding the difference between accessibility guidelines and standards (see chapter 4);
- deciding whether there is a need to come to an agreement on the standardization of guidelines and standards (see chapter 3);
- understanding the underpinning principles of different accessibility design approaches and the differences between them (see chapter 7);
- understanding the strengths and weaknesses of accessibility design, filter, transformation, validation and evaluation tools and developing criteria to help decide or justify their use (see chapter 7);
- understanding what should be included in an effective accessibility policy and deciding how it might be successfully integrated into other more mainstream policies (see chapter 10).

In addition, there is evidence that the accessible e-learning community is attempting to re-appropriate reification through more local processes. For example:

- re-framing and adapting generic accessibility guidelines to suit more specific or local purposes and contexts (see chapter 4 for organisation, service, disability, media and technology specific accessibility guidelines);
- developing procedures for evaluating the accessibility of an end-product that involve manual as well as automatic procedures and tools (see chapter 7);

- developing procedures and tools for evaluating accessibility of a service (see chapter 10).

This re-appropriation of reification is significant in that it may help to overcome what Wenger called the 'double-edged' sword of reification where reification produces inertia rather than action. Certainly the confusion and frustration over how to interpret the WCAG-1 (Witt and McDermott 2002) will cause some to give up at the first hurdle. Meanwhile, the confusion and debate surrounding the appropriate use of accessibility validation and evaluation tools such as Bobby, A-Prompt and LIFT and whether or not they are valid and reliable means not only that designers are unsure whether tools will help them to develop their practice but that users are unsure whether they can trust claims of accessibility. As (Seale 2003c: 310) argues:

> The Bobby logo displayed a statement of the values of accessibility and had become something that people could point to and strive for. Yet as reification it did not capture the richness of what is understood by accessibility because it could be appropriated in misleading ways and therefore be a false representation of what it was intended to reflect.

In the formative years of the accessible e-learning community, reification probably prevailed over participation. However the more recent attempts to re-appropriate reification by re-framing and adapting tools and procedures would suggest that the balance between reification and participation may soon be restored through the interactive negotiation and sharing of experiences about how best to re-frame and adapt the tools and procedures which the community has inherited.

Developing a coherent community

Wenger describes three dimensions by which practice is a source of coherence for a community: mutual engagement, joint enterprise and shared repertoire. The accessible e-learning community appears to be made up of a constellation of stakeholder practices (students, lecturers, learning technologists, student support services, staff developers and senior managers). A review of past practice has produced very few examples of how these different stakeholders have been mutually engaged in developing 'accessible' online learning material (e.g. Middling and Bostock 2002). But there appears to be some agreement that these communities should be working together to develop a range of strategic partnerships (chapter 9) and teams willing to take on a collective responsibility for accessible e-learning (chapter 10).

Wenger's example of a community of practice that has arisen in response to some outside mandate has some resonance for the accessible e-learning community who might perhaps see legislation such as SENDA and guidelines such as WCAG as outside mandates that have been imposed on the community. If, as evidence suggests, the accessible e-learning community is attempting to produce a practice to deal with what it understands to be its enterprise, its practice as it unfolds will belong to the community, even though it might have been prompted by external drivers such as guidelines and legislation.

According to Wenger, the shared repertoire of a community of practice includes routines, words, tools, ways of doing things, stories, gestures, symbols, genres, actions or concepts that the community has produced or adopted in the course of its existence, and which have become part of its practice. The findings within this book suggest that the accessible e-learning community has started to develop a shared 'accessibility' repertoire, but that it is by no means complete. The accessible e-learning community has tools and procedures (legislation, guidelines, standards, policies and automated evaluation tools) but what it doesn't have is:

- actions: not everyone within this community is using these tools and procedures;
- ways of doing things: not everyone within this community understands what the 'way of doing things' is (e.g. how to interpret and implement these tools and procedures meaningfully) and there is disagreement over whether there should be 'one best way' or a range of 'acceptable ways' that can be adapted to suit different purposes and contexts;
- stories: the literature within this community is predominantly recording arguments about why tools and procedures should be used and is failing to record detailed stories (case studies, rich descriptions) of how these tools and procedures are being used and adapted in local contexts;
- concepts: in order for a coherent practice to emerge and develop, the community needs to develop its conceptualisations of what best practice is and what factors influence that practice.

Whilst we might be close to having a near to complete set of tools, we are nowhere near to having a complete set of routines, ways of doing things, stories or concepts which will help us to use the tools effectively.

Creating links between communities

There is evidence to suggest that links between the different stakeholder communities are being made (or could be made) through boundary objects and brokers.

Boundary objects

Artefacts such as accessibility related legislation (e.g. Section 508, SENDA 2001) and the Web Content Accessibility Guidelines could be viewed as boundary objects which may create links between communities in the sense that multiple communities refer to them in the literature when trying to negotiate or define theirs and others' practice (see Table 13.2). Although it is interesting to note that some stakeholder communities (staff developers and senior managers) do so less than others. The attention given to these boundary objects by accessibility consultants and experts is significant when we come to consider the role of brokers.

Brokers

Wenger argues that 'brokers' can create connections between communities. The job of brokering is a complex one, involving processes of translation, co-ordination and alignment between perspectives. Brokers need to have legitimacy so that they can influence the development of practice, be able to link practices by facilitating transaction between them and be secure in living on the boundaries of practices.

Within the accessible e-learning community there are examples of different stakeholder groups taking on an obvious brokerage role. The two most notable examples are that of disability officers (staff working within student support services who have a specialist knowledge of disability and/or technology) and staff developers (including educational developers). Disability officers are a natural choice for the role of broker in that they have a history of providing a focal point for disability issues by raising awareness throughout an institution (Hall and Tinklin 1998); acting as a 'broker between the student and the relevant department' (Stefani 2000) and facilitating academic staff to take on board the role of supporting disabled students (Wray 2002). Examples of disability officers acting in a brokerage role within higher education institutions in relation to accessibility include:

- facilitating meetings between disabled students and computer services (Marhsall and Cunneen 2001);
- involving academic staff in assistive technology assessments (Leung *et al.* 1999);
- collaborating with faculty and administration to move forward on new technology initiatives (Michaels *et al.* 2002).

The strategic nature of such brokering activities has the potential to spread the responsibility for meeting the needs of disabled students beyond the 'disability office' to the whole of the institution. As Edwards (2000) argues:

No longer does funding need to be isolated to one office. No longer does the responsibility for the educational requirements for students who have a disability need to be accepted by a small number of people. Now, the system becomes accountable and accessible for all members of the community with students frequently not needing to identify for 'special' services.

Despite the obvious advantages of disability officers acting as 'brokers' and attempting to encourage accessible e-learning practices by crossing the boundaries of different communities, there are some problems with disability officers acting as 'brokers'. These problems relate to: insecurities over professional identity; lack of legitimacy and power; and the risk of isolation. There is some evidence to suggest that disability officers as a whole group (particulary in the UK) may not be secure enough in their own identity to fulfil this brokerage role at the moment. Draffan (1999) speaking at the inaugural conference of the National Association of Disability Officers said:

> People working in this profession have a problem in that they don't know what they are called: disability officers, disability advisers, disability co-ordinators . . . It is not easy if you belong to the faculty of a university, to the British Dyslexia Association, to the Royal College of Speech Therapists, and to the National Federation of Access Centres, as they all have different views of what you should be.

Disability officers may also lack the legitimacy or power to influence strategic and policy issues. For example, in a survey of higher education disability co-ordinators Parker (2000) found some evidence that co-ordinators did not feel highly regarded by academic staff. Parker called for training, advice and guidance in many of the tasks that coordinators undertake, to enable them to feel competent and confident in the role and to achieve the status and authority necessary to do the job expected of them. Reporting on the roles of disability officers within the UK, McCabe (2002) found that the role of a disability officer can be an isolated one, with 55 per cent of respondents stating that they were the only disability officer within their institution. So even if a disability officer is secure in their identity and highly regarded by their institution the effectiveness of their brokerage role may be influenced by their sheer lack of numbers within an institution.

To a lesser extent, staff and educational developers have also been identified as having the potential to take on a 'brokerage role' within the accessible e-learning community. For example Phipps (2002: 6) argues:

> In order to engage with the process of systemic change, developers must act in a brokerage role with all the staff providing perspectives that can inform strategic policy and decisions. Staff and educational developers must be the catalysts that get technical, disability and lecturing staff into a dialogue and then act as a rapportuer to the senior management teams, providing contextualized input to all policies in their institution.

Examples of this brokerage role in action include:

- an educational developer and student counsellor working in partnership with staff from different disciplines to determine their understanding of the concept of the curriculum, their definition and understanding of 'accessibility' and their notion of disability (Stefani 2000);
- development of staff development programmes jointly between Staff Development teams, Disability Services, and departments (Middling and Bostock 2002);
- the collaboration of the Higher Education Staff Development Agency with the Disability Rights Commission, The National Bureau for Students with Disabilities, Universities UK, Universities Scotland, Higher Education Wales and Scottish Higher Education Funding Council to produce a Staff Development Good Practice Guide (Disability Rights Commission 2003).

In all of these examples staff and educational developers appear to be collaborating with disability advocates in order to broker connections between academics and their students. The collaboration between staff and educational developers and disability advocates (e.g. disability officers) may in part be effective because the staff and educational developer may provide the perceived legitimacy that disability officers lack. Developers may also be perceived as central service providers as opposed to a marginalized peripheral service (such as disability support services).

Whoever the brokers are in the accessible e-learning community it is essential that they work to blur some of the boundaries between different communities. When the boundaries between different communities are softened, then other boundaries can be challenged or blurred, for example, the boundaries between mainstream and specialist service provision.

Boundary practices

Seale (2003c) argues that the growth of 'boundary practices' could potentially link different communities in some way. So for example:

- involving the user in the accessibility design process (making connections between student, lecturer and learning technologists communities) suggests a boundary practice for which disability officers working within student support services might be brokers;
- disseminating information about good or best practice in accessible e-learning (making connections between student, lecturer, learning technologist, student support services and senior manager communities) suggests a boundary practice for which staff developers might be brokers.

Conclusion

Wenger's Communities of Practice Theory prompt us to consider socio-cultural responses to accessibility and to explore the role that communities and individuals within those communities can have in developing accessible e-learning practice, if they all have a shared enterprise. The idea that connections need to be made between the different stakeholder communities that make up the constellation of accessible e-learning practice is compelling in that there is growing evidence that these stakeholder communities need to work together and that the boundaries between the communities are not unbreachable. Changes in practice are often difficult, complex and uncomfortable and so require people who can champion the cause, mediate the tensions and broker the changes. Wenger's concept of brokers is therefore appealing in that it gives a role to those people who are already committed to change, are knowledgeable and have a real potential to influence changes in practice.

Like Activity Theory, Communities of Practice also focuses on the influence of rules and tools (artefacts) on the development of practice. Unlike Activity Theory, Communities of Practice does not deal in any great detail with conflicts and contradictions and the influence this may have on the development of practice. This may be a potential weakness of the theory as tension and conflict appears to be an inherent element of accessible e-learning practice. For example, Neville and Burmeister (2003) identified that web content accessibility, as a topic and as a practice, is wide-ranging, with many varied and, at times, conflicting considerations. Some conflicts are local to a community and other conflicts cross the borders of communities.

Despite its weaknesses, Wenger's theory of Communities of Practice has a huge contribution to make to the development of accessible e-learning practice by encouraging practitioners to shift their attention away from reification (focusing on guidelines, legislation and validation and repair tools) and towards participation (how the community can use those tools to develop practice). Seale (2004) uses the example of Virtual Learning Environments (VLEs) to demonstrate the need for such a shift, arguing that now we have guidelines for designing accessible VLEs (Pearson and Koppi 2001) and tools for designing VLE interfaces (Smith 2002) we can perhaps move towards describing different ways of using VLEs with disabled students (Woodford and Bradley 2004) as well as exploring different pedagogical approaches to supporting disabled students in their use of VLEs (ALERT 2005). Such descriptions may contribute to a rounder, fuller picture of accessibility practices.

Chapter 14

Conclusions

Building bridges

> Meaning is constructed as an ideological bridge between the people having the dialogue. During the dialogue, the construction of meaning is ongoing and changing. If people do not meet in dialogue, the bridge of meaning between the participants is not constructed, and confrontation will not take place.
>
> (Schenker and Scadden 2002)

Introduction

Despite the powerful drivers for making e-learning accessible that have emerged over the last five to six years, it is still possible to read a report that condemns the perceived 'inaccessibility' of e-learning experiences that we are offering our students with disabilities. Proposed reasons and solutions for this inaccessibility offer an overly simplistic view of accessible e-learning in higher education:

Reason 1 Staff in higher education are prejudiced against disabled students and therefore happy to discriminate against them.
Solution 1 We'll threaten staff with punishment and guilty consciences so they won't dare discriminate against disabled students.

Reason 2 Staff in higher education are ignorant of the issues and therefore unwittingly discriminate against disabled students.
Solution 2 We'll create guidelines and tools and tell staff in higher education that if they use these it will be virtually impossible for them to discriminate against disabled students ever again.

In recognition that accessible e-learning in higher education is more complex than this, the chapters in this book have provided an in-depth exploration of what we currently know about the development and maintenance of accessible e-learning in higher education and have discussed future developments.

Understanding the 'here and now' of accessible e-learning

One striking picture that emerges from this in-depth exploration is one of existing disconnections and potential connections. The chapters in Part 1 provided a picture of disconnections that currently exist. There are disconnections between:

- practitioners' understanding of disability and the lived experience of being a disabled student in higher education (chapter 2);
- e-learning and students with disabilities (chapter 3);
- drivers for change and individual practitioners (chapter 4).

Chapter 2 explored how definitions and understandings of disability can influence the way people respond to people with disabilities and organize services to meet their needs which impacts directly on people with disabilities. Chapter 3 discussed how e-learning has the potential to meet the needs of students with disabilities, and how that potential is currently not being met to the full, leading to a gap or a divide between students with disabilities and successful e-learning experiences. Chapter 4 described the drivers for accessible e-learning, such as legislation, guidelines and standards and considered the difficulties individual practitioners have in applying guidelines and standards to their own contexts and practices.

The chapters in Part 2 offered a glimpse of the potential connections that might exist or need to be nurtured within higher education. There are potential connections between:

- disabled students and a positive e-learning experience (chapter 5);
- practitioners and aspects of accessibility that are most relevant and meaningful to them (chapters 6 and 7);
- stakeholders in the same community or service (chapter 8);
- stakeholders in different communities or services (chapter 9);
- individual stakeholders, the communities or services in which they are located and the institutions in which they work (chapter 10).

Chapter 6 considered how it might be more fruitful for lecturers to focus on the pedagogical rather than technical aspects of accessibility. Chapter 7 argued that learning technologists may benefit from understanding and questioning the underpinning philosophy and the background history of accessibility guidelines, standards and tools available to them so that they can more confidently adopt a design approach that is meaningful to them and appropriate for the context in which they are working. In chapter 8, the contribution of both generic and specialists stakeholders to the delivery of student support services was explored. Chapter 9 concluded that staff developers will need to be strategic in terms of the partnerships they form with stakeholders from other services or communities. Chapter 10, looked at how the way that institutions develop responses to external drivers such as legislation (e.g. accessibility policies) will influence the way services are organized as well as the way individual stakeholders work with one another.

The exploration of disconnections and connections that exist within accessible e-learning practice has also identified factors that have the potential to make, broker or mediate connections. The chapters in Part 3 explored what mediates institutional, community and individual responses to the drivers for accessible e-learning. Chapter 11 explored the extent to which the interpretation, application and enforcement of accessibility rules (contained within legislation, guidelines and standards) is a socio-political issue and is mediated by issues of alignment, conflict, power, autonomy, negotiation and equality. Chapters 12 and 13 explored the extent to which the application of accessibility rules and tools is a socio-cultural issue and is mediated by how the community understands tools, rules, roles and responsibilities. Chapter 13 discussed the extent to which individual stakeholders may have a crucial role to play in brokering connections between different stakeholder communities.

Exploring the future of accessible e-learning

The descriptions of what we know about current accessible e-learning practice are multi-layered and complex. There may be value therefore in seeking to draw from these descriptions a conceptualisation of accessible e-learning practice that:

- offers a simplified way of representing what we know about accessible e-learning;
- highlights what we know, what we don't know and what we need to know;
- offers new or different ways of thinking about accessible e-learning in the future.

Conceptualisations often emerge through the use of metaphors, theories and models to analyse and reflect on current and best practice. In the accessible e-learning community there are very few metaphors, theories and models that have been developed to try and describe, explain and develop practice. There is a need however for conceptual tools which reflect the existence and potential of disconnections and connections and the factors and people that influence these relationships. Conceptual tools also need to take into account the stakeholders of accessible e-learning practice (individual and community), the context in which they are operating and the drivers and mediators that have the potential to influence stakeholder responses to the need to develop accessible e-learning. This chapter will explore the extent to which new and existing metaphors, models and theories can help to develop our conceptualisations of accessible e-learning practice, in particular to strengthen our understanding of what 'best' practice might entail.

Metaphors as conceptual tools for exploring the future of accessible e-learning

Integral to the concept of accessibility, is the concept of access. In thinking about the concept of access, different but related stakeholder communities have focused on access to a space, access to a function or 'access to the other side'. Within the Internet and online learning community conceptualisation of accessibility is frequently geographically framed in terms of access to 'information space' where access is conceptualized in similar terms to access to a building, garden, street or town. Within the assistive technology and human computer interaction communities conceptualisations of assistance introduce a different understanding of access where assistance is about assisting access to the different functions of a system (Wandke 2005). The inability of a user to access the functions of a system is frequently represented by the metaphor of a divide or a gap, suggesting a large physical distance between the user and the system.

Within the accessibility community the physicality of access is repeated in conceptualisations of access that focus on bridging the gap or the digital divide (Sanda 2003; Snaprud and Aslaksen 2004), so that disabled people can get from one side to another. In seeking to represent the connection between two sides, or the need to make connections between two sides, the bridge metaphor has been used to conceptualize the relationship between users and technologies (Purcell and Grant 2004; Cook and Gladhart 2002) as well as the relationship between developers and technologies (Draffan and Rainger 2004; Regan 2004a,b).

The rainbow bridge as a metaphor for accessible e-learning

The bridge as a metaphor is useful in that it reflects what we understand about disconnections and connections, but we also need a metaphor that reflects what we are beginning to understand about who should and could help to avoid disconnections and make connections, thus bridging the gap or divide that is perceived to exist. One such metaphor that could help us do this is the metaphor of a rainbow bridge.

The rainbow bridge is understood and embraced in several European, North American and Asian cultures. For example, in Norse mythology the rainbow bridge (*Bifrost*) is a bridge that connects heaven (*Asgard*) and earth (*Midgard*). The Rainbow Bridge is also known as *Antahkarana*, a Sanskrit term, which translated literally 'means that which acts or works between'. It is like a spiritual filament of light that bridges the physical and the spiritual.

Just as the rainbow bridge is understood by the many cultures of the world, the many stakeholders of the accessible e-learning community may also understand it.

A strong attraction of the rainbow bridge as a metaphor is the similarities that can be drawn between Asgard and accessibility and Midgard and inaccessibility. The goal for accessible e-learning practice is to cross the bridge from Midgard to Asgard: from inaccessibility to accessibility.

The colours of the rainbow

The multitude of different colours in a rainbow is often equated to different cultures, races or religions and so the rainbow can be used to symbolize the co-operation or collaboration of different people and cultures: a diverse group of people united in working together for a common purpose. For Clement and Shade (2000) the rainbow metaphor is a useful tool for conceptualising universal access to information because it simultaneously suggests unity and diversity. Although the coloured layers can be distinguished from each other, there are no definitive boundaries between them. They are intrinsically related to one another and integral to the whole. No single strand is sufficient; all are necessary. In terms of accessible e-learning, this is appealing when thinking about the stakeholders and their role in promoting accessible e-learning (see Figure 14.1).

It is universally accepted that there are six colours of the rainbow: red, orange, yellow, green, blue and purple (whilst is it popular to break purple into two separate colours, indigo and violet, there is little scientific evidence

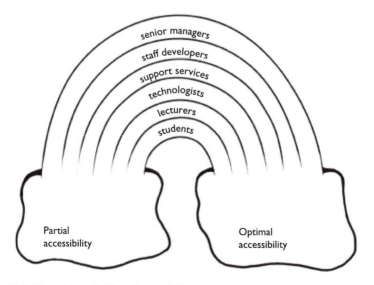

Figure 14.1 The rainbow bridge of accessibility.

for their existence). The six colours of the rainbow can be equated to the six stakeholders identified in this book: students, lecturers, learning technologists, support staff, staff developers and senior managers.

The metaphor of a rainbow bridge is therefore useful in that it helps us to conceptualize who needs to be involved in achieving the goals of accessible e-learning practice and to argue that the development of successful accessible e-learning practices will require these diverse stakeholders to unite towards a common goal. No one stakeholder can produce accessible e-learning on their own; it requires all six to work together as a unit, team or community.

The pot of gold at the end of the rainbow

Mythology and folklore frequently refer to a pot of gold that is buried at the end of the rainbow. However, as we all know, it is impossible to get to the end of a rainbow, because it always moves as you approach it. Thus, it is impossible to find the pot of gold. If we liken accessibility to that pot of gold, it too is impossible to achieve in the sense that both perfect design solutions and fully accessible e-learning resources probably do not exist. Hull (2004) argues that it is trying to make a website accessible to everyone that is next to impossible. While Kelly *et al.* (2005: 52) argue that there is 'no one-size fits all' solution. Using the rainbow bridge as metaphor may therefore encourage us to think about the 'pot of gold' and the achievability and appropriateness of the goals for which we are striving. For example, we may wish to question our quest for 100 per cent, full or complete accessibility. Sloan and Stratford (2004) suggest that:

> the term 'fully accessible' is very ambitious and easily disproved in many cases. 'Optimally accessible' is a far more appropriate goal for which to aim . . . accessibility to disabled people should extend beyond the minimum condition of being able to access information, it should be looking towards making the experience of accessing and using information worthwhile and beneficial.

The rainbow bridge metaphor can therefore be used, to build on the arguments made in chapter 4 about there being no one right way to meet the diverse e-learning needs of disabled students, and to encourage practitioners to accept that successfully crossing the rainbow bridge does not mean:

- crossing from multiple design solutions to one design solution; it probably means crossing from fixed design solutions to adaptable design solutions;
- crossing from inaccessible to accessible, it probably means crossing from partial accessibility to optimal accessibility.

Different views of the rainbow

A rainbow is a set of physical drops of water that reflect the light in a certain way. However, no two people see exactly the same rainbow, because they each occupy different positions in space, select different rays of light and thus different drops of water to look at. In this sense, a rainbow is a terribly personal phenomenon. Just as different people will see different rainbows depending on their standpoint, different people will view accessibility in different ways depending on their viewpoint. Stakeholders will hold different viewpoints regarding the rationale for making e-learning accessible. For example:

> Often people become interested in Web accessibility for a specific reason, unaware that there are other reasons for accessible design. Some people come to the topic because of regulatory requirements for accessibility, others because they consider it the 'right' thing to do. Few are initially aware of business reasons for accessibility. Even for audiences who are strongly motivated by one rationale, it can be helpful to introduce information supporting other rationales to increase the likelihood that they can secure accessibility commitments from colleagues in their organizations who have different perspectives.
>
> (Brewer *et al.* 1998)

Stakeholders may also hold different viewpoints about the solutions to making e-learning accessible. For example:

> the same issue will attract different solutions, depending on the viewpoint of the actor. In a Web development community, a single issue such as whether all tables should be linearised, will be understood differently, depending on whether the actor is a policy maker, a developer, a commissioning agent or a community member with vision-impairment.
>
> (Nevile and Burmeister 2003)

The chapters in Part 2 explored in depth the different viewpoints and perspectives of the key stakeholders in accessible e-learning. In some cases these different viewpoints may bring conflict that requires resolving (Nevile and Burmeister 2003). The contribution of the rainbow bridge metaphor however, is that it encourages us to accept the value that different viewpoints bring. While different people may see different 'rainbows', they usually all believe they are seeing a thing of beauty and wonderment. Different stakeholders might have different viewpoints about rationales and solutions, but for the most part, they believe that accessibility is a goal worth striving for. As long as there is agreement that a bridge needs to be built, it does not matter too much that there is disagreement about how the bridge should be built and what it should look like. If there is agreement about the goal (to build a bridge) then people will work together to resolve conflict and out of this conflict resolution new practices and knowledge (how to build a bridge) will emerge.

Crossing the rainbow bridge

For many, the journey over the rainbow bridge is a journey into higher awareness and understanding. The rainbow bridge is a useful metaphor for accessible e-learning in that it encourages us to think about what higher awareness or understanding needs to be obtained in order for accessible e-learning practice to be developed. For example:

- an understanding that there is a complex relationship between e-learning, students and disability: what is a barrier to e-learning for one disabled student, will not be a barrier to another, what is a facilitator of e-learning for a disabled student might also be a facilitator for a non-disabled student;
- an awareness that universal design can apply to the design of instruction as well as to design of accessible e-learning and that accessible e-learning might be one valuable outcome from universal instructional design (see chapter 6);
- an understanding that there is less difference between the different approaches to designing for accessibility than one might first imagine (see chapter 7);
- an awareness that the way services which support disabled students in their use of e-learning are organized and staffed will highlight tensions between the mainstream and the specialist and be seen to reflect attitudes to and models of disability (see chapter 8);
- an understanding that the extent to which meaningful learning that changes practice is the outcome of staff development programmes and activities will depend on the methods, strategies and partnerships that are adopted (see chapter 9);
- an awareness that the development of institutional accessibility policies that have the potential to impact on practice requires leadership and strategic involvement of key stakeholders (see chapter 10).

Models as conceptual tools for exploring the future of accessible e-learning

Three models that have been proposed to explain accessibility and e-learning are the Web Accessibility Integration Model (Lazar *et al.* 2004), the Composite Practice Model (Leung *et al.* 1999) and the Holistic Model (Kelly *et al.* 2005). The scope of the Web Accessibility Integration Model is very limited in that it only focuses on one aspect of e-learning; the various influences on the development of an accessible website. In doing so, the focus is narrowed to just the website developer and their client. It does, however, place their interaction within a societal context of policies, laws and guidelines.

Leung *et al.* (1999) developed a composite practice model to describe and explain current practice in regard to assistive technology service delivery in post-secondary educational settings across Australia. Whilst the focus of this model is as narrow as that of Lazar *et al.* what it does do effectively is highlight the contribution of a range of stakeholders including: administrators, student services, lecturers, librarians, IT services and assistive technology specialists. Kelly *et al.* (2005) propose a holistic model for e-learning accessibility, which laudably places the learner at the centre of the development process. This model focuses predominantly on the context in which accessible e-learning is developed, arguing that local cultural, political and social factors need to be taken into account. In doing so, however, it ignores the perspectives of stakeholders other than the student and perhaps the lecturer.

A proposal for a contextualized model of accessible e-learning practice in higher education institutions

Whilst these three models focus on different stakeholders (developer, AT specialist, student) what they all have in common is that they include the context in which the stakeholders are operating. A new model of accessible e-learning practice is proposed therefore, that takes into account:

- the stakeholders;
- the context: drivers and mediators;
- how the relationship between the stakeholders and the context influences the responses they make and the accessible e-learning practices that develop (see Figure 14.2).

The extent to which e-learning material and resources is accessible will be influenced by how all the stakeholders within a higher education institution respond to external drivers for accessibility such as legislation, guidelines and standards. This response will be mediated by stakeholders' views and understandings of: disability, accessibility and inclusion; duty and responsibility; autonomy and freedom; teamwork and community. The accessible e-learning practices that develop out of these responses will vary depending on the stakeholders and the context in which they are operating but essentially centres on taking ownership and control as well as developing personal meaning from externally imposed impersonal mandates.

Legislation will not on its own change accessible e-learning practice within a higher education institution because the stakeholders have to translate

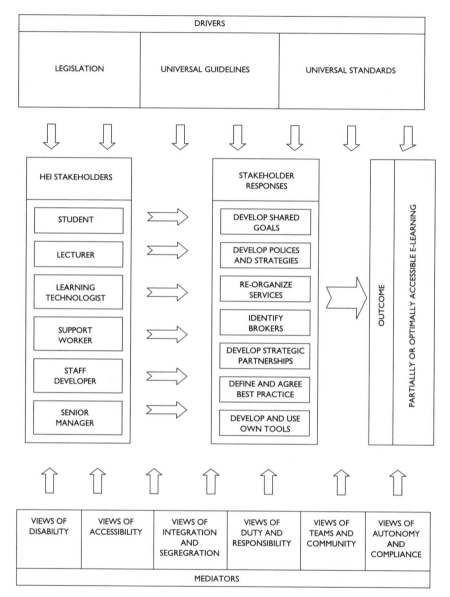

Figure 14.2   A contextualized model of accessible e-learning practice in higher education.

legislation into polices and strategies that are meaningful to them in the context in which they are working. Universal accessibility guidelines on their own will not change accessible e-learning practice within a higher education institution because the stakeholders have to adapt and develop the guidelines into guidelines (and tools) that are meaningful to them in the context in which they are working. Universal accessibility standards on their own will not change accessible e-learning practice within a higher education institution because the stakeholders have to define and agree what the benchmarks of best practice might be in the context in which they are working.

What a model such as this stresses is that there is a 'gap' between the drivers for accessible e-learning and their desired outcome (accessible e-learning material). The gap between drivers and outcome needs to be 'bridged' by accessible e-learning practices and the stakeholders within a higher education institution help to bridge that gap.

An accessibility reference model

The proposed contextualized model of accessible e-learning practice is not a process or task based model in that in does not detail the development of accessible e-learning from the initial conception to delivery. In the general field of e-learning there is a growing acknowledgement that the development of e-learning involves the linkage of numerous roles, processes and resources and is necessarily complex and difficult to conceptualize. Work is starting however, through the E-Learning Framework (a joint initiative of the UK's Joint Information Services Committee and Australia's Department of Education, Science and Training), on the development of reference models that attempt to conceptualize the complexity of e-learning. Reference models attempt to map or represent the domain of e-learning through the software, projects, standards and use cases of which it is composed. A reference model is therefore an abstract task model of what has to be accomplished to meet the user's needs, described in a way that is independent of how it is accomplished. For example, the team developing the assessment reference model envisage that their model will include: a domain definition that will describe the scope of the assessment domain, including evidence that gives an overview of current practices, processes and systems; a set of use cases that describe common solution patterns in the assessment domain area; and service profile definitions for both existing services and those that need to be developed for the assessment domain area, their scope, behaviour and data (see http://www.frema.ecs.soton.ac.uk/).

In mapping different domains within e-learning, such as assessment and learning activity authoring, it is hoped that reference models will facilitate a common understanding of the components of the domain and their interfaces as well as provide a map for service development (what organisational and technical architecture is required to make things happen). It is possible to imagine that it could be very useful to have a reference model that helps accessibility stakeholders plan service development by:

- describing the scope of the accessibility domain and giving an overview of current practices, processes and systems;

- offering a set of use cases that describe common solution patterns in the accessibility domain area;
- offering service profile definitions for both existing services and those that need to be developed for the accessibility domain area, their scope, behaviour and data.

However, at the moment accessibility does not exist as a separate domain within the E-Learning Framework (see http://www.elframework.org/) and until all the reference models are published it is difficult to tell the extent to which accessibility will be integrated into their descriptions, definitions, cases and profiles. However, in the early days of reference model development it would not necessarily hurt to distill out a separate accessibility reference model and then figure out later how it relates to other models in the e-learning framework.

Theories and frameworks as conceptual tools for exploring the future of accessible e-learning

The chapters in Part 3 explored how useful three theories or frameworks were in helping to develop an understanding of accessible e-learning: the Institutional Change Framework, Activity Theory and the Communities of Practice Theory. Each theory offers a unique contribution to our potential understanding of accessible e-learning practice:

- The institutional change framework prompts us to think about the influence of rules on practice and the potential conflicts that rules can cause when people or teams who have different responses to and relationships with the rules.
- Activity Theory prompts us to think about 'division of labour' and how different roles and responsibilities for accessible e-learning are decided.
- Communities of Practice prompts us to think about whether accessible e-learning practice is located in several different communities that need to be brought together in order for a fuller and more successful practice to develop.

There are a lot of similarities between the three theories. For example, all three theories are theories of practice. Each one views practice in some way as a purposive activity that has objectives and goals. All three also explore how practice at some level is mediated and influenced by rules. For the Institutional Change Framework institutional practice is mediated by formal and informal rules. For Activity Theory individual practice is mediated by rules. For Communities of Practice theory, the meaning that communities find in rules may influence community practice. All three theories, in different ways also get us to focus on connections. Konur's application of the

Institutional Change Framework prompts us to consider the connection between individuals and teams and the extent to which individuals co-operate and compete to help their team meet the goal of accessible e-learning. Activity Theory encourages us to explore the connections between individuals and communities, how those connections can be influenced and the impact this has on achieving the objective of accessible e-learning. Communities of Practice theory gives us the notion of different communities forming connections between each other and how brokers have a role in encouraging and facilitating those connections to be built and maintained.

A tentative framework for exploring and understanding future accessible e-learning practice

This analysis of the contribution of the three theories to understanding accessible e-learning practice enables a tentative framework for exploring and understanding accessible e-learning practice to be proposed. It may therefore be beneficial if any future exploration of the future development of accessible e-learning took into consideration:

- *Purposive activity* the extent to which accessible e-learning practice is a purposive activity with a clear objective, an objective that is focused on meeting the needs of disabled students;
- *Shared enterprise* the extent to which the different stakeholder communities are connected by a shared enterprise and work together towards achieving the same objective;
- *Personal and collective meaning* the extent to which the different stakeholders (individual and communities) work towards developing their own meaning through interpretation and adaptation of external or universal rules, tools and approaches or procedures;
- *Roles and responsibilities* the extent to which communities decide a clear 'division of labour' and allocate different roles and responsibilities and the impact of this on the success of accessible e-learning practice;
- *Brokering of connections* the extent to which individual stakeholders can broker connections between different stakeholder communities and the impact of these connections on the success of accessible e-learning practice.

Conceptualizing best practice in accessible e-learning

Seale (2004) has argued that the accessibility research and practice literature has been overly focused on the product of accessibility practices (e-learning materials and resources) rather than the process by which they are produced. This book has attempted to address the balance by focusing, through the eyes of key stakeholders, on the practice rather than the product. In doing so, one of the key conclusions that have been drawn is that it would be useful for practitioners to have access to detailed accounts (sets of routines, ways of doing things, stories or cases) of how other practitioners have:

- interpreted the accessibility legislation, guidelines and standards and the different judgements they have made regarding the implementation or adaptation of these;
- developed procedures ('rules of practice') for using or adapting accessibility tools;
- developed strategic and working relationships with other practitioners (stakeholders).

Whilst some descriptions of accessibility practice do exist, they do not exist in abundance. Without rich and detailed descriptions of practice we cannot produce a definitive conceptualisation of what constitutes best practice. For example, Nevile and Burmeister (2003) argue that 'richly scripted scenarios' can be used instructively to help stakeholders problem solve and develop their practice. The exploration of practice within this book suggests some possible indicators of best practice, indicators such as flexibility, adaptability, user involvement or planning from the start. More work needs to be done, however, in order to produce a widely agreed and evidence-based set of indicators.

From indicators to service development tools

Once we have a set of indicators of best practice it should be possible to use these to help to develop and improve accessible e-learning practice. But not practice at an individual level, rather practice at a service level. There has been a great disconnection in the current accessibility field in that legislation is aimed at changing practice at an institutional level, whilst guidelines and standards appear to be aimed at changing practice at an individual level. There is nothing aimed at the 'gap', there is nothing aimed at changing practice at the service level. Whilst individual practitioners are employed by an institution, their work is organized, structured and influenced at a service (department, unit, school, faculty) level. If we want to improve accessible e-learning practice we need to bridge the gap between the individual practitioner and the drivers for change and pay attention to what needs to happen at a service level for practice to develop into 'best practice'.

An index of accessibility

Seale (2004) argued that indicators of best practice could be used to develop an 'index of accessibility', comparable to the 'Index for Inclusion' produced by the inclusive education community (Booth and Ainscow 2000). The Index for Inclusion is a resource or tool that invites schools to identify barriers to learning and participation and invites them to reduce those barriers by addressing cultures, policies and practices (Vaughn 2002). The review and analysis of accessibility practices in higher education contained within this book suggests that there may be value in identifying barriers to the design and implementation of accessible electronic materials (e.g. lack of user involvement, resistance to a perceived loss of creative freedom) and exploring how changes or adaptations to cultures, policies or practices might reduce these barriers. In addition, indicators of the accessibility of higher education services and systems might help to structure future discussion and debate concerning accessibility in higher education.

A service auditing tool

In addition to producing indices of accessibility, indicators of best practice may also be used to develop more formal service auditing tools, tools that are more encompassing and less specialised than those that exist at the moment. An investigation of the research literature reveals that two very specialist auditing tools currently exist; one of which audits the accessibility of campus computers, the other audits the quality of assistive technology services. Fossey *et al.* (2004) describe the development of the Accessibility of Campus Computers: Disability Services Scale (ACCDSS). The 19 six-point Likert scaled items which comprise the scale inquire about the situation at the respondents' institution, campus or sector and evaluate the adequacy of campus-based computer technologies, resources, training, policies, personnel and services as well as the adequacy of rehabilitation sector support to meet the needs of students with disabilities. A key criterion item used for validation inquired about how well, overall, the computer and/or adaptive computer technology needs of students with disabilities are met at the respondent's institution. The scale is scored for four subscales: Access To Adaptive Computers, Infrastructure and Collaboration, Academic Inclusion, and Adaptive Technology Competence. Fossey *et al.* (2004) argue that the ACCDSS fills an important void in addressing the evaluation of computer accessibility.

McNairn and Zabala (2005) describe the Quality Indicators for Assistive Technology Services (QIAT) tool. QIAT is a set of descriptors of critical elements related to major functions involved in the provision of assistive technology services. Currently, quality indicators have been developed for six functions including Administration, Consideration, Assessment of Assistive Technology Need, Documentation in the Individualized Education Program (IEP) Intervention and Evaluation of Effectiveness. Recently, two additional critical elements on Transition and Professional Development have been added to the QIAT matrix. The primary purpose of QIAT is to support thoughtful development, provision and evaluation of assistive technology services for students with disabilities, regardless of where the services are provided or the specific model used to support service provision. QIAT also supports the idea that the services should address not only the needs of students, but also the needs of people who work with students who require assistive technology devices and services. The QIAT is primarliy school based and focuses predominantly on assessment of AT needs (QIAT 2003). Nevertheless, some of the quality indicators may apply to colleges and universities. For example:

- assistive technology devices and services are considered for all students with disabilities regardless of type or severity of disability;
- the IEP team has the knowledge and skills to make informed assistive technology decisions;
- the IEP team uses a collaborative decision-making process based on data about the student environment and tasks to determine assistive technology needs;
- decisions regarding the need for assistive technology devices and services are made based on access to the curriculum and the student's IEP goals and objectives.

Whilst the ACCDSS and QIAT may be too specialist to apply to the delivery of accessible e-learning services as a whole, some of the principles that underpin these tools may be useful when looking at how to transform indicators of best practice into an auditing tool, principles that certainly reflect some of the key messages contained within this book:

- auditing a service involves looking at resources, personnel, training and polices;
- auditing a service involves evaluating the extent to which disabled students' needs are met;
- a quality service will be student-centred, collaborative and knowledgeable in all its activities.

In thinking about how useful it is to audit or evaluate accessible e-learning service delivery, it is possible to see that services would be resistant to having to undergo yet another quality assurance exercise on top of all the others that they are required to undertake by their institutions and by external funding agencies. Therefore any audit tool that is developed will probably need to be developed by and for service providers, probably with a view to using it as an informal self-development tool. Bridging the gap between what should happen and what is happening may therefore require practitioners to take some control and ownership over the process of developing 'best practice'.

Conclusions

To date, a huge amount of literature has focused almost exclusively on accessibility legislation, guidelines and standards and the rules contained within them. One of the major problems of such an approach is that it has drawn practitioners into thinking that their objective is to comply with rules. It is not. Their objective should be to address the needs of students. The danger of only focusing on rules is that it can constrain thinking and therefore practice. The purpose of this book has been to expand thinking beyond that of how to comply with rules, towards how to meet the needs of students with disabilities, within the local contexts in which practitioners are working. In thinking about how to meet the needs of students with disabilities, practitioners will need to develop their own tools. These tools might be adaptations of accessibility guidelines, user case studies, evaluation methodologies or metaphors, models and theories.

Another key message of this book is that accessible e-learning practice will not develop through the actions of individual practitioners or stakeholders alone. Accessible e-learning practice will develop and progress when all the different stakeholders join to work together. It is hoped that this book will facilitate interaction and discussion between the different stakeholders of accessible e-learning and that through a 'meeting of dialogue' (Schenker and Scadden 2002) bridges can be built:

- between legislation, guidelines and standards and their potential users;
- between individual practitioners and the institutions in which they work;
- between the different stakeholder practices;
- between theory, practice and research.

References

Abascal, J., Arrue, M., Fajardo, I., Garay, N. and Tomas, J. (2004) The use of guidelines to automatically verify web accessibility. *Universal Access in the Information Society*, 3, 71–79.

Abecasis, H. and Fernandes, J. (2002) The national initiative for people with special needs in the Information Society – the elderly, people with disabilities and long-term bed-ridden. Paper presented at WUAUC '01, Alcacer do Sol, Portugal, 22–25 May 2002.

Academic Staff Development in Support of Disabled Students Project (2002) Project Summary. Online. Available HTTP: <http://www.nottingham.ac.uk/ssc/staff/randd_asdsds/summary.html> (accessed 5 October 2005).

Accessibility in Learning Environments and Related Technologies (ALERT) (2005) Guidelines on using VLEs with disabled students. Online. Available HTTP: <http://www.dur.ac.uk/alert/guidelines/pdf/alert_allVLEguidelines.pdf> (accessed 5 October 2005).

Adams, M. and Brown, P. (2000) 'The times they are a changing': developing disability provision in UK higher education. Paper presented at Pathways 5 Conference, Canberra, Australia, 6–8 December 2000.

Akoumianakis, D. and Stephanidis, C. (1999) Propogating experience-based accessibility guidelines to user interface development. *Ergonomics*, 42, 10, 1283–1310.

Alexander, D. (2002) WebCT Accessibility Audit. Paper presented at AusWeb02. Online. Available HTTP: <http://ausweb.scu.edu.au/aw02/papers/refereed/alexander/index.html> (accessed 5 October 2005).

Alexander, D. (2003a) How accessible are Australian University websites? Paper presented at AusWeb03. Online. Available HTTP: <http://ausweb.scu.edu.au/aw03/papers/alexander3/paper.html> (accessed 5 October 2005).

Alexander, D. (2003b) Redesign of the Monash University web Site: a case study in user-centred design methods. Paper presented at AusWeb03. Online. Available HTTP: <http://ausweb.scu.edu.au/aw03/papers/alexander/paper.html> (accessed 5 October 2005).

Alexandraki, C., Paramythis, A., Maou, N. and Stephanidis, C. (2004) web accessibility through adaptation. In K. Klaus, K. Miesenberger, W. Zagler and D. Burger (eds) *Computers Helping People with Special Needs*. Proceedings of 9th International Conference. Berlin Heidelberg: Springer-Verlag, pp. 302–309.

Amtman, D., Harris, M. and Witzel, J. (2005) Introduction to accessible information technology in education: a webcourse. Paper presented at CSUN '05, Los Angeles,

17–19 March 2005. Online. Available HTTP: <www.csun.edu/cod/conf/2005/proceedings/2390.htm> (accessed 5 October 2005).

Anderson, A. (2004) Supporting web accessibility policies: creating a campus e-culture of inclusion at UW-Madison. Paper presented at CSUN '04. Online. Available HTTP: <http://www.csun.edu/cod/conf/2004/proceedings/20.htm> (accessed 5 October 2005).

Arch, A. (2002) Dispelling the myths – web accessibility is for all. Paper presented at AusWeb '02. Online. Available HTTP: <http://ausweb.scu.edu.au/aw02/papers/refereed/arch/paper.html> (accessed 5 October 2005).

Arch, A. M. J. and Burmeister, O. K. (2003) Australian experiences with accessibility policies post Sydney Olympic Games. *Information Technologies and Disabilities Journal*, 9, 2. Online. Available HTTP: <http://www.rit.edu/~easi/itd/itdv09n2/arch.htm> (accessed 5 October 2005).

Arch, A., Celic, S., Faulkner, S. and Hardy, B. (2003) Getting started with accessibility assessments. Paper presented at AusWeb03. Online. Available HTTP: <http://ausweb.scu.edu.au./aw03/papers/arch2/paper.html> (accessed 5 October).

Arditi, A. (2004) Adjustable typography: an approach to enhancing low vision text accessibility. *Ergonomics*, 47, 5, 469–482.

Asuncion, J. V., Fichten, C., Fossey, M. E. and Barile, M. (2002) Dialoguing with developers and suppliers of adaptive computer technologies: data and recommendations. *Universal Access in the Information Society*, 1, 177–196.

Australian Government Attorney-General Department (1992) Disability Discrimination Act 1992. Online. Available HTTP: <http://scaleplus.law.gov.au/html/pasteact/0/311/top.htm> (accessed 5 October 2005).

Australian Vice Chancellor's Committee (2004) Guidelines on information access for students with print disabilities. Online. Available HTTP: <http://www.avcc.edu.au/documents/publications/GuidelinesOnInfoAccessForStudentsWithDisablilities.pdf> (accessed 5 October 2005)

Axtell, R. and Dixon, J. M. (2002) Voyager 2000: a review of accessibility for persons with visual disabilities. *Library Hi Tech*, 20, 2, 141–147.

Bain, K., Basson S. H., Wald, M. (2002) Speech recognition in university classrooms: Liberated Learning Project. Paper presented at ASSETS 2002, the Fifth International ACM SIGCAPH Conference on Assistive Technologies, Edinburgh, Scotland.

Ball, S. (2002) The view from Europe: a TechDis perspective on how European initiatives will impact on education, technology and disabilities. In L. Phipps, A. Sutherland and J. Seale (eds) *Access All Areas: Disability, Technology and Learning*. Oxford :ALT/TechDis, pp. 10–13.

Ball, S. and Rousell, J. (2004) Virtual disability: simulations as an aid to lecturers' understanding of disability. In K. Klaus, K. Miesenberger, W. Zagler and D. Burger (eds) *Computers Helping People with Special Needs*. Proceedings of 9th International Conference, pp. 589–596, Berlin, Heidelberg: Springer-Verlag.

Banes, D. and Seale, J. (2002) Accessibility and Inclusivity in further and higher education: an overview. In L. Phipps, A. Sutherland and J. Seale (eds) *Access All Areas: Disability, Technology and Learning*. Oxford: ALT/TechDis, pp. 1–5.

Banks, R., Lazzaro, J. L. and Noble, S. (2003) Accessible e-learning: policy and practice. Paper presented at CSUN '03. Online. Available HTTP: <http://www.csun.edu/cod/conf/2003/proceedings/139.htm> (accessed 5 October 2005).

Banks, R., Coombs, E. and Coombs, N. (2005) Accessible powerpoint on the web: tools that can help. Paper presented at CSUN '05, Los Angeles, 17–19 March 2005. Online. Available HTTP: <http://www.csun.edu/cod/conf/2005/proceedings/2402. htm> (accessed 05.10.05)

Barab, S., Schatz, S. and Scheckler, R. (2004). Using activity theory to conceptualize online community and using online community to conceptualize activity theory. *Mind, Culture, and Activity*, 11, 1, 25–47.

Barstow, C. (2003) Making online learning accessible: update on activities of the IMS accessibility working group. Paper presented at CSUN '03. Online. Available HTTP: <http://www.csun.edu/cod/conf/2003/proceedings/138.htm> (accessed 5 October 2005).

Becker, S. A. (2004) E-government visual accessibility for older adult users. *Social Sciences Computer Review*, 22, 1, 11–23.

Bennett, U. (2002) Disabled by design. *Disability and Society*, 17, 7, 809–823.

Bilotta, J. A. (2005) Over-done: when web accessibility techniques replace true inclusive user centred design. Paper presented at CSUN '05, Los Angeles, 17–19 March 2005. Online. Available HTTP: <http://www.csun.edu/cod/conf/2005/proceedings/ 2283.htm> (accessed 5 October 2005).

Blankfield, S. and Martin, L. (2002) Are we getting it right? A widening participation project. Online. Available HTTP: <http://www.lancashirecompact.ac.uk/ reportspapers/gettingitright.pdf> (accessed 5 October 2005).

Blankfield, S., Davey, J. and Sackville, A. (2002) Supporting students with dyslexia in the effective use of C&IT in their academic studies. Online. Available HTTP: <http://www.edgehill.ac.uk/TLD/research/sedafinalreport.pdf> (accessed 5 October 2005).

Bleach, K. and Zavoli, V. (2005) Powerpoint presentations design by and accessible to people who are blind. Paper presented at CSUN '05. Online. Available HTTP: <http:// www.csun.edu/cod/conf/2005/proceedings/2189.htm> (accessed 5 October 2005).

Boess, S. and Lebbon, C. S. (1998) Integrating participant research with product design education. Paper presented at IDATER '98, Loughborough. Online. Available HTTP: <http://www.lboro.ac.uk/departments/cd/docs_dandt/idater/ downloads98/boess98.pdf> (accessed 5 October 2005).

Bohman, P. (2003a) Introduction to web accessibility. Online. Available HTTP: <http://www.webaim.org/intro/> (accessed 5 October 2005).

Bohman, P. (2003b) Visual vs cognitive disabilities. Online. Available HTTP: <http://www.webaim.org/techniques/articles/vis_vs_cog?templatetype=3> (accessed 5 October 2005).

Bohman, P. (2003c) Fast track to web accessibility using a template-based design strategy. Paper presented at CSUN '03. Online. Available HTTP: <http:// www.csun.edu/cod/conf/2003/proceedings/233.htm> (accessed 5 October 2005).

Bohman, P. R. (2003d) University web accessibility policies: a bridge not quite far enough. Online. Available HTTP: <http://www.webaim.org/coordination/articles/ policies-pilot> (accessed 5 October 2005).

Bohman, P. and Anderson, S. (2005) A conceptual framework for accessibility tools to benefit users with cognitive disabilities. Paper presented at WWW2005, 10 May 2005, Chiba, Japan. Online. Available HTTP: <http://www.webaim.org/ techniques/articles/framework/> (accessed 5 October 2005.

Booth, T. and Ainscow, M. (2000) Breaking down the barriers: the Index for Inclusion. Online. Available HTTP: <http://inclusion.uwe.ac.uk/csie/index-inclusion-summary.htm> (accessed 5 October 2005).

Borchert, M. and Conkas, M. (2003) A web accessibility testing case study: QUT library. Paper presented at AusWeb '03, Gold Coast, 5–9 July 2003. Online. Available HTTP: <http://ausweb.scu.edu.au/aw03/papers/borchert2/paper.html> (accessed 5 October 2005).

Borland, J. and James, S. (1999) The learning experience of students with disabilities in Higher Education. A case study of a UK University. *Disability and Society*, 14, 1, 85–101.

Bostock, S. (2002) Designing websites that are accessible to all. *Educational Developments*, 3, 3, 18–19.

Brajnik, G. (2000) Automatic web usability evaluation: what needs to be done? Paper presented at the 6th conference on Human Factors and the Web. Online. Available HTTP: <http://www.dimi.uniud.it/giorgio/papers/hfweb00.html> (accessed 5 October 2005).

Brajnik, G. (2001) Towards valid quality models for websites. Paper presented at 7th Conference on Human Factors and the Web. Online. Available HTTP: <http://www.dimi.uniud.it/giorgio/papers/hfweb01.html> (accessed 5 October 2005).

Brajnik, G. (2004) Comparing accessibility evaluation tools: a method for tool effectiveness. *Universal Access to the Information Society*, 3, 252–263.

Brewer, J. (2002) Developing organizational policies on web accessibility. Online. Available HTTP: <http://www.w3.org/WAI/impl/pol.html> (accessed 5 October 2005).

Brewer, J. (2004) Review Teams for Evaluating web Site Accessibility. Online. Available HTTP: <http://www.w3.org/WAI/eval/reviewteams.html> (accessed 5 October 2005).

Brewer, J. and Horton, S. (2002) Implementation plan for web accessibility. Online. Available HTTP: <http://www.w3.org/WAI/impl/> (accessed 5 October 2005).

Brewer, J., Dardailler, D. and Vanderheiden, G. (1998) Toolkit for promoting accessibility. Paper presented at CSUN '98. Online. Available HTTP: <http://www.dinf.ne.jp/doc/english/Us_Eu/conf/csun_98/csun98_057.htm> (accessed 5 October 2005).

Bryant, E. (2005) The user experience: a case study of website accessibility and usability. Paper presented at CSUN '05, Los Angeles, 17–19 March 2005. Online. Available HTTP: <http://www.csun.edu/cod/conf/2005/proceedings/2331.htm> (accessed 5 October 2005).

Buck, D. V. (2004) Developing a web accessibility policy – improve access and ensure implementattion. Paper presented at CSUN '04. Online. Available HTTP: <http://www.csun.edu/cod/conf/2004/proceedings/87.htm> (accessed 5 October 2005).

Burgstahler, S. (2002a) Distance learning: the library's role in ensuring access to everyone. *Library Hi Tech*, 20, 4, 420–432.

Burgstahler, S. (2002b) Distance learning: universal Design, universal Access. *Educational Technology Review*, 10, 1. Online. Available HTTP: <http://www.aace.org/pubs/etr/issue2/burgstahler.cfm> (accessed 5 October 2005).

Burgstahler, S. and Cook, D. (2005) Promoting accessible technology within post-secondary computing organizations: dos and don'ts. Paper presented at CSUN '05, Los Angeles, 17–19 March 2005. Online. Available HTTP: <http://www.csun.edu/cod/conf/2005/proceedings/2394.htm> (accessed 5 October 2005).

Burgstahler, S., Corrigan, B. and McCarter, J. (2004) Making distance learning courses accessible to students and instructors with disabilities: a case study. *Internet and Higher Education*, 7, 233–246.

Burzagli, L., Emiliani, P. L. and Graziani, P. (2004) Accessibility in the field of education. In C. Stary and C. Stephanidis (eds) *Proceedings of UI4All 2004*, Lecture Notes in Computer Science, Volume 3196. Berlin Heidelberg: Springer-Verlag, pp. 235–241.

Byerley, S. L. and Chambers, M. B. (2002) Accessibility and usability of web-based library databases for non-visual user. *Library Hi Tech*, 20, 2, 169–178.

Byrne, J. (2004) An example: UK university accessible web design plan. Online. Available HTTP: <http://www.mcu.org.uk/show.php?contentid=85> (accessed 5 October 2005).

Caldwell, B., Chisholm, W., Vanderheiden, G. and White, J. (2004) web Content Accessibility Guidelines 2.0: W3C Working Draft, 19 November 2004. Online. Available HTTP: <http://www.w3.org/TR/WCAG20/> (accessed 5 October 2005).

Carey, K. (2005) All Passion Spent? *Ability*, 56, Winter, 25.

Chancellor's Office of California Community Colleges (1999) Distance education: access guidelines for students with disabilities. Online. Available HTTP: <http://www.htctu.net/publications/guidelines/distance_ed/distedguidelines.pdf> (accessed 5 October 2005).

Chief Ministers Department (2004) ACT Government Website policy. Online. Available HTTP: <http://www.publishing.act.gov.au/pdfs/P09_0504_Website_Policy.pdf > (accessed 5 October 2005).

Chisholm, W. and Brewer, J. (2005) web Content Accessibility Guidelines 2.0: Transitioning your website. Paper presented at CSUN '05, Los Angeles, 17–19 March 2005. Online. Available HTTP: <http://www.csun.edu/cod/conf/2005/proceedings/2355.htm> (accessed 5 October 2005).

Chisholm, W. and Kasday L. (2003) Evaluation, repair, and transformation tools for web content accessibility. Online. Available HTTP: <http://www.w3.org/WAI/ER/existingtools.html> (accessed 5 October 2005).

Chisholm, W., Vanderheiden, G. and Jacobs, I. (1999) web Content Accessibility Guidelines 1.0: W3C Recommendation, 5 May 1999. Online. Available HTTP: <http://www.org/TR/WAI-WEBCONTENT/> (accessed 5 October 2005).

Clement, A. and Shade, L. R. (2000) The access rainbow: conceptualizing universal access to the information/communication infrastructure. In M. Gurstein (ed.) *Community Informatics: Enabling Communities with Information and Communication Technologies*. Hershey, PA: Idea Group Publishing, pp. 32–51.

Clement-Lorford, F. (2005) Slightly long winded but please bear with it as I need the advice. Dyslexia JISCMAIL Archives. Online. Available HTTP: <http://www.jiscmail.ac.uk/cgi-bin/webadmin?A2=ind0506&L=dyslexia&T=0&F=&S=&X=&P=8718> (accessed 5 October 2005).

Cobham, E., Coupe, C., Broadbent, E. and Broadbent, S. (2001) *Evaluation of the Process of Identifying the Provision of Assistive Technology, Study Strategies and Support for Students with Disabilities in Higher Education and the Value of this Intervention on their Education and their Lives*. Ashley-Under-Lyne: Broadbent and Co.

Colwell, C., Scanlon, E. and Cooper, M. (2002) Using remote laboratories to extend access to science and engineering. *Computers and Education*, 38, 65–76.

Cook, A. and Hussey, S. (1995) *Assistive Technologies: Principles and Practice*. St Louis, MO: Mosby.

Cook, R. A. and Gladhart, M. A. (2002) A survey of online instructional issues and strategies for postsecondary students with learning disabilities. *Information Technology and Disabilities*, 8, 1. Online. Available HTTP: <http://www.rit.edu/~easi/itd/itdv08n1/gladhart.htm> (accessed 5 October 2005).

Coombs, N. (2000) Assistive technology in third level and distance education. Online. Available HTTP: <http://www.rit.edu/~nrcgsh/arts/dublin.htm> (accessed 5 October 2005).

Coombs, N. (2002) Accessible E-Learning: Infrastructure and Content. In K. Miesenberger, J. Klaus and W. Zagler (eds) *Proceedings of ICCHP 2002*, Lecture Notes in Computer Science, Volume 2398. Berlin Heidelberg: Springer-Verlag, pp. 133–135.

Cooper, M., Valencia, L. P. S., Donnelly, A. and Sergeant, P. (2000) User interface approaches for accessibility in complex World-Wide Web applications – an example approach from the PEARL project. Paper presented at the 6th ERCIM Workshop, 'User Interfaces for All'. Online. Available HTTP: <http://ui4all.ics.forth.gr/UI4ALL-2000/files/Position_Papers/Cooper.pdf> (accessed 5 October 2005).

Corbett, J. (2001) Is equity compatible with entitlement? Balancing inclusive values and deserving needs. *Support for Learning*, 16, 3, 117–121.

Craven, J. (2000) Electronic Access for All: awareness in creating accessible websites for the university library. Online. Available HTTP: <http://www.dmag.org.uk/resources/casestudies/cravenfull.asp> (accessed 5 October 2005).

Craven, J. (2003a) Access to electronic resources by visually impaired people. *Information Research*, 8, 4. Online. Available HTTP: <http://informationr.net/ir/8-4/paper156.html> (accessed 5 October 2005).

Craven, J. (2003b) Accessibility and usability of websites. *Update Magazine*. May. Online. Available HTTP: <http://www.cilip.org.uk/publications/updatemagazine/archive/archive2003/may/update0305d.htm> (accessed 5 October 2005).

Darcy, S. (2003) The politics of disability and access: the Sydney 2000 Games experience. *Disability and Society*, 18, 6, 737–757.

Davies, M. (2003) The Special Educational Needs and Disability Act 2001 – The implications for higher education. *Education and the Law*, 15, 1, 19–27.

Department for Education and Schools (DfES) (2002) *Get on with IT: the Post-16 E-learning Strategy Task Force Report*. London: Department for Education and Skills.

Diaper, D. and Worman, L. (2003) Two falls out of three in the automated accessibility assessment of world wide websites: A-Prompt v. Bobby. Online. Available HTTP: <http://dec.bournemouth.ac.uk/staff/ddiaper/hci2003sub.pdf> (accessed 5 October 2005).

Disability Rights Commission (DRC) (2002) Disability Discrimination Act 1995 Part 4: Code of Practice for providers of post-16 education and related services. Online. Available HTTP: <http://www.drc.org.uk/uploaded_files/documents/2008_187_DDA_Pt4_Code_of_Practice_for_Post_16_education.doc> (accessed 5 October 2005).

Disability Rights Commission (DRC) (2003) The Disability Discrimination Act Part 4: Staff Development Good Practice Guide. Online. Available HTTP: <http://www.drc-gb.org/publicationsandreports/publicationhtml.asp?id=208&docsect=0&section=e> (accessed 5 October 2005).

Disability Rights Commission (DRC) (2004) The web: access and inclusion for disabled people. Online. Available HTTP: <http://www.drc-gb.org/publicationsandreports/2.pdf> (accessed 5 October 2005).

Dix, A. (2001) The right mind? *SIGHCI Bulletin*. February, p. 6. Online. Available HTTP: <http://www.comp.lancs.ac.uk/computing/users/dixa/hci-education/sigchibulletin/2001-jan-right-mind.html> (accessed 5 October 2005).

Dixon, M. (2004) Disability as a vehicle for identifying hidden aspects of human activity: inclusive design and dyslexia in educational software development. In C. Stary and C. Stephanidis (eds) *Proceedings of UI4All 2004*. Lecture Notes in Computer Science, Volume 3196. Berlin Heidelberg: Springer-Verlag, pp. 254–261.

Dobson, M., LeBlanc, D. and Burgoyne, D. (2004) Transforming tensions in learning technology design: operationalising activity theory. *Canadian Journal of Learning Technology*, 30, 1. Online. Available HTTP: <http://www.cjlt.ca/content/vol30.1/cjlt30–1_art2.html>(accessed 5 October 2005).

Downie, A. (2000) The microchip revolution improving opportunities for students who have disabilities. Paper presented at Pathways 5 Conference, Canberra, Australia, 6–8 December 2000.

Downie, A. (2004) The Pros and Cons of PDF files. Paper presented at the Round Table Conference on Print Disability, Sydney 2004.

Doyle, C. and Robson, K. (2002) Designing accessible curriculum. Online. Available HTTP: <http://www.techdis.ac.uk/resources/files/curricula.pdf> (accessed 5 October 2005).

Draffan, E. A. (1999) In-service professional development. Paper presented at the NADO Inaugural Conference, 29 March 1999. University of Lincolnshire and Humberside. Online. Available HTTP: <http://nado.org.uk/events/inauguration/draffen.html> (accessed 5 October 2005).

Draffan, E. A. (2002) Dyslexia and technology. In L. Phipps, A. Sutherland and J. Seale (eds) *Access All Areas: Disability, Technology and Learning*. Oxford: ALT/TechDis, pp. 24–28.

Draffan, E. A. and Corbett, R. (2001) Implementing a web-accessible database. *The Electronic Library*, 19, 5, 342–348.

Draffan, E. A. and Rainger, P. (2004) Can we exclude disability when we talk about accessibility and assistive technology? Paper presented at CSUN '04. Online. Available HTTP: <http://www.csun.edu/cod/conf/2004/proceedings/215.htm> (accessed 5 October 2005).

Duchateau, S., Boulay, D., Tchang-Ayo, C. and Burger, D. (2002) A strategy to achieve the accessibility of public websites. In K. Miesenberger, J. Klaus and W. Zagler (eds) *Proceedings of ICCHP 2002*, Lecture Notes in Computer Science, Volume 2398. Berlin Heidelberg: Springer-Verlag, pp. 58–60.

Edwards, M. (2000) Wising up: strategies for moving towards an inclusive model of service provision for higher education students with disabilities. Paper presented at Pathways 5 Conference, Canberra, Australia, 6–8 December 2000.

Equal Access to Software and Information (EASI) (n. d.) Accessible E-learning. Online. Available HTTP: <http://easi.cc/dl/whatis.htm > (accessed 5 October 2005).

Emerson, V., Kozak, J. and Cutway, S. (2003) Where did today's designers learn about universal design? Paper presented at CSUN '04. Online. Available HTTP: <http://www.csun.edu/cod/conf/2003/proceedings/283.htm > (accessed 5 October 2005).

Engeström, Y. (1987) *Learning by Expanding: An Activity-theoretical Approach to Developmental Research.* Helsinki: Orienta-Konsultit.

Ethical Media (2004) Disability organisations fail to meet challenge on accessibility. Online. Available HTTP: <http://www.ethicalmedia.com/stories/disability50/> (accessed 5 October 2005).

European Commission (2002) A review of legislation relevant to accessibility in Europe. Online. Available HTTP: <http://europa.eu.int/comm/employment_social/knowledge_society/eacc_rev_leg.pdf> (accessed 5 October 2005).

European Commission (2005) eAccessibility. Online. Available HTTP: <http://europa.eu.int/information_society/policy/accessibility/com_ea_2005/a_documents/cec_com_eacc_2005.html> (accessed 5 October 2005).

Evans, S. (2002) E learning a level playing field? Paper presented at New Visions: Moving Toward an Inclusive Community. 11th ICEVI World Conference. 27 July–2 August 2002. Noordwijkerhout, The Netherlands. Online. Available HTTP: <http://www.icevi.org/publications/ICEVI-WC2002/papers/09-topic/09-evans.htm> (accessed 5 October 2005).

Fain, W. B. and Bursa, D. (2005) Using the '508 Assistant' to support the design and procurement of accessible technology. Paper presented at CSUN '05, Los Angeles, 17–19 March 2005. Online. Available HTTP: <http://www. csun.edu/cod/conf/2005/proceedings/2111.htm> (accessed 5 October 2005).

Faulkner, S. and Arch, A. (2003) Accessibility testing software compared. Paper presented to AusWeb '03. Online. Available HTTP: <http://ausweb.scu.edu.au/aw03/papers/arch/paper.html> (accessed 5 October 2005).

Feingold, L. (2004) Legal issues for CSUN participants: using disability rights laws to make information and information technology more accessible. Paper presented at CSUN '04. Online. Available HTTP: <http://www. csun.edu/cod/conf/2004/proceedings/154.htm> (accessed 5 October 2005).

Feingold, L. and Creagan, T. (2005) Advocacy strategies – using the law to increase accessibility of electronic and information technology and telecommunications. Paper presented at CSUN '05, Los Angeles, 17–19 March 2005. Online. Available HTTP: <http:// www.csun.edu/cod/conf/2005/proceedings/2337.htm> (accessed 5 October 2005).

Feingold, L. and Earl, C. (2005) web accessibility and the law: recent legal development and advocacy strategies. Paper presented at CSUN '05, Los Angeles, 17–19 March 2005. Online. Available HTTP: <http://www.csun.edu/cod/conf/2005/proceedings/2116.htm> (accessed 5 October 2005).

Ferreira, H. and Freitas, D. (2004) Enhancing the accessibility of mathematics for blind people: The AudioMath Project. In K. Klaus, K. Miesenberger, W. Zagler, and D. Burger (eds) *Computers Helping People with Special Needs.* Proceedings of 9th International Conference. Berlin Heidelberg: Springer-Verlag, pp. 678–685.

Fichten, C. S., Barile, M., Asuncion, J., Judd, D., Alapin, I., Reid, E., Lavers, J., Genereux, C., Guimont, J-P. and Schipper, F. (1999) A comparison of postsecondary students with disabilities and service providers' views about computer and information technologies. Paper presented at CSUN '99. Online. Available HTTP: <http://www.csun.edu/cod/conf/1999/proceedings/session0254.htm> (accessed 5 October 2005).

Fichten, C. S., Asuncion, J. V., Barile, M., Fossey, M. and de Simone, C. (2000) Access to educational and instructional computer technologies for post-secondary students with disabilities: lessons from three empirical studies. *Journal of Educational Media*, 25, 3, 2000.

Fichten, C. S., Asuncion, J. V., Robillard, C., Fossey, M. E. and Barile, M. (2003) Accessible computer technologies for students with disabilities in Canadian higher education. *Canadian Journal of Learning and Technology*, 29, 2. Online. Available   HTTP: <http://www.cjlt.ca/content/vol29.2/cjlt29–2_art-1.html> (accessed 5 October 2005).

Finkelstein, V. (1993) Disability: a social challenge or an administrative responsibility. In J. Swain, V. Finkelstein, S. French and M. Oliver (eds) *Disabling Barriers – Enabling Environments*. London: Sage.

Flowers, C., Bray, M. and Algozzine, R. F. (2001) Content accessibility of community college websites. *Community College Journal of Research and Practice*, 25, 475–485.

Flowers, C. P., Bray, M., Furr, S. and Algozzine, R. F. (2002) Accessibility of counselling education programs' websites. *Journal of Technology in Counseling*, 2, 2. Online.   Available   HTTP: <http://jtc.colstate.edu/vol2_2/flowersbray.htm> (accessed 5 October 2005).

Folds, D. J. and Fain, W. B. (2005) Case studies of accessibility approaches among electronic and information technology manufacturers. Paper presented at CSUN '05, Los Angeles, 17–19 March 2005. Online. Available HTTP: <http://www.csun.edu/cod/conf/2005/proceedings/2208.htm> (accessed 5 October 2005).

Foley, A. R. (2003a) Integrating accessible design into the educational web design process. *Meridian*, 6, 1. Online. Available HTTP: <http://www.ncsu.edu/meridian/win2003/accessibility/> (accessed 5 October 2005).

Foley, A. R. (2003b) Distance, disability and the commodifcation of education: web accessibility and the construction of knowledge. *Current Issues in Comparative Education*, 6, 1, 1–16.

Fossey, M. E., Asuncion, J. V., Fichten, C., Lamb, D., Robillard, C. and Barile, M. (2004) Presenting the accessibility of campus computing for students with disabilities scale. Paper presented at CSUN '04. Online. Available HTTP: <http://www.csun.edu/cod/conf/2004/proceedings/338.htm> (accessed 5 October 2005).

French, D. and Valdes, L. (2002) Electronic accessibility: United Sates and international perspectives. *Educational Technology Review*, 10, 1 Online. Available HTTP: <http:// www.aace.org/pubs/etr/issue2/French-a.cfm> (accessed 5 October 2005).

Friesen, N. and Cressman, D (2005) The politics of e-learning standardization. *Ipseity*, 7 July 2005. Online. Available HTTP: <http://ipseity.blogsome.com/2005/07/07/the-politics-of-e-learning-standardization/> (accessed 5 October 2005).

Fuller, M., Healey, M., Bradley, A. and Hall, T. (2004a) Barriers to learning: a systematic study of the experience of disabled students in one university. *Studies in Higher Education*, 29, 3, 303–318.

Fuller, M., Bradley, A. and Healey, M. (2004b) Incorporating disabled students within an inclusive higher education environment. *Disability and Society*, 19, 5, 455–468.

Gappa, H., Nordbrook, Mohamad, Y. and Velasco, C. A. (2004) Preferences of people with disabilities to improve information presentation and information retrieval inside Internet Services – results of a user study. In K. Klaus, K. Miesenberger, W. Zagler and D. Burger (eds) *Computers Helping People with Special Needs*. Proceedings of 9th International Conference. Berlin Heidelberg: Springer-Verlag, pp. 296–301.

Gardiner, V. and Anwar, N. (2001) Providing learning support for students with mobility impairments undertaking fieldwork and related activities. Cheltenham: Geography Discipline Network. Online. Available HTTP: <http://www.glos.ac.uk/gdn/disabil/mobility/index.htm> (accessed 5 October 2005).

Gay, G. and Harrison, L. (2001) Inclusion in an electronic classroom – accessible courseware study. Paper presented at CSUN '01. Online. Available HTTP: <http://www.csun.edu/cod/conf/2001/proceedings/0188gay.htm> (accessed 5 October 2005).

Gay, G., Harrison, L., Richards, J. and Trevinarus, J. (1999) Courseware accessibility study. Online. Available HTTP: <http://snow.utoronto.ca/initiatives/crseval/crseval.html> (accessed 5 October 2005).

Gheerawo, R., Lebbon, C. and Donahue, S. (2004) Inclusive design in practice: working with students and educators. Paper presented at Designing for the 21st Century III, 7–12 December, 2004, Rio de Janeiro, Brazil. Online. Available HTTP: <http://www.designfor21st.org/proceedings/proceedings/project_hhrc_gheerawo.html> (accessed 5 October 2005).

Gonzales, J., Macias, M., Rodriguez, R. and Sanchez, F. (2003) Accessibility metrics of web pages for blind end-users. In J. M. Cueva Lovelle (ed.) *Proceedings of ICWE 2003, Lecture Notes in Computer Science*, Volume 2722. Berlin Heidelberg: Springer-Verlag, pp. 374–383.

Goodman, G., Tiene, D. and Luft, P. (2002) Adoption of assistive technology for computer access among college students with disabilities. *Disability and Rehabilitation*, 24, 1/2/3, 80–92.

Grott, R. (1999) Technology only goes so far: solutions through advocacy and resource teams (S.T.A.R.T). Paper presented at CSUN '99. Online. Available HTTP: <http://www.csun.edu/cod/conf/1999/proceedings/session0127.htm> (accessed 5 October 2005).

Guarino-Reid, L. and Pisocky, G. (2005) Techniques for creating accessible PDF files using Adobe Acrobat. Paper presented at CSUN '05, Los Angeles, 17–19 March 2005. Online. Available HTTP: <http://www.csun.edu/cod/conf/2005/proceedings/2403.htm> (accessed 5 October 2005).

Guenaga, M. L., Burger, D. and Oliver, J. (2004) Accessibility for e-Learning Environments. In K. Klaus, K. Miesenberger, W. Zagler and D. Burger (eds) *Computers Helping People with Special Needs*. Proceedings of 9th International Conference. Berlin Heidelberg: Springer-Verlag, pp. 157–163.

Gulliksen, J. and Harker, S. (2004) The software accessibility of human-computer interfaces – ISO Technical Specification. *Universal Access in the Information Society*, 3, 6–16.

Gulliksen, J., Andersson, H. and Lundgren, P. (2004) Accomplishing universal access through system reachability – a management perspective. *Universal Access in the Information Society*, 3, 96–101.

Gunderson, J. and May, M. (2005) W3C user agent accessibility guidelines test suite version 2.0 and implementation report. Paper presented at CSUN '05, Los Angeles, 17–19 March 2005. Online. Available HTTP: <http://ww.csun.edu/cod/conf/2005/proceedings/2363.htm> (accessed 5 October 2005).

Hackett, S., Parmanto, B. and Zeng, X. (2004) Accessibility of Internet Websites through time. Paper presented at ASSETS '04, Atlanta, Georgia, 18–20 October.

Haines, A. and Molenaar, S. (2000) Breaking down the barriers: a team approach to learning development. Paper presented at the Pathways 5 National Conference, Canberra, Australia, 6–8 December 2000.

Hall, J. and Tinklin, T. (1998) Students first: the experiences of disabled students in higher education. *SCRE Research Report No. 85.* The Scottish Council for Research in Education. Online. Available HTTP: <http://www.scre.ac.uk/resreport/pdf/085.pdf> (accessed 5 October 2005).

Hanson, V. L. and Richards, J. T. (2004) A web accessibility service: update and findings. Paper presented at ASSETS '04, 18–20 October, Atlanta, Georgia. Online. Available HTTP: <http://www.research.ibm.com/people/v/vlh/HansonASSETS04.pdf> (accessed 5 October 2005).

Harniss, M. and Amtman, D. (2005) An awareness video on the need for accessible information technology in education. Paper presented at CSUN '05, Los Angeles, 17–19 March 2005. Online. Available HTTP: <http://www. csun.edu/cod/conf/2005/proceedings/2393.htm> (accessed 5 October 2005).

Harris, C. and Oppenheim, C. (2003) The provision of library services for visually impaired students in UK further education libraries in response to the Special Educational Needs and Disability Act (SENDA). *Journal of Librarianship and Information Science*, 35, 4, 243–257.

Harrison, L. (2002) Access to online learning: the role of the courseware authoring tool developer. *Library Hi Tech*, 20, 4, 433–440.

Hassell, J. (2005) BBC New Media Accessibility Checklist v 0.2. Online. Available HTTP: <http://www.bbc.co.uk/guidelines/newmedia/accessibility/> (accessed 5 October 2005).

Haverty, R. (2005) New accessibility model for Microsoft Windows. Paper presented at CSUN '05, Los Angeles, 17–19 March 2005. Online. Available HTTP: <http://www.csun.edu/cod/conf/2005/proceedings/2428.htm> (accessed 5 October 2005).

Healey, M., Roberts, C., Jenkins, A. and Leach, J. (2001) Issues in providing learning support for disabled students undertaking fieldwork and related activities. Cheltenham: Geography Discipline Network, University of Gloucestershire.

Heath, A. (2003) The accessibility jigsaw puzzle. *The Learning Citizen Newsletter*, 4, 9–12.

Heath, A. (2005) Eportfolio and Accessibility. Online. Available HTTP: <http://axelrod.plus.com/moin/EpAccess> (accessed 5 October 2005).

Henderson, P. (2002) Physical disability and technology. In L. Phipps, A. Sutherland and J. Seale (eds). *Access All Areas: Disability, Technology and Learning*. Oxford: ALT/TechDis, pp. 29–32.

Herrell, A. (2001) Accessibility: The politics of design. Online. Available HTTP: <http://www.evolt.org/article/Accessibility_The_politics_of_design/4090/5034/> (accessed 5 October 2005).

Herrington, M. (2000) The organic model of staff development in relation to disability. Online. Available HTTP: <http://www.nottingham.ac.uk/ssc/staff/randd_asdsds/organic.html> (accessed 5 October 2005).

Higher Education Statistics Agency (HESA) (2002) *Students in Higher Education Institutions*. Cheltenham: HESA.

Hinn, M. (1999) Evaluating the accessibility of web-based instruction for students with disabilities. Paper presented at the Annual Meeting of the Association for Educational Communications and Technology, February 1999, Houston, Texas. Online.

Available HTTP: <http://access.ed.uiuc.edu/AECT/Eval/AECT_Hinn.PDF> (accessed 5 October 2005).

HMSO (1995) Disability Discrimination Act. Online. Available HTTP: <http://www.legislation.hmso.gov.uk/acts/acts1995/Ukpga_19950050_en_1.htm> (accessed 5 October 2005).

HMSO (2001) The Special Educational Needs and Disability Act. Online. Available HTTP: <http://www.legislation.hmso.gov.uk/acts/acts2001/20010010.htm> (accessed 5 October 2005).

Ho, A. (2004) To be labelled, or not be labelled: that is the question. *British Journal of Learning Disability*, 32, 86–92.

Holloway, S. (2001) The experience of higher education from the perspective of disabled students. *Disability and Society*, 16, 4, 597–615.

Horton, S. (2002) Accessibility: how to use the web to reach a diverse student body. Online. Available HTTP: <http://www.dartmouth.edu/~shorton/wesleyan/accessibility.pdf> (accessed 5 October 2005).

Horwath, J. (2002) Evaluating opportunities for expanded information access: a study of the accessibility of four online databases. *Library Hi Tech*, 20, 2, 199–206.

Hricko, M. (2003) Implementing accessibility standards in the campus technology plan. Paper presented at the Ohio Learning network, 3–4 March 2003, Easton, Ohio. Online. Available HTTP: <http://www.oln.org/conferences/OLN2003/papers/Implementing_Accessibility_Standards_in_the_Campus_Technology_Plan.pdf> (accessed 5 October 2005).

Hudson, W. (2003) Public accommodation: the US Web accessibility jigsaw. *SIGCHI Bulletin* (January/February), p. 8.

Hull, L. (2004) Accessibility: it's not just for disability any more. *Interactions*, March–April 2004, 36–41.

Human Rights and Equal Opportunity Commission (HREOC) (2002) World Wide Web Access: Disability Discrimination Act Advisory Notes. Online. Available HTTP: <http://www.hreoc.gov.au/disability_rights/standards/www_3/www_3.html> (accessed 5 October 2005).

Hunziker, D. (2004) web accessibility: a model for implementing campus-wide standards and increasing awareness. Online. Available HTTP: <http://www.csun.edu/cod/couf/2004/proceedings/128.htm> (accessed 5 October 2005).

Hurst, D. and Smerdon, B. (2000) Post secondary students with disabilities: enrolment, services and persistence. Online. Available HTTP: <http://nces.ed.gov/pubs2000/2000092.pdf> (accessed 5 October 2005).

IBM (2004) web Accessibility Checklist. Online. Available HTTP: <http://www-306.ibm.com/able/guidelines/web/accessweb.html> (accessed 5 October 2005).

IMS Global Learning Consortium (2003) IMS Learner Information Package Access for LIP Best Practice Implementation Guide. Version 1.0 Final Specification. Online. Available HTTP: <http://www.imsglobal.org/accessibility/acclipv1p0/imsacclip_bestv1p0.html> (accessed 5 October 2005).

IMS Global Learning Consortium (2004a) IMS AccessForAll Meta-data Overview. Online. Available HTTP: <http://www.imsglobal.org/accessibility/accmdv1p0/imsaccmd_oviewv1p0.html> (accessed 5 October 2005).

IMS Global Learning Consortium (2004b) IMS Guidelines for Developing Accessible Learning Applications. Version 1.0 White Paper. Online. Available HTTP: <http://www.imsglobal.org/accessibility/#accguide> (accessed 5 October 2005).

Income Data Services (2000) *Monitoring the Disability Discrimination Act 1995*. First interim report to the Department of Education and Employment. London: Income Data Services.

Issroff, K. and Scanlon, E. (2002) Using technology in higher education: an Activity Theory perspective. *Journal of Computer Assisted Learning*, 18, 1, 77–83.

Ivory, M. Y., Mankoff, J. and Le, A. (2003) Using automated tools to improve website usage by users with diverse abilities. *IT and Society*, 1, 3, 195–236.

Iwarsson, S. and Stahl, A. (2003) Accessibility, usability and universal design – positioning and definition of concepts describing person–environment relationships. *Disability and Rehabilitation*, 25, 2, 57–66.

Jacko, J. A. and Hanson, V. L. (2002) Universal access and inclusion in design. *Universal Access to the Information Society*, 2, 1–2.

Jacobs, S. (2005) Market forces driving the design of more accessible information and communications technology (ICT). Paper presented at CSUN '05, Los Angeles, 17–19 March 2005. Online. Available HTTP: <http://www. csun.edu/cod/conf/ 2005/proceedings/2269.htm> (accessed 5 October 2005).

Jahankhani, H., Lynch, J. A. and Stephenson, J. (2002) The current legislation covering e-learning provisions for the visually impaired in the EU. In M. H. Shafazand and A. M. Tjoa (eds) *Proceedings of EurAsia-ICT 2002*, Lecture Notes in Computer Science, Volume 2510. Berlin Heidelberg: Springer-Verlag, pp. 552–559.

Jeffels, P. and Martson, P. (2003) Accessibility of online learning materials. Online. Available HTTP: <http://www.scrolla.hw.ac.uk/papers/jeffelsmarston.html> (accessed 5 October 2005).

Johnson, A. and Ruppert, S. (2002) An evaluation of accessibility in online learning management systems. *Library Hi Tech*, 20, 4, 441–451.

Johnson, K. L., Brown, S., Amtmann, D. and Thompson, T. (2003) web accessibility in post-secondary education: legal and policy considerations. *Information Technology and Disabilities*, 9, 2. Online. Available HTTP: <http://www.rit.edu/~easi/itd/ itdv09n2/johnson.htm> (accessed 5 October 2005).

Jones, A. and Tedd, L. A. (2003) Provision of electronic information services for the visually impaired: an overview with case studies from three institutions within the University of Wales. *Journal of Librarianship and Information Science*, 35, 2, 105–113.

Jordan, M. (2005) Strategies for building accessible learning web applications and games with Macromedia Flash MX. Paper presented at CSUN '05, Los Angeles, 17–19 March 2005. Online. Available HTTP: <http://www.csun.edu/cod/conf/ 2005/proceedings/2330.htm> (accessed 5 October 2005).

Katseva, A. (2004) The case for pervasive accessibility. Paper presented at CSUN '04. Online. Available HTTP: <http://www.csun.edu/cod/conf/2004/proceedings/ 114.htm> (accessed 5 October 2005).

Kavanagh, J. (2005) DRC Airs doubts on auto test. *Ability*, 57, 7.

Keates, S. and Clarkson, P. J. (2003) Countering design exclusion: bridging the gap between usability and accessibility. *Universal Access to the Information Society*, 2, 215–225.

Keats, R. E. (2003) Report of a survey of the staff development needs of teaching staff in higher education in relation to disabled students. Online. Available HTTP: <http://www.open.ac.uk/cater/pics/d12809.doc> (accessed 5 October 2005).

Keegan, S. (2004) Creating accessible adobe PDF documents: authoring techniques for accessible electronic materials. Paper presented at CSUN '04. Online. Available HTTP: <http://www.csun.edu/cod/conf/2004/proceedings/223.htm> (accessed 5 October 2005).

Keller, S., Owens, J. and Parker, C. (2000) Improving online access for people with disabilities. Paper presented at 8th European Conference on Information Systems (ECIS2000), Vienna, Austria, July 2000. Online. Available HTTP: <http://www.deakin.edu.au/buslaw/infosys/docs/workingpapers/archive/Working_Papers_2000/2000_19_Keller.pdf> (accessed 5 October 2005).

Keller, S., Braithwaite, R., Owens, J. and Smith, K. (2001) Towards universal accessibility: including users with a disability in the design process. Paper presented at the 12th Australasian Conference on Information Systems, Southern Cross University, New South Wales.

Kelly, B. (2002a) WebWatch: an accessibility analysis of UK university entry points. *Ariadne*, 33. Online. Available HTTP: <http://www.ariadne.ac.uk/issue33/web-watch/> (accessed 5 October 2005).

Kelly, B. (2002b) Bobby analysis of JISC 5/99 project entry points. Online. Available HTTP: <http://www.ukoln.ac.uk/qa-focus/surveys/web-10–2002/bobby/> (accessed 5 October 2005).

Kelly, B., Phipps, L. and Swift, E. (2004) Developing a holistic approach for e-learning accessibility. *Canadian Journal of Learning and Technology*, 30, 3. Online. Available HTTP: <http://www.cjlt.ca/content/vol30.3/kelly.html> (accessed 5 October 2005).

Kelly, B., Phipps, L., Sloan, D., Petrie, H. and Hamilton, F. (2005) Forcing standardization or accommodating diversity? A framework for applying the WCAG in the real world. Paper presented at the 2005 International Cross Disciplinary Workshop on Web Accessibility (W4A), Manchester, UK.

Kipar, N. (2005) Newsletter contribution. Online. Available HTTP: <http://newsletter.alt.ac.uk/e_article000429330.cfm?x=b11.0.w> (accessed 20 January 2006).

Kirkpatrick, A. and Thatcher, J. (2005) Web accessibility error prioritisation. Paper presented at CSUN '05, Los Angeles, 17–19 March 2005. Online. Available HTTP: <http://www.csun.edu/cod/conf/2005/proceedings/2341.htm> (accessed 5 October 2005).

Klein, D. and Thompson, K. (2005) Accessible video in a diverging web environment. Paper presented at CSUN '05, Los Angeles, 17–19 March 2005. Online. Available HTTP: <http://www.csun.edu/cod/conf/2005/proceedings/2243.htm> (accessed 5 October 2005).

Klein, D., Myhill, W., Hansen, L., Asby, G., Michaelson, S. and Blank, P. (2003) Electronic doors to education: study of high school website accessibility in Iowa. *Behavioural Sciences and the Law*, 21, 27–49.

Koivunen, M.-R. (2003) Accessibility and ubiquitous computing. Paper presented at CSUN '03. Online. Available HTTP: <http://www.csun.edu/cod/conf/2003/proceedings/70.htm> (accessed 5 October 2005).

Koivunen, M.-R. (2004) Accessibility of web collaboration technologies. Paper presented at CSUN '04. Online. Available HTTP: <http://www.csun.edu/cod/conf/2004/proceedings/273.htm> (accessed 5 October 2005).

Konicek, K., Hyzny, J. and Allegra, R. (2003) Electronic reserves: the promise and challenge to increase accessibility. *Library Hi Tech*, 21, 1, 102–108.

Konur, O. (2000) Creating enforceable civil rights for disabled students in higher education: an institutional theory perspective. *Disability and Society*, 15, 7, 1041–1063.

Konur, O. (2002) Access to e-learning in higher education by disabled students: current public policy issues. Paper presented at Networked Learning Conference, Sheffield, 25–26 March, 2002. Online. Available HTTP: <http://www.shef.ac.uk/nlc2002/proceedings/papers/18.htm> (accessed 5 October 2005).

Kowalsky, R. and Fresko, B. (2002) Peer tutoring for college students with disabilities. *Higher Education Research and Development*, 21, 3, 259–271.

Kraithman, D. and Bennett, S. (2004) Case study: blending chalk, talk and accessibility in an introductory economics module. *Best Practice*, 4, 2, 12–15.

Kramer, H. (2004) 508 in the University Environment. Paper presented at CSUN '04. Online. Available HTTP: <http://www.csun.edu/cod/conf/2004/proceedings/276.htm> (accessed 5 October 2005).

Kretchmer, S. B. and Carveth, R. (2003) Analyzing recent Americans with disabilities act-based accessible information technology court challenges. *Information Technology and Disabilities*, 9, 2. Online. Available HTTP: <http://www.rit.edu/~easi/itd/itdv09n2/kretchmr.htm> (accessed 5 October 2005).

Kunzinger, E., Snow-Weaver, A., Bernstein, H., Collins, C., Keates, S., Kwit, P., Laws, C., Querner, K., Murphy, A., Sacco, J. and Soderston, C. (2005) Ease of access – a cultural change in the IT product design process. Paper presented at CSUN '05, Los Angeles, 17–19 March 2005. Online. Available HTTP: <http://www.csun.edu/cod/conf/2005/proceedings/2512.htm> (accessed 5 October 2005).

Kurniawan, S. H. (2002) How Accessible are Web information resources for students with disabilities? In K. Miesenberger., J. Klaus and W. Zagler (eds) *Proceedings of ICCHP 2002*, Lecture Notes in Computing Science, Volume 2398. Berlin Heidelberg: Springer-Verlag, pp. 756–757.

Kuutti, K. (1996) Activity theory as a potential framework for human–computer interaction research. In B. Nardi (ed.) *Context and Consciousness: Activity Theory and Human–Computer Interaction*. Cambridge, MA: The MIT Press, pp. 17–44.

Lagace, Y. (2004) An accessible personal assistant for the blind. Paper presented at CSUN '04. Online. Available HTTP: <http://www.csun.edu/cod/conf/2004/proceedings/274.htm> (accessed 5 October 2005).

Lakey, M. (2002) The development of an institutional Web policy: a case study. In L. Phipps, A. Sutherland and J. Seale (eds). *Access All Areas: Disability, Technology and Learning*. Oxford: ALT/TechDis, pp. 78–81.

Lambert, J. B. (2001) Discreet silence: disability in postgraduate education. Paper presented at the Innovation and Links: Research Management and Development and Postgraduate Education Conference, Auckland, 26–27 November. Online. Available HTTP: <http://www.aut.ac.nz/conferences/innovation/papersthemetwo/lambertpapertwo.pdf> (accessed 5 October 2005).

Lamshed, R., Berry, M. and Armstrong, L. (2003) Keys to access: accessibility conformance in VET. Online. Available HTTP: <http://www.flexiblelearning.net.au/projects/resources/accessibility-conformance.doc> (accessed 5 October 2005).

Lazar, J. (2003) Improving Web accessibility through service–learning partnerships. *Information Systems Education Journal*, 1, 33. Online. Available HTTP: <http://isedj.org/1/33/ISEDJ.1(33).Lazar.pdf> (accessed 5 October 2005).

Lazar, J., Beere, P., Greenidge, K. D. and Nagappa, Y. (2003) Web accessibility in the

Mid-Atlantic States: a study of 50 homepages. *Universal Access in the Information Society*, 2, 331–341.

Lazar, J., Dudley-Sponaugle, A. and Greenidge, K.-D. (2004) Improving web accessibility: a study of webmaster perceptions. *Computers in Human Behaviour*, 20, 269–288.

Lemon, G. and Wilcock, J. (2003) Accessibility of UK government Web sites investigated. Online. Available HTTP: <http://www.accessify.com/articles/accessibility-of-uk-government-websites.asp> (accessed 5 October 2005).

Leung, P., Owens, J., Lamb, G., Smith, K., Shaw, J. and Hauff, R. (1999) Assistive technology: meeting the technology needs of students with disabilities in post-secondary education. Online. Available HTTP: <http://www.dest.gov.au/archive/highered/eippubs/eip99–6/eip99_6.pdf> (accessed 5 October 2005).

Leverton, S. (2002) Monitoring the Disability Discrimination Act (Phase 2). A study carried out on behalf of the Department for Work and Pensions. Online. Available HTTP: <http://www.dwp.gov.uk/asd/asd5/IH91.pdf> (accessed 5 October 2005).

Lewis, K. L., Bronstad, P. M., Barron, B. and Hays, J. (2004) web usage strategies: individuals with learning disabilities and individuals with visual impairments. Paper presented at CSUN '04. Online. Available HTTP: <http://www.csun.edu/cod/conf/2004/proceedings/219.htm> (accessed 5 October 2005).

Linder, D. and Gunderson, J. (2003) Publishing Accessible WWW presentations from PowerPoint slide presentations. Paper presented at CSUN '03. Online. Available HTTP: <http://www.csun.edu/cod/conf/2003/proceedings/174.htm>   (accessed 5 October 2005).

Lindsay, K. (2004) Asking for the moon? A critical assessment of Australian disability discrimination laws in promoting inclusion for students with disabilities. *International Journal of Inclusive Education*, 8, 4, 373–390.

Lockley, S. (2001) Dyslexia and higher education: accessibility issues. Online. Available   HTTP: <http://www.heacademy.ac.uk/resources.   asp?process=full_record&section=generic&id=416> (accessed 5 October 2005).

Ludi, S. (2002) Access for everyone: introducing accessibility issues to students in Internet programming courses. Paper presented at the 32nd ASEE/IEEE Frontiers in Education Conference, 6–9 November, Boston, MA. Online. Available HTTP: -<http://fie.engrng.pitt.edu/fie2002/papers/1559.pdf> (accessed 5 October 2005).

Luke, R. (2002) Access*Ability*: Enabling technology for lifelong learning inclusion in an electronic classroom-2000. *Educational Technology and Society*, 5, 1, 148–152.

Manouselis, N., Panagiotou, K., Psichidou, R. and Sampson, D. (2002) Issues in designing web-based environments for learning communities with special educational needs. Paper presented at ICALT '02, Kazan Russia, September 9–12, 2002. Online. Available HTTP: <http://www.ask.iti.gr/Uploads/Files/Publications/En_Pubs/Man_etal_ICALT02_draft.pdf> (accessed 5 October 2005).

Marshall, K. and Cunneen, N. (2001) Using technology to improve access. Paper presented at Progress Through partnerships conference, New Zealand. Online. Available   HTTP: <http://services.admin.utas.edu.au/adcet/Articles/marshall&cunneen.doc> (accessed 5 October 2005).

May, Mark (2003) Comparing the roles and interrelationships of the W3C web accessibility guidelines. Paper presented at CSUN '03. Online. Available HTTP: <http://www.csun.edu/cod/conf/2003/proceedings/73.htm> (accessed 5 October 2005).

May, Michael (2003) Accessible GPS for the blind: what are the current and future frontiers? Paper presented at CSUN '03. Online. Available HTTP: <http://www.csun.edu/cod/conf/2003/proceedings/140.htm> (accessed 5 October 2005).

McAvinia, C. and Oliver, M. (2004) Developing a managed learning environment using 'Roundtables': an activity theoretic perspective. *Interactive Learning Environments*, 12, 3, 209–225.

McCabe, E. (2002) NADO Technical Briefing 1/2001: Disability Officers in Higher Education. Online. Available HTTP: <http://nado.org.uk/pubs/techbrief.html> (accessed 5 October 2005).

McCarthy, D. (2001) Accessibility and legislation in higher education. *Interactions*, 5, 3. Online. Available HTTP: <http://www. warwick.ac.uk/ETS/interactions/vol5no3/McCarthy.htm> (accessed 5 October 2005).

McCord, S. K., Frederiksen, L. and Campbell, N. (2002) An accessibility assessment of selected web-based health information resources. *Library High Tech*, 20, 2, 188–198.

McEwan, T., Cairncross, S. and MacLean, A. (2003) Good practice for all. Paper presented at Napier staff conference. Online. Available HTTP: <http://www.ed.napier.ac.uk/staffconference/june2003/papers/mcewan.doc> (accessed 5 October 2005).

McInnery, J., McNamee, L. and Roberts, T. (2003) Usability, accessibility and equity: understanding the anomalies in online learning. Paper presented at AusWeb '03. Online. Available HTTP: <http://ausweb.scu.edu.au/aw03/papers/roberts/paper.html> (accessed 5 October 2005).

McMullen, B. (2002) WARP: web Accessibility Reporting Project – Ireland 2002 baseline study. Online. Available HTTP: <http://eaccess.rince.ie/white-papers/2002/warp-2002–00/warp-2002–00.pdf> (accessed 5 October 2005).

McNairn, P. and Zabala, J. (2005) A team training model based on the quality indicators for assistive technology. Paper presented at CSUN '05, Los Angeles, 17–19 March 2005. Online. Available HTTP: <http://www.csun.edu/cod/conf/2005/proceedings/2132.htm> (accessed 5 October 2005).

Michaels, C. A., Prezait, F. P., Mavaboto, S. M. and Jackson, K. (2002) Assistive and instructional technology for college students with disabilities: a national snapshot of post secondary service providers. *Journal of Special Education Technology*, 17, 1. Online. Available HTTP: <http://jset.univ.edu/17.1/michaels/michaels.pdf> (accessed 5 October 2005).

Middling, T. and Bostock, S. (2002) Accessibility: implications for teaching staff and staff developers. *Educational Developments*, 3, 3, 8–9.

Milani, A. A. (1996) Disabled students in higher education, administrative and judicial enforcement of disability law. *Journal of College and University Law*, 22, 989–1043.

Mirabella, V., Kimani, S. Gabrielli, S. and Catarci, T. (2004) Accessible e-learning material: a no-frills avenue for didactical experts. *New Review of Hypermedia and Multimedia*, 10, 2, 165–180.

Nardi, B. (1996) Activity theory and human–computer interaction. In B. Nardi (ed.) *Context and Consciousness: Activity Theory and Human–Computer Interaction*. Cambridge, MA: MIT Press, pp. 7–16.

Neumann, Z. (2002) Visual impairment and technology. In L. Phipps, A. Sutherland and J. Seale (eds) *Access All Areas: Disability, Technology and Learning*. Oxford: ALT/TechDis, pp. 16–18.

Nevile, L. and Burmeister, O. K. (2003) Acting accessibility: scenario-based consideration of Web content accessibility for development and publishing communities. Paper presented at the 12th International World Wide Conference, Budapest, 20–24 May 2003. Online. Available HTTP: <http://www2003.org//cdrom/papers/alternate/P306/p306nevile.pdf> (accessed 5 October 2005).

Nicolle, C. and Darzentas, J. (2003) The IDCNET approach: educating students and professionals in 'Design for All'. Online. Available HTTP: <http://www.bcs.org.uk/disability/icat/papers/paper6.pdf> (accessed 5 October 2005).

Nicolle, C., Osman, Z., Black, K. and Lysley, A. (2004) Learning from Internet requirements of people with communication needs. In K. Miesenberger, J. Klaus and W. Zagler (eds) *Proceedings of ICCHP 2002*, Lecture Notes in Computer Science, Volume 3118. Berlin Heidelberg: Springer-Verlag, pp. 183–186.

Nielson, J. (2002) Top ten guidelines for home page usability. Online. Available HTTP: <http://www.useit.com/alertbox/20020512.html> (accessed 5 October 2005).

North, D. C. (1993) Institutions and credible commitment. Online. Available HTTP: <http://econwpa.wustl.edu:8089/eps/eh/papers/9412/9412002.pdf> (accessed 5 October 2005).

North, D. C. (1994a) Institutional change: a framework of analysis. Online. Available HTTP: <http://econwpa.wustl.edu/eps/eh/papers/9412/9412001.pdf> (accessed 5 October 2005).

North, D. C. (1994b) Institutional competition. Online. Available HTTP: <ftp://ftp.sinica.edu.tw/pub/doc/econ-wp/eh/papers/9411/9411001.pdf> (accessed 5 October 2005).

O'Connor, B. (2000) E-learning and students with disabilities: from outer edge to leading edge. Keynote speech presented at Networking 2000. Online. Available HTTP: <http://www.flexiblelearning.net.au/nw2000/main/key04.htm> (accessed 5 October 2005).

O'Grady, L. and Harrison, L. (2003) Web accessibility validation and repair: which tool and why? *Library Hi Tech*, 21, 4, 463–470.

O'Gribin, N. (2004) Accessible Java using JAAPI. Online. Available HTTP: <http://www.computing.dundee.ac.uk/projects/dmag/resources/design_articles/accessiblejava.asp> (accessed 5 October 2005).

Oliver, M. (1990) *The Politics of Disablement*. Basingstoke: MacMillan and St Martin's Press.

Olney, M. F. and Brockelman, K. F. (2003) Out of the disability closet: strategic use of perception management by select university students with disabilities. *Disability and Society*, 18, 1, 35–50.

Opitz, C. (2002) Online course accessibility: a call for responsibility and necessity. *Educational Technology Review*, 10, 1. Online. Available HTTP: <http://www.aace.org/pubs/etr/issue2/optiz-x1.cfm> (accessed 5 October 2005).

Opitz, C., Savenye, W. and Rowland, C. (2003) Accessibility of State Department of Education home pages and special education pages. *Journal of Special Education Technology*, 18, 1 Online. Available HTTP: <http://jset.unlv.edu/18.1/opitz/first.html> (accessed 5 October 2005).

Oravec, J. (2002) Virtually accessible: empowering students to advocate for accessibility and support universal design. *Library Hi Tech*, 20, 4, 452–461.

Ormerod, M. (2002) Developing an accessible distance taught MSc. Online. Available

HTTP: <http://www.hefce.ac.uk/pubs/hefce/2002/02%5F48/02%5F48c3.pdf> (accessed 5 October 2005).

Ortner, D., Batusic, M. and Miesenberger, K. (2004) Postgraduate course on accessible design. In K. Klaus, K. Miesenberger, W. Zagler and D. Burger (eds) *Computers Helping People with Special Needs*. Proceedings of 9th International Conference. Berlin Heidelberg: Springer-Verlag, pp. 183–186.

Ouellett, M. L. (2004) Faculty development and universal instructional design. *Equity and Excellence in Education*, 37, 135–144.

Owens, J. and Keller, S. (2000) MultiWeb: Australian contribution to Web accessibility. Paper presented at the 11th Australasian Conference on Information Systems, Brisbane, Australia. Online. Available HTTP: <http://www.deakin.edu.au/infosys/docs/workingpapers/archive/Working_Papers_2000/2000_18_Owens.pdf.> (accessed 5 October 2005).

Owens, J., Leung, P., Lamb, G., Smith, K., Shaw, J. and Hauff, R. (1999) Assistive technology issues for students with disabilities and university staff who work with them. Paper presented at HERDSA Annual International Conference, Melbourne, 12–15 July 1999. Online. Available HTTP: <http://www.herdsa.org.au/branches/vic/Cornerstones/pdf/Owens.PDF> (accessed 5 October 2005).

Paciello, M. G. (2000) *Web Accessibility for People with Disabilities*. Kansas: CMP Books.

Paciello, M. G. (2005) Enhancing accessibility through usability inspections and usability testing. Paper presented at CSUN '05, Los Angeles, 17–19 March 2005. Online. Available HTTP: <http://www.csun.edu/cod/conf/2005/proceedings/2509.htm> (accessed 5 October 2005).

Paolucci, P. (2004) Should online course design meet accessibility standards? *Educational Technology and Society*, 7, 1, 6–11.

Parker, V. (1997) The Disability Discrimination Act 1995, disability statement and the effect on higher education for students with special needs in England. *Research in Post-Compulsory Education*, 2, 1, 89–101.

Parker, V. (2000) Developing a code of practice for disability coordinators. *European Journal of Special Needs Education*, 15, 3, 275–284.

Parker, V. (2001) Staff development and curricular inclusion in higher education. *Research in Post-Compulsory Education*, 6, 1, 105–112.

Parkin, J. (2001) Exams and DSA for DB. Message posed to the Deaflink JISC Mailing list. Online. Available HTTP: <http://www.jiscmail.ac.uk/cgi-bin/webadmin?A2=ind01&L=deaflink&T=0&F=&S=&P=477> (accessed 5 October 2005).

Parsons, A. (2000) A level playing field. *Learning Technology*, 2, 4. Online. Available HTTP: <http://lttf.ieee.org/learn_tech/issues/october2000/#level> (accessed 5 October 2005).

Patterson, K. and Ellis, A. (2002) Design and navigation: a survey of Australian university homepages. Paper presented at AusWeb '02. Online. Available HTTP: <http://ausweb.scu.edu.au/aw02/papers/refereed/patterson/paper.html> (accessed 5 October 2005).

Peacock, S., Ross, D. and Skelton, J. (2002) Improving staff awareness of accessibility legislation for online teaching and learning materials: a case study. In L. Phipps, A. Sutherland and J. Seale (eds) *Access All Areas: Disability, Technology and Learning*. Oxford: ALT/TechDis, pp. 56–60.

Pearson, E. J. and Koppi, T. (2001) Inclusion and online learning opportunities: designing for accessibility. *Association for Learning Technology Journal*, 10, 2, 17–28.

Pearson, E. J. and Koppi, T. (2003) Developing inclusive practices: evaluation of a staff development course in accessibility. *Australian Journal of Educational Technology*, 19, 3, 275–292.

Perkins, A. and Haverty, R. (2005) Windows accessibility today and tomorrow. Paper presented at CSUN '05, Los Angeles, 17–19 March 2005. Online. Available HTTP: <http://www.csun.edu/cod/conf/2005/proceedings/2426.htm> (accessed 5 October 2005).

Perks, J. (2003) DRAGON in my exams. *British Journal of Educational Technology*, 34, 1, 103–104.

Phillips, C. (2004) A technical look at accessibility through assistive technology in post-secondary settings. Paper presented at CSUN '04. Online. Available HTTP: <http://www.csun.edu/cod/conf/2004/proceedings/263.htm> (accessed 5 October 2005).

Phipps, L. (2002) Are you reasonably adjusted? *Educational Developments*, 3, 4, 6.

Phipps, L., Witt, N. and McDermott, A. P. (2002) To Logo or Not to Logo? Online. Available HTTP: <http://www.techdis.ac.uk/index.php?p=3_8_8> (accessed 5 October 2005).

Phipps, L., Harrison, S., Sloan, D. and Willder, B. (2004) Developing and publicising a workable accessibility strategy. *Ariadne*, 38. Online. Available HTTP: <http://www.ariadne.ac.uk/issue38/phipps/> (accessed 5 October 2005).

Phipps, L., Witt, N. and Kelly, B. (2005) Towards a pragmatic framework for accessible e-learning. *Ariadne*, 44. Online. Available HTTP: <http://www.ariadne.ac.uk/issue44/phipps/> (accessed 5 October 2005).

Piket-May, M. J. and Avery, J. P. (2001) First year students can do e-teams: experiences with a first year engineering design course and the Handi Swing. Online. Available HTTP: <http://www.nciia.net/proceed_01/Piket-May%20materials.pdf> (accessed 5 October 2005).

Pilling, D., Barret, P. and Floyd, M. (2004) Disabled people and the Internet. Experiences, barriers and opportunities. Report for the Joseph Rowntree Foundation, City University, London, UK. Online. Available HTTP: <http://www.jrf.org.uk/bookshop/eBooks/1859351867.pdf> (accessed 5 October 2005).

Pliner, S. M. and Johnson, J. R. (2004) Historical, theoretical and foundational principles of universal instructional design. *Equity & Excellence in Education*, 37, 105–113.

Poulson, D. and Nicolle, C. (2004) Making the Internet accessible for people with cognitive and communication impairments. *Universal Access in the Information Society*, 3, 48–56.

Powell, N., Moore, D., Gray, J., Finlay, J. and Reaney, J. (2004) Dyslexia and learning programming. *Italics*, 13, 2. Online. Available HTTP: <http://www.ics.ltsn.ac.uk/pub/italics/Vol3–2/dyslexia.pdf> (accessed 5 October 2005).

Powlik, J. J. and Karshmer, A. I. (2002) When accessibility meets usability. *Universal Access in the Information Society*, 1, 217–222.

Pulichino, J. (2005) The e-learning accessibility and Section 508 report. The Elearning Guild. Online. Available HTTP: <http://www.elearningguild.com/pdf/1/jan05survey-accessibility.pdf> (accessed 5 October 2005).

Purcell, S. L. and Grant, D. (2004) Assistive technology solutions: IT's all about curriculum access! Paper presented at CSUN '04. Online. Available HTTP: <http://www.csun.edu/cod/conf/2004/proceedings/141.htm> (accessed 5 October 2005).

QIAT Consortium (2003) Quality indicators for assistive technology services in schools. Online. Available HTTP: <http://www.qiat.org> (accessed 5 October 2005).

Quick, D., Lehmann, J. and Deniston, T. (2003) Opening doors for students with disabilities on community college campuses: what have we learned? What do we still need to know? *Community College Journal of Research and Practice*, 27, 815–827.

Rainger, P. (2003) A dyslexic perspective on e-content accessibility. Online. Available HTTP: <http://www.techdis.ac.uk/seven/papers/dyslexia-index.html> (accessed 5 October 2005).

Reed, P. S., Gardner-Bonneau, D. and Isensee, S. (2004) Software accessibility standards and guidelines: progress, current status and future developments. *Universal Access to the Information Society*, 3, 30–37.

Regan, B. (2004a) The tension between a wide and narrow UI. Online. Available HTTP: <http://weblogs.macromedia.com/accessibility/archives/2004/11/index.cfm> (accessed 5 October 2005).

Regan, B. (2004b) web accessibility and design: a failure of the imagination. Paper presented at Designing for the 21st Century III. Online. Available HTTP: <http://www.designfor21st.org/proceedings/proceedings/plenary_regan.html> (accessed 5 October 2005).

Regan, B. (2005a) Accessible web authoring with Macromedia Dreamweaver MX 2004. Paper presented at CSUN '05, Los Angeles, 17–19 March 2005. Online. Available HTTP: <http://www.csun.edu/cod/conf/2005/proceedings/2405.htm> (accessed 5 October 2005).

Regan, B. (2005b) Flash accessibility. Online. Available HTTP: <http://weblogs.macromedia.com/accessibility/archives/2005/02/index.cfm> (accessed 5 October 2005).

Reid, L. G., Denham, J. and Eghtesadi, K. (2005) Accessibility of next generation Adobe Acrobat software for blind and visually impaired users. Paper presented at CSUN '05, Los Angeles, 17–19 March 2005. Online. Available HTTP: <http://www.csun.edu/cod/conf/2005/proceedings/2379.htm> (accessed 5 October 2005).

Richards, J. T. and Hanson, V. L. (2004) web accessibility: a broader view. Paper presented to WWW 2004, May 17–22, New York.

Riemer-Reiss, M. L. and Wacker, R. R. (1999) Assistive technology use and abandonment among college students with disabilities. *International Electronic Journal for Leadership in Learning*, 3, 23. Online. Available HTTP: <http://www.ucalgary.ca/~iejll/volume3/riemer.html> (accessed 5 October 2005).

Ritchie, H. and Blanck, P. (2003) The promise of the Internet for disability: a study of on-line services and Web site accessibility at Centers for Independent Living. *Behavioural Sciences and the Law*, 21, 5–26.

Roer-Strier, D. (2002) University students with learning disabilities advocating for change. *Disability and Rehabilitation*, 24, 17, 914–924.

Rosenbaum, S., Wilson, C. E., Jokela, T., Rohn, J. A., Smith, T. B. and Vredenburg, K. (2002) Usability in practice: user experience lifecycle – evolution and revolution. Paper presented at CHI, 20–25 April 2002. Minneapolis, Minnesota, USA Online. Available HTTP: <http://www.kessu. oulu.fi/p898rosenbaum.pdf> (accessed 5 October 2005).

Rothberg, M., Almasy, E., Cheetham, A., Kirkpatrick, A. and Treviranus, J. (2005)

Accessible e-learning demonstrations using IMS Accessibility Specifications. Paper presented at CSUN 2005. Online. Available HTTP: <http://www.csun.edu/cod/conf/2005/proceedings/2328.htm> (accessed 5 October 2005).

Roulstone, A. (2003) The legal road to rights? Disabling premises, *Obiter Dicta* and the Disability Discrimination Act 1995. *Disability and Society*, 18, 2, 117–131.

Rowland, C. (2000) Accessibility of the Internet in postsecondary education: meeting the challenge. Paper presented at Universal Web Accessibility Symposium 31 October 2000. San Antonio Texas. Online. Available HTTP: <http://www.webaim.org/coordination/articles/meetchallenge> (accessed 5 October 2005).

Rowland, C. (2004) Cognitive disabilities Part 2: conceptualizing design considerations. Online. Available HTTP: <http://www.webaim.org/techniques/articles/conceptualize/?templatetype=3> (accessed 5 October 2005).

Russell, C. (2003) Access to technology for the disabled: the forgotten legacy of innovation? *Information & Communication Technology Law*, 12, 3, 237–246.

Saito, S., Fukuda, K., Takagi, H. and Asawaka, C. (2005) aDesigner: visualizing blind usability and simulating low vision visibility. Paper presented at CSUN '05, Los Angeles, 17–19 March 2005. Online. Available HTTP: <http://www.csun.edu/cod/conf/2005/proceedings/2631.htm> (accessed 5 October 2005).

Sajka, J. and Roeder, J. (2002) *PDF and Public Documents: A White Paper*. New York: American Foundation for the Blind.

Sampson-Wild, G. and Burmeister, O. K. (2001) The continuing evolution of best practice principles in designing for web accessibility. Paper presented at OZCHI 2001, Churchlands, WA, Australia.

Sams, L. and Yates-Mercer, P (2000) The web for students and staff with disabilities: visual impairments, dyslexia and motor impairment. Online. Available HTTP: <http://www.soi.city.ac.uk/~db522/disinhe/Print%20the%20entire%20article%20final.htm> (accessed 5 October 2005).

Sanda, J. (2003) eCollege accessibility: the on-campus benefits of accessible e-learning. Paper presented at CSUN '03. Online. Available HTTP: <http://www.csun.edu/cod/conf/2003/proceedings/98.htm> (accessed 5 October 2005).

Sanders, E. (2000) Working as a Disability Liaison Officer in England, 1997–1999. Paper presented at Pathways 5 Conference, Canberra, Australia, 6–8 December.

Schenker, K. T. and Scadden, L. A. (2002) The design of the accessible distance education environments that use collaborative learning. *Information Technology and Disabilities*, 8, 1. Online. Available HTTP: <http://www.rit.edu/~easi/itd/itdv08n1/scadden.htm> (accessed 5 October 2005).

Scherer, M. (2004) *Connecting to Learn: Educational and Assistive Technology for People with Disabilities*. Washington DC: American Psychological Society.

Schmetzke, A. (2001) Web accessibility at university libraries and schools. *Library Hi Tech*, 19, 1, 35–49.

Schmetzke, A. (2002a) Web site accessibility at 56 North American Universities: 2002 survey data on libraries and library schools. Online. Available HTTP: <http://library.uwsp.edu/aschmetz/Accessible/nationwide/Survey2002/contents2002.htm> (accessed 5 October 2005).

Schmetzke, A. (2002b) The accessibility of online library resources for people with print disabilities: research and strategies for change. In K. Miesenberger, J. Klaus and W. Zagler (eds) *Proceedings of ICCHP 2002*, Lecture Notes in Computer Science, Volume 2398. Berlin Heidelberg: Springer-Verlag, pp. 390–397.

SciVisum (2004) *Web Accessibility Report*. Kent, UK: SciVisum Ltd.

Scott, G. (2001) Supporting students with disabilities: what training and development do library staff in higher education require? *Impact*, 4, 2. Online. Available HTTP: <http://www.careerdevelopmentgroup.org.uk/impact/0301/ideas.htm> (accessed 5 October 2005).

Scott, S. S., McGuire, J. M. and Foley, T. E. (2003) Universal design for instruction: a framework for anticipating and responding to disability and other diverse learning needs in the college classroom. *Equity and Excellence in Education*, 36, 1, 40–49.

Seale, J. (2002) So what does all this mean for me? In L. Phipps, A. Sutherland and J. Seale (eds) *Access All Areas: Disability, Technology and Learning*. Oxford: ALT/TechDis, pp. 82–86.

Seale, J. (2003a) Supporting the development of e-learning accessibility practices: new and emergent roles for staff developers. In G. Crisp, D, Thiele, I. Scholten, S. Barker and J. Baron (eds) *Proceedings of the 20th Annual Conference of the Australasian Society for Computers in Tertiary Education*, pp. 458–464. Online. Available HTTP: <http://www.ascilite.org.au/conferences/adelaide03/docs/pdf/458.pdf> (accessed 5 October 2005).

Seale, J. (2003b) The challenge of researching accessibility practices within higher education: an exploration of 'shared enterprises' or 'political games'? Paper presented at NZARE and AARE 2003 Conference, 28 November–2 December, Auckland, New Zealand. Online. Available HTTP: <http://www.aare.edu.au/03pap/sea03251.pdf> (accessed 5 October 2005).

Seale, J. (2003c) In search of an enterprise of accessibility: communities, practices, boundaries and constellations. In J. Cook and D. McConnell (eds) *Research Proceedings of the 10th Association for Learning Technology Conference* (ALT-C 2003). Oxford: Association for Learning Technology, pp. 299–313.

Seale, J. (2004) The development of accessibility practices in e-learning: an exploration of communities of practice. *Association for Learning Technology Journal*, 12, 1, 51–63.

Selwyn, N. (2003) ICT for All? Access and use of public ICT sites in the UK, *Information, Communication & Society*, 6, 3, 350–375.

Selwyn, N. and Gorard, S. (2003) Reality bytes: examining the rhetoric of widening educational participation via ICT, *British Journal of Educational Technology*, 34, 2, 169–181.

Shaw, J. (2003) Bedding down for the long haul – philosophy of service delivery for students who have a disability or a chronic medical condition. Online. Available HTTP: <http://www.eophea.anu.edu.au/Jenny%20Shaw2003.pdf> (accessed 5 October 2005).

Shelvin, M., Kenny, M. and Mcneela, E. (2004) Participation in higher education for students with disabilities: an Irish perspective. *Disability & Society*, 19, 1, 15–30.

Shillock, E. (2004) The Disability Discrimination Act Part 4. Working with partner institutions – a good practice guide. Online. Available HTTP: <http://nado.org.uk/documents/dda4.html> (accessed 5 October 2005).

Shneiderman, B. and Hochheiser, H. (2001) Universal usability as a stimulus to advanced interface design. *Behaviour & Information Technology*, 20, 5, 367–376.

Slatin, J. (2002) The imagination gap: making web-based instructional resources accessible to students and colleagues with disabilities. *Currents in Electronic*

Literacy, Spring 2002, 6. Online. Available HTTP: <http://www.cwrl.utexas.edu/currents/spring02/slatin.html> (accessed 5 October 2005).

Slatin, J. M. (2005) Overview of the general techniques for web content accessibility guidelines 2.0. Paper presented at CSUN '05, Los Angeles, 17–19 March 2005. Online. Available HTTP: <http://www.csun.edu/cod/conf/2005/proceedings/2382.htm> (accessed 5 October 2005).

Sloan, D. (2000) How to uncover a website's accessibility barriers. Online. Available HTTP: <http://www.dmag.org.uk/resources/design_articles/howtojudge.asp> (accessed 5 October 2005).

Sloan, D. and Stratford, J. (2004) Producing high quality materials on accessible multimedia. Paper presented at the ILTHE Disability Forum, Anglia Polytechnic University, 29 January. Online. Available HTTP: <http://www.heacademy.ac.uk/embedded_object.asp?id=21627&filename=Sloan_and_Stratford> (accessed 5 October 2005).

Sloan, D., Rowan, M., Booth, P. and Gregor, P. (2000) Ensuring the provision of accessible digital resources. *Journal of Educational Media*, 25, 3, 203–216.

Sloan, D., Gregor, P., Booth, P. and Gibson, L. (2002) Auditing accessibility of UK higher education web sites. *Interacting With Computers*, 14, 313–325.

Sloan, M. (2001) Web accessibility and the DDA. *Journal of Information, Law and Technology*. Online. Available HTTP: <http://www2.warwick.ac.uk/fac/soc/law/elj/jilt/2001_2/sloan/> (accessed 5 October 2005).

Smith, J. (2005) Accessibility of live/real-time web-based multimedia for the deaf and hard of hearing. Paper presented at CSUN '05, Los Angeles, 17–19 March 2005. Online. Available HTTP: <http://www.csun.edu/cod/conf/2005/proceedings/2336.htm> (accessed 5 October 2005).

Smith, J. and Bohman, P. (2004) Evaluating website accessibility: a seven step process. Paper presented at CSUN '04. Online. Available HTTP: <http://www.csun.edu/cod/conf/2004/proceedings/203.htm> (accessed 5 October 2005).

Smith, J. and Lyman, M. (2005) A policy implementation model for increasing web accessibility. Paper presented at CSUN '05, Los Angeles, 17–19 March 2005. Online. Available HTTP: <http://www.csun.edu/cod/conf/2005/proceedings/2335.htm> (accessed 5 October 2005).

Smith, S. (2002) Dyslexia and Virtual Learning Environment Interfaces. In L. Phipps., A. Sutherland and J. Seale (eds) *Access All Areas: Disability, Technology and Learning*. Oxford: ALT/Jisc/TechDis, pp. 50–53.

Snaprud, M. H. and Aslaksen, F. (2004) The European Internet Accessibility Observatory (EIAO): aspects of internationalisation. Paper presented at Designing for the 21st Century III. Online. Available HTTP: <http://www.designfor21st.org/proceedings/proceedings/project_aslaksen_internet.html> (accessed 5 October 2005).

Southern Higher and Further Education Consortium (2001) Information, Communication and Learning Technologies and widening participation. Online. Available HTTP: <http://www.soton.ac.uk/~shec/Section1shfecwapICTadvicedocument.html> (accessed 5 October 2005).

Spindler, T. (2004) The accessibility of web pages for mid-sized college and university libraries: *Reference and User Services Quarterly*, 42, 2, 149–154.

Stefani, L. (2000) How accessible is your curriculum? Online. Available HTTP: <http://www.heacademy.ac.uk/resources. asp?process=full_record&section=generic&id=419> (accessed 5 October 2005).

Stein, E. W., Manco, M. P. and Manco, S. A. (2001) A knowledge-based system to assist university administrators in meeting disability act requirements. *Expert Systems with Applications*, 21, 65–74.

Stephanidis, C. (2005) Towards an on-line community promoting design for all in Europe. Paper presented at CSUN '05, Los Angeles, 17–19 March 2005. Online. Available HTTP: <http;//www.csun. edu/cod/conf/2005/proceedings/2151.htm> (accessed 10 March 2005).

Stephanidis, C., Paramythis, A., Akoumianakis, D. and Sfyrakis, M. (1998). Self-adapting web-based systems: towards universal accessibility. In C. Stephanidis and A. Waern (eds) *Proceedings of the 4th ERCIM Workshop 'User Interfaces for All'* Stockholm: European Research Consortium for Informatics and Mathematics, pp. 19–21.

Steyaert, J. (2005) Web based higher education, the inclusion/exclusion paradox. *Journal of Technology in Human Services*, 23, 1, 67–68.

Stiles, M. J. (2001) Disability access to Virtual Learning Environments. Online. Available HTTP: <http://www.dmag.org.uk/resources/casestudies/stilesfull.asp> (accessed 5 October 2005).

Stratford, J. and Sloan, D. (2005) Skills for Access: putting the world to rights for accessibility and multimedia. *ALT Online Newsletter*, 15 July. Online. Available HTTP: <http://newsletter.alt.ac.uk/e_article000428038.cfm?x=b11,0,w> (accessed 5 October 2005).

Tagaki, H., Asakawa, C., Fukudu, K. and Maeda, J. (2004) Accessibility designer: visualizing usability for the blind. Paper presented at ASSETS '04, 18–20 October, 2004, Atlanta, Georgia.

Taylor, G. and Palfreman-Kay, J. M. (2000) Helping each other: relations between disabled and non-disabled students on Access programmes. *Journal of Further and Higher Education*, 24, 1, 39–53.

TechDis (n.d.) Scenarios relating to staff development, accessibility and resource creation. Online. Available HTTP: <http://www.techdis.ac.uk/index. php?p=9_7_20040511011156> (accessed 5 October 2005).

TechDis (2004) TechDis guidelines for the development of e-content. Online. Available HTTP: <http://www.techdis.ac.uk/resources/files/DraftVersionTechDis-GuidelinesinRTF.rtf> (accessed 5 October 2005).

Thatcher, J. (2004) web accessibility – what not to do. Paper presented at CSUN '04. Online. Available HTTP: <http://www.csun.edu/cod/conf/2004/proceedings/80.htm> (accessed 5 October 2005).

The Learning Federation (2003) Accessibility specification for content development. Online. Available from: <http://www.thelearningfederation.edu.au/tlf2/sitefiles/images/documents/Accessibility_Specification_V2_0.pdf> (accessed 5 October 2005).

Theofanos, M. F. and Redish, J. (2003) Guidelines for accessible and usable websites: observing users who work with screen readers. *Interactions*, 10, 6, 38–51. Online. Available HTTP: <http://www.redish.net/content/papers/InteractionsPaper-AuthorsVer.pdf> (accessed 5 October 2005).

Theofanos, M., Kirkpatrick, A. and Thatcher, J. (2004) Prioritizing web accessibility evaluation data. Paper presented at CSUN '04. Online. Available HTTP: <http://www.csun.edu/cod/conf/2004/proceedings/145.htm> (accessed 5 October 2005).

Thompson, T. (2004a) Accessing PDAs in the classroom. Paper presented at CSUN

'04. Online. Available HTTP: <http://www.csun.edu/cod/conf/2004/proceedings/227.htm> (accessed 5 October 2005).

Thompson, T. (2004b) 2004 Survey on Access Technology in Higher Education. Online. Available HTTP: <http://staff.washington.edu/tft/athen/> (accessed 5 October 2005).

Thompson, T. (2005) Universal design and web accessibility: unexpected beneficiaries. Paper presented at CSUN '05, Los Angeles, 17–19 March 2005. Online. Available HTTP: <http://www.csun.edu/cod/conf/2005/proceedings/2392.htm> (accessed 5 October 2005).

Thompson, T., Burgstahler, S. and Comden, D. (2003) Research on Web accessibility in higher education. *Information Technology and Disabilities*, 9, 2. Online. Available HTTP: <http://www.rit.edu/~easi/itd/itdv09n2/thompson.htm> (accessed 5 October 2005).

Tierney, J. (2002) University students take complaints to Anti-Discrimination Commissioner. Australian Broadcasting Corporation, TV programme transcript. Online. Available HTTP: <http://www.abc.net.au/7.30/content/2002/s460046.htm> (accessed 5 October 2005).

Tinklin, T., Riddell, S. and Wilson, A. (2004) Policy and provision for disabled students in higher education in Scotland and England: the current state of play. *Studies in Higher Education*, 29, 5, 637–657.

US Department of Labour (1973a) Section 504, Rehabilitation Act of 1973. Online. Available HTTP: <http://www.dol.gov/oasam/regs/statutes/sec504.htm> (accessed 5 October 2005).

US Department of Labour (1973b) Section 508, Rehabilitation Act of 1973. Online. Available HTTP: <http://www.dol.gov/oasam/regs/statutes/sec508.htm> (accessed 5 October 2005).

US Department of Justice (1990) American with Disabilities Act. Online. Available HTTP: <http://www.usdoj.gov/crt/ada/pubs/ada.txt> (accessed 5 October 2005).

Vanderheiden, G. C. (1996) Universal design. What it is and what it isn't. Online. Available HTTP: <http://trace.wisc.edu/docs/whats_ud/whats_ud.htm> (accessed 5 October 2005).

Vanderheiden, G. C. (1997) Anywhere, anytime (+anyone) access to the next generation WWW. *Computer Networks and ISDN Systems*, 29, 1439–1446.

Vaughn, M. (2002) An index for inclusion. *European Journal of Special Needs Education*, 17, 2, 197–201.

Waddell, C. (1998) Applying the ADA to the Internet: a Web accessibility standard. Paper presented at National Conference of American Bar Association, 'In pursuit of a blueprint for disability law and policy'. Online. Available HTTP: <http://www.icdri.org/CynthiaW/applying_the_ada_to_the_internet.htm> (accessed 5 October 2005).

Waddell, C. (1999) The growing digital divide in access for people with disabilities: overcoming barriers to participation in the digital economy. Online. Available HTTP: <http://www.icdri.org/CynthiaW/the_digital_divide.htm> (accessed 5 October 2005).

Waddell, C. (2004) Electronic textbooks. US accessibility laws and issues. Paper presented to CSUN '04. Online. Available HTTP: <http://www.csun.edu/cod/conf/2004/proceedings/221.htm> (accessed 5 October 2005).

Waddell, C. D. (2005) Litigation and legislation trends in accessible IT and telecommunications. Paper presented at CSUN '05, Los Angeles, 17–19 March 2005. Online. Available HTTP: <http://www.csun.edu/cod/conf/2005/proceedings/2406.htm> (accessed 5 October 2005).

Waddell, C. D. and Hardy, B. (2004) Developments in global accessible ICT policy and law. Paper presented at CSUN '04. Online. Available HTTP: <http://www.cun.edu/cod/conf/2004/proceedings/97.htm> (accessed 5 October 2005).

Wald, M. (2002) Hearing disability and technology. In L. Phipps, A. Sutherland and J. Seale (eds) *Access All Areas: Disability, Technology and Learning*. Oxford: ALT/TechDis, pp. 19–23.

Wall, P. S. and Sarver, L. (2003) Disabled student access in an era of technology, *The Internet and Higher Education*, 6, 3, 277–284.

Wandke, H. (2005) Assistance in human–machine interaction: a conceptual framework and a proposal for a taxonomy. *Theoretical Issues in Ergonomics Science*, 6, 2, 129–155.

Waterfield, J. and Hurst, A. (2000) It's not what you do, it's the way that you do it. Paper presented at the Pathways 5 National Conference, Canberra, Australia, 6–8 December 2000.

Wattenberg, T. (2004) Beyond legal compliance: communities of advocacy that support accessible online learning. *The Internet and Higher Education*, 7, 123–139.

WebAIM (n.d.a) Constructing a POUR Website. Part 1: putting people at the center of the process. Online. Available HTTP: <http://www.webaim. org/techniques/articles/pour/people> (accessed 10 October 2005).

WebAIM. (n.d.b) The important of leadership. If not you, who? Online. Available HTTP: <http://www.webaim.org/coordination/articles/imp_of_leadership?templatetype=3> (accessed 5 October 2005).

Web Accessibility Initiative (WAI) (2004) Statement on Web access report from UK Disability Rights Commission. Online. Available HTTP: <http://www.w3.org/2004/04/wai-drc-statement.html> (accessed 5 October 2005).

Wenger, E. (1998) *Communities of practice: learning, meaning and identity*. Cambridge: Cambridge University Press.

Wilder, B. (2002) Disability legislation: implications for learning technologists in the UK. In L. Phipps., A. Sutherland and J. Seale (eds) *Access All Areas: Disability, Technology and Learning*. Oxford: ALT/TechDis, pp. 6–9.

Wilson, A., Ridell, S. and Tinklin, T. (2002) Disabled students in higher education. Finding from key informant interviews. Online. Available HTTP: <http://www.ces.ed.ac.uk/Disability/Papers/KeyInfrm.pdf> (accessed 5 October 2005).

Wimberley, L., Reed, N. and Morris, M. (2004) Postsecondary students with learning disabilities: barriers to accessing education-based information technology. *Information Technology and Disabilities*, 10, 1. Online. Available HTTP: <http://www.rit.edu/~easi/itd/itdv10n1/wimberly.htm> (accessed 5 October 2005).

Winberg, F. (1999) Discount accessibility engineering: haven't we met before? Paper presented at INTERACT '99, Edinburgh, Great Britain. Online. Available HTTP: <http://cid.nada.kth.se/pdf/cid_75.pdf> (accessed 5 October 2005).

Witt, N. A. J. and McDermott, A. P. (2002) Achieving SENDA-compliance for Web Sites in further and higher education: an art or a science? In L. Phipps, A. Sutherland and J. Seale (eds). *Access All Areas: Disability, Technology and Learning*. Oxford: ALT/TechDis, pp. 42–49.

Witt, N. and McDermott, A. (2004) Web site accessibility: what logo will we use today? *British Journal of Educational Technology*, 35, 1, 45–56.

Woodford, R. and Bradley, S. (2004) Using Virtual Learning Environments to support students with dyslexia. *ALT Newsletter*, 45, 7.

World Health Organisation (WHO) (2001) International Classification of Functioning, Disability and Health. Online. Available HTTP: <http://www3.who.int/icf/icftemplate.cfm> (accessed 5 October 2005).

Wray, M. (2002) Online learning to deliver staff development materials about disabled students. *Interactions*, 6, 3. Online. Available HTTP: <http://www.warwick.ac.uk/ETS/interactions/vol6no3/wray.htm> (accessed 5 October 2005).

Wright, L. and Stephenson, J. (2002) Issues around the use of WebCT in on-line learning for dyslexic students at the University of East London. Paper presented at the Scholarship of Teaching and Learning Conference 2002. Online. Available HTTP: <http://www.uel.ac.uk/sdel/internal_resources/docs/SoTL_Paper01.doc> (accessed 5 October 2005).

Yu, H. (2003) Web Accessibility and the law: issues in implementation. In M. Hricko (ed.) *Design and Implementation of web Enabled Teaching Tools*. Ohio: Kent State University.

Index